A Practical Guide to Earned Value Project Management

A Practical Guide to Earned Value Project Management

Charles I. Budd, MDv, PMP

Charlene S. Budd, PhD, CPA, CMA, CFM, PMP

MANAGEMENTCONCEPTS

〈〈〈
MANAGEMENTCONCEPTS

8230 Leesburg Pike, Suite 800
Vienna, VA 22182
(703) 790-9595
Fax: (703) 790-1371
www.managementconcepts.com

Printed in the United States of America

Library of Congress Cataloging-in-Publication Data

Budd, Charles I., 1936–
   A practical guide to earned value project management / Charles I. Budd,
   Charlene S. Budd.
       p.   cm.
   Includes bibliographical references and index.
   ISBN 1-56726-167-1
   1. Project management. I. Budd, Charlene S., 1938– II. Title.
   HD69.P7583 2005
   658.4'04—dc22

                                                              2005050491

About the Authors

Charles I. Budd (Chuck) is a Principal of U/S Management Systems in Waco, Texas. His career began in computer programming and grew into executive management. He has been CEO of Financial Information Trust in Des Moines, President of International Computer Systems, Inc., in Akron, President of Technology Connections, Inc., in Atlanta, Senior Project Manager for Softlab Enabling Technologies also in Atlanta, and Operations Vice President for Intercontinental Computing, Inc., in Kansas City.

He is a Project Management Professional and currently is developing project management automation tools, consulting on information systems projects, conducting seminars, and writing with his co-author, Charlene Budd. He has taught webinar classes and conducted workshops and presentations around the world. Some of his international consulting engagements included major Y2K remediation projects in the United States, Germany, and South Africa, where he first began using earned value management concepts.

Chuck is active in several civic volunteer organizations, the Project Management Institute, and information systems organizations. He is a graduate of Baldwin-Wallace College, has been certified a Systems Analyst by the Foundation for Administration Research, attended graduate classes at Drake University, and has a graduate degree from Baylor University.

Charlene Spoede Budd, PhD (Charli), is Professor Emeritus of Accounting at Baylor University, where she has taught graduate management accounting and graduate project management classes. She has a PhD in business administration and holds certifications as a CPA, CMA, CFM, PMP, and all six professional categories of the Theory of Constraints.

Her research has been published primarily in practitioner journals and she has been awarded three Certificates of Merit for articles (one of which explained why multi-project management is an essential skill for management accountants) published in *Strategic Finance*. She also has published in *Today's CPA, The Counselor*, other journals, and many conference proceedings. She has written two accounting textbooks and currently she and co-author Charles Budd are working on two other books.

Charli is active in several professional organizations, including the American Institute of CPAs, the American Accounting Association, the Financial Executives Institute, and the Project Management Institute. She also is an active member of the Finance and Metrics Committee of the TOC-ICO (Theory of Constraints International Certification Organization) and currently is assisting the AICPA in developing questions and simulations for the Business Environment component of the new computerized CPA examinations.

Table of Contents

FIGURES

Preface

If a project sponsor has dictated that your project must adhere to the requirements of the Earned Value Management System (EVMS), you need to read this book. If you want to learn the mechanics of the system that is much-discussed and well-accepted in knowledgeable project management circles, you will want to read this book. If your organization is seeking to increase its project management maturity, you should read this book.

Many project managers initially are opposed to implementing EVMS. Change in any form is often feared. After all, if project managers are successful to some degree without EVMS, they naturally will wonder how successful they will be in a new environment that uses EVMS. Project managers who are accustomed to and comfortable with their particular system may now feel that their every move will be studied microscopically and that they will be compelled to waste time explaining their every action. But consider this: If you are extremely competent, don't you want top management to recognize your value based on criteria other than your ability to promote yourself?

This practical guide provides two perspectives on EVMS: an academic perspective to give you insight into the mechanics of the system, and a practical perspective to assist you in its everyday implementation and use.

We have heard several complaints that the requirements of EVMS are too complicated, too detailed, and too difficult to understand. It is our intent to walk you through the EVMS criteria in a way that will clarify the requirements and untangle any complications. *A Practical Guide to Earned Value Project Management* will not only bring the EVMS requirements into your world, but also will guide you in applying additional successful project management techniques and tools.

We have also heard comments that some of the EVMS requirements overlap, some are too "picky," and some are just not necessary in the commercial and industrial worlds. These comments remind us of one of our project management workshops sponsored by an organization that brought us in because their projects were never completed on time, produced within budget, or delivered to all original specifications. When we presented some basic project management processes, a few of the participants responded that they were too simple to be of value and that the organization's abilities were too highly developed to need those particular methods. With that attitude, it is no wonder that their projects were unsuccessful!

There are always individuals who want to shortcut the requirements of any proven system. That is not to say that EVMS does not have shortcomings, because it does. We will point out weak and sometimes treacherous aspects, but our purpose is to guide you on a practical route through EVMS and to give you some no-nonsense ideas for ways to meet its criteria and complete your projects successfully.

EVMS is a highly effective project management tool, but it is not a completely stand-alone project management system. Project managers need much more in their tool bag. So before we begin to discuss the details of EVMS, we will review project management in general. We realize that most of our readers already have good project management skills, so some information will seem very basic. For that reason we will only skim the surface; however, it is our hope that these discussions will introduce unfamiliar topics or stimulate your interest in a well-known topic. You may find a nugget or two—or perhaps even a real gem—to engage you while you mull over the problems of your current project.

Most of our readers are accomplished project managers who, for any number of reasons, want to learn about EVMS criteria and how they can conform to its detailed requirements while still completing their projects. We will do our best to give you this knowledge. However, we also will offer occasional insights and discussions that we consider to be important, but sometimes overlooked, aspects of successful project management.

This is not a project management "how to" book. Many books and classes are available on the techniques for successful project management. While virtually all these books and classes use earned value concepts, however, few discuss the EVMS criteria and even fewer offer project managers practical advice on interpreting and using the criteria to manage their projects.

You don't need to be an expert in accounting or even have had any college accounting classes to understand EVMS. We will guide you step-by-step through everything you need to understand the requirements. Checkpoints throughout the material (called "gates" in project management terminology) will allow you to review your progress and retrace your steps if necessary. Anticipating that some readers will be involved in EVMS projects that will be audited (internally or by a government agency) for compliance with all 32 criteria, we will cover the entire set.

Throughout the book, we try to communicate our perspective in a straightforward manner. Figures and tables are provided to enable readers to grasp concepts readily through visual depictions instead of through many paragraphs of text.

Chapter 1 provides the book's purpose and organization; Chapter 2 sets the stage with background information; Chapter 3 introduces and provides our general analysis of EVMS; and Chapter 4 details the requirements of an EVMS implementation. The 32 criteria of EVMS are discussed in detail in Chapters 5 through 11. Chapter 12 deals with the closing process and the unfortunate, but necessary, subject of terminating a project. Other resources provided include a bibliography, a glossary of key terms, the 32 criteria presented in numerical order (Appendix A), and the answers and solutions to problems from the chapter reviews (Appendix B).

We hope that you will find our travel together through the Earned Value Management System to be enlightening, interesting, and beneficial.

Charles I. Budd

Charlene S. Budd

Introduction

Part I is a condensed introduction to the many facets of project management. If you are an experienced project manager, you may choose to skip selected portions of this introduction. However, even seasoned project managers can gain some valuable insights from these first two chapters.

The purpose of this book and its organization are discussed in Chapter 1. Background on general project management is presented in Chapter 2. Obviously, project managers need more than knowledge of EVMS to be successful. While we do not purport to present a comprehensive treatment of project management, we will try to broaden your understanding of the project management environment. Besides discussing what it takes to be a successful project manager and project team, we will also briefly address project life cycles, the project management office, and the stages of project management maturity.

CHAPTER 1

Background and Motivation

Most project managers are passionate about accomplishing challenging objectives, but lack similar passion in the areas of detailed planning, reporting progress, or explaining their success or failure in meeting baseline targets. Projects often prove difficult because they are striving to accomplish their targets while working through previously uncharted territory without dedicated resources. Therefore, a good deal of a project manager's time may be spent in negotiations to acquire what is needed.

People intimately involved in a project have knowledge that others do not possess. Sometimes we take advantage of this information asymmetry to protect the project or the project team or to buy ourselves more time for solving problems and reaching project goals. Regardless of the project manager's or team's feeling about the project, its continuation depends on communication with owners and other interested parties about the project's status. At the present time, an earned value management system is the accepted methodology for objectively communicating progress compared with the established project baseline and related cost estimates.

OUR BASIC PREMISE

While your company may be an exception, most organizations do not have a well-organized and functioning project office that controls the entry of projects into the system and tracks progress on all active projects from charter to close. It is widely accepted that projects are unique and inherently risky. Nevertheless, rather than being subject to controls commensurate with their risk, they are usually not even subject to the same degree of internal controls that is applied to repetitive operations having far less risk.

Projects traditionally have populated the twilight area between current reality and desired future position. We usually know where we are and where we would like to be, but sometimes we don't know exactly how to get there. That's where projects enter the picture. Rather than being coordinated into an integrated organizational portfolio, projects typically have been "sold" independently, either by clients or by the heads of various organizational divisions. We are not suggesting that projects are promoted for nefarious reasons, but merely that divisional responsibilities drive spirited competition for funding.

Once projects are approved and funded, progress is generally not well tracked by project owners. For the most part, project metrics are rudimentary and primarily involve milestone achievement, budget consumption, and subjective progress reporting by the project manager.

THE THREE BASIC PARAMETERS OF PROJECT MANAGEMENT

Project management revolves around the three basic project characteristics: scope, schedule, and budget. EVMS provides the metrics for comparing what has been planned with what has been completed within these three parameters (see Figure 1.1). While EVMS establishes very precise organizational and reporting requirements, it does not prescribe how the project must be managed. It allows the flexibility of using a variety of project management processes as long as they meet the required criteria. While the critical path method is most common, it is not generally

	SCOPE	SCHEDULE	BUDGET
PLAN	What are the deliverables?	When are they due?	How much will it cost?
PROGRESS	What tasks have been completed?	How long has it taken to complete the work accomplished?	How much money have we spent to complete the tasks reported as finished?
PROJECTION	Will all project specifications be met?	When will the project be completed?	What is the estimated total cost at completion?

FIGURE 1.1   Basic Project Metrics

required; newer methods, such as critical chain, are permitted and sometimes encouraged.

BUSINESS CHANGES

Several recent events have encouraged organizations to restrain their "everyone-for-themselves" mentality concerning project management. Our increased pace means that we don't have time for a major failure. We can't spend months working on a project, bring it to a successful but delayed conclusion, and find that the environment has changed so that the deliverables no longer have value. A project like that should have been speeded up, if possible, or killed early enough to transfer its resources to projects with better prospects. Without critical project information, decision makers charged with global project responsibility sometimes operate blindly.

Some projects may hold the life or death of the organization in their successful completion. Others have profound influence on the company's future success. Those projects may have an effect on an entity's financial reporting. If so, stringent internal controls dictated by the recent Sarbanes-Oxley Act (SOX) (Sarbanes and Oxley 2002), which became effective in November 2004, might apply. Even if the projects currently do not meet the law's *financial operations* internal control criteria, they might meet them in the future. EVMS offers internal controls that in all likelihood will meet SOX requirements according to the Securities and Exchange Commission (SEC).

THE NEED FOR A COST AND SCHEDULE CONTROL SYSTEM

Recognizing the problem of poor project performance and having dealt repeatedly with the shock of overruns and underperformances, the federal government more than 40 years ago commissioned the development of a project measurement system based on a standard cost model. This system became known as Cost/Schedule Control Systems Criteria (C/SCSC). Private industry found the requirements cumbersome and suggested a revision in the mid 1990s. The new criteria were formally named the Earned Value Management System and in 1996 the government formally adopted 32 revised EVMS criteria. The American National Standards Institute Guidelines for EVMS, ANSI/EIA-748-1998, were issued in 1998.

For many years, private governmental contractors have been required to use EVMS on large government projects. Operations performed by the U.S. government for itself, such as repair depots and other project-oriented work, are rapidly implementing earned value metrics that affect total funding. Because it offers enhanced control features, many companies are now interested in employing EVMS for nongovernmental work.

Meanwhile, the accounting profession has had its own problems over the past few years with scandals that have prompted investors to demand more transparency from corporations. SOX established the Public Company Accounting Oversight Board (PCAOB) to rein in auditing firms by instituting rigorous control over their activities. One of the Board's first pronouncements, formally approved by the SEC (U.S. Securities and Exchange Commission 2003, 96), establishes exactly how public accounting firms must audit internal controls. If an external or internal auditor decides to look at your project, you must be prepared to show adequate internal controls.

Part of the reason many corporations are not forthcoming about their plans is that they don't want to provide their competitors with information about their strategies. Nor does top management want to risk embarrassment by public strategic failures resulting from either commissioning the wrong projects or having the projects' deliverables not further the organization's strategic initiatives. However, in light of recent scandals and public attention in the media, corporations are being pressured to be more candid about the status of their future plans. And if the boss gets pressured, you know it won't be long before the project manager begins to feel the heat!

The biggest impetus to the intense spotlight on project control is the enactment of SOX. While the act itself emphasizes internal control over *financial processes*, the final rules issued by the SEC introduce a newly defined term, *disclosure controls and procedures*. This term expands the concept of internal controls over financial reporting into the broader area of controls and procedures over disclosure of material financial and nonfinancial information in public reports. Disclosure controls and procedures will likely encompass project performance.

PROJECT MANAGEMENT MATURITY

The project management profession has recognized the need to improve. Its response to dismal internal control over projects has been to detail the formal steps of organizational maturity in managing and delivering projects. Project management maturity models have been devised to standardize and improve an organization's ability to implement its strategy by consistently delivering successful projects.

While organizations are aware of the various versions of the project maturity model, most organizations are located at the lowest steps of the model's progression. For example, consider a typical five-level model. Those at Level 1 have a project management process, but not a generalized structured process and standards. To achieve Level 2, it is necessary to achieve Level 1 and have standard project metrics in place. To reach Level 3, the organization must possess standards and institutionalized processes that involve project metrics and must evaluate performance among projects.

An organization must adopt either earned value or comparable metrics to master Levels 2 and 3 of project management maturity. Only after achieving Level 3 (necessitating that the requirements of Levels 1 and 2 also have been met) can an organization attempt Levels 4 and 5, which tackle continuous improvement efforts. These last levels offer tremendous benefits to organizations—especially those that arrive there before their competitors!

Thus, implementing EVMS is a worthy goal for you and your organization. However, even though EVMS is useful for reporting general progress to persons outside the project team, it does not solve all project management problems and, in certain cases, creates problems of its own. For example, EVMS was developed as an extension of a standard cost system. Attempting to manage a project via EVMS metrics alone can be disastrous. In subsequent chapters, we will discuss exactly how to comply with EVMS and still successfully manage your project work. Along the way, we will present additional ideas and project management tools that can be used profitably with EVMS.

LOOKING FOR VALUE IN ALL THE WRONG PLACES

It is especially true in difficult economic times that organizations must be very careful about investments in new initiatives and very hardnosed about return on those investments. Projects must realize their objectives; however, achieving project success does not have to be a complicated process. Success is not about mastering complicated theories or finding and adopting the latest business fad. Project success is about discipline—being able to stick to a tried and proven process, starting with a well-planned project.

No project plan can be considered complete without having some way of measuring how well the project earns its expected value. One recommended approach is for project plans to have their deliverables explicitly included in the project's baseline. The number of additional tasks that fully utilize the deliverables in the manner intended may be surprising.

It's all about value—perceived or real. In the movie, "Trading Places," Dan Ackroyd played a character who lost his job and had to pawn his wristwatch. No matter how hard he tried to convince the pawnbroker that the watch was actually worth thousands of dollars, the pawnbroker's response was, "In Philadelphia, it's worth 50 bucks." You may not have sold your project initially, but you have to continually sell yourself and your work on your projects. One way to do that compellingly and objectively is with EVMS. Keep in mind that even though EVMS informs others about your work, you must still use good project management judgment and skills.

We face immense pressure to take shortcuts so we can deliver value faster. The upshot is that there is no time to fully plan our activities. Following EVMS requirements will give you the opportunity to overcome most deficiencies in planning and controlling your projects. EVMS helps justify our value by requiring careful definition of the program objective, directing continual focus on ongoing project costs, and incorporating very stringent progress measurement processes.

OUR SAMPLE PROJECT

To maintain continuity and to facilitate understanding of the requirements of EVMS concepts, we have created a common baseline project. We have attempted to keep the sample project simple enough for illustration purposes yet realistic enough to enable you to translate the concepts into your own project environment.

Many exciting projects are being managed all over the world. For example, some very intriguing ones are being conducted or considered through a program called the Intelligent Manufacturing Systems (IMS), an international research and development program designed to develop the next generation of manufacturing and processing technologies. Other projects are underway to deliver medical miracles or to explore uncharted areas of the earth and the universe. While these projects are exciting, they also are extremely complex. Of necessity, our sample project must be both simple to understand and one to which we can all relate. While we will look at several historical projects—some of which are very complex—we will use our sample project to illustrate important points.

The sample project will be to install a new information technology (IT) system—specifically, a customer relations management (CRM) system. In this project, CRM is intended to give our sample organization complete access to and control over all information about customers and prospects. We expect the system to automate all the day-to-day tasks for our sales and marketing professionals as well as our office and field customer service, to interface with production, and to integrate with our other back-office systems. Many companies that have attempted to install this system have found it to be extremely challenging—a "mission impossible" without a happy ending.

An entire CRM implementation from conception to completion would be too complex for our simple illustration so we will use a subproject. Our assumptions are that a new CRM software system has been researched, approved, purchased, customized, and tested. A new data store has been defined and created for the required information elements. Our project is called "Project

CRM: The Final Step." It is intended to train the users, install the hardware, distribute the workstation software, and provide a support system.

> This brief user-friendly introduction to EVMS for project managers promises to make your study as painless as possible. This chapter establishes the need for EVMS from internal control and return-on-investment perspectives.
>
> While change is always difficult, it need not be tortuous. There are benefits to be gained from implementing EVMS—and even greater benefits from implementing it correctly! Many of the EVMS concepts are simply good business practices that can easily be employed in other environments. While you may love your work now, at some point you will want to broaden your horizons by moving into another position. Your knowledge of EVMS will serve you well whether you remain a project manager or move to a higher level of management.

DISCUSSION QUESTIONS

1. Discuss with your colleagues some major project management failures of which you have personal knowledge. Try to establish the root cause of the failures.

2. List some factors you believe would create a major project success.

3. At what level of project management maturity is your organization and where does it aspire to be?

4. Why are you interested in learning about EVMS?

5. What impact do you think the Sarbanes-Oxley Act has on project management?

6. Why do you believe it is difficult to deliver a project on time, within budget, and with full specifications intact?

CHAPTER 2

Project Management

Before we begin to discuss the application of the Earned Value Management System (EVMS) to projects, we will review some basic project management principles to ensure a common starting point. Experienced project managers may elect to browse this chapter for any nuggets of useful information. A common understanding of projects and their management provides the basic structure required to support EVMS.

Using project methods has become the more recognized way to perform an organization's work. After all, the work of most top executives primarily involves projects. The Project Management Institute, headquartered in the United States, and several comparable organizations in other parts of the world are dedicated to project management achieving professional status through programs and constant updating of materials. In addition, many other professions recognize the desirability of project management knowledge. For example, in their monograph of the future of accounting education, Albrecht and Sack (2000, 57) reveal that accounting practitioners rated project management as one of the top 10 technical skills that new accounting graduates should have.

A PROJECT

A project is a unique production event in the life of an individual or organization. While similar events may have been accomplished in the past, the type of event, the people working on it, the deliverables, the environment in which it takes place, or all of these elements, differentiate this event. A project can be as small as trying a new dinner recipe or as complex as constructing a space station—they all take planning, organization, and control. R. E. Westney, an engineer, stated his definition of a project that we really like: "A project can be defined as the work required to take an opportunity and convert it into an asset" (2001, 128).

Setting out activities in an orderly way to accomplish a goal is the result of an *orderly thought process* that has been occurring as long as humankind has been recording history. Thomas P. Hughes (1998) wrote about four incredibly complex projects in his book, *Rescuing Prometheus*. Hughes describes Prometheus as a mythological second creator and uses this reference to describe the transformation of our world from a natural state to a technological one. As these four enormous projects progressed, new ways of managing activities had to be developed. If your project seems overwhelming at times, read about some of the trials and accomplishments of the SAGE air-defense project, the Atlas missile project, the Boston Central Artery/Tunnel project, and the development of the Internet. From these projects came the inspiration for new technology, new organizational structures, and new management styles.

Most studies show that the majority of projects do not meet at least one criterion for the estimates of their original cost, schedule, or expected result. Indeed, the Boston project described by Hughes was popularly christened the "Big Dig" and later the "Big Leak." It became infamous for its cost overruns and unsatisfactory management. Project goals will not be realized if the efforts to meet them are unrealistic, not approved, underestimated, not planned, or if the project is not given adequate resources. Managing a project requires extensive planning and careful management using a consistent system.

There is a tremendous amount of material published about project management. The material is becoming fairly well-defined as associations such as the Project Management Institute (www.pmi.org), the Association of Project Management (www.apm.org.uk), and the International Project Management Association (www.ipma.ch/intro) publish and continue to update their bodies of knowledge on project management.

A project is a temporary and unique activity. Projects are generally undertaken by extensions of the organization that existed before and after the duration of the project. As we will see in Chapter 6, which discusses project organization, this typical organizational approach means that a project rarely has fully committed and full-time resources. Projects are not production-oriented even though they may have a production component. They begin and end to fulfill a particular need. The features "temporary" and "unique" describe not only the project, but also its organizational *system*. The resources assigned to a project do not usually make up a permanent functional unit, but are linked together in a constantly changing and evolving way.

THE PROJECT CHARTER

Many activities and documents are part of a project. The project charter is both one of the first and one of the most important. It is the primary agreement between the organization requesting a product or service and the organization providing that product or service. The charter identifies the project stakeholders and the project team's roles, responsibilities, and accountabilities. In other words, it's about who will do what for whom.

The project manager should develop the project charter in cooperation with the project sponsor. However, it is not uncommon for the project manager to draft the charter for the sponsor's signature. The charter ensures clear communication about what is to be accomplished, the timeframe in which it will be completed, and the resource support that the project team can expect. The charter provides an overview created at the project's initiation—prior to any detailed planning—and is approved by the key stakeholders.

It provides a brief description of the scope of the project and its objectives. Detailed specifications will be developed later after the charter is approved. Because the project charter typically becomes the basic reference document for large and/or complex projects, it also should discuss how the project will be structured and the processes for mitigating potential risks, resolving issues, and managing project changes.

There are some generally accepted components that a project charter should contain. We have compiled an outline of typical items that should be included (see Figure 2.1), but the size and complexity of the project will dictate the amount of detail for each of the entries. Your organization may have a template for constructing a project charter. If not, you may have to create a charter from scratch. We recommend that even a small project list some information for each of the standard headings shown in Figure 2.1, even if that information only cites a standard procedure.

Charters for large and complex projects undoubtedly will require the use of brief summaries and references to other documents that contain the detailed information. Charters for such projects also may contain information that could be considered to be a part of the project planning that is completed after the initial project is approved. Examples include a Gantt chart, work breakdown structure, organizational breakdown structure, risk analysis and management, project control methodologies (including required progress reporting), quality control activities, plans for project support activities such as training and documentation assistance, project facilities and resource requirements, required interim approvals, and change control procedures. While these elements are project requirements, they more logically may be shown in the project charter as planning deliverables.

PROJECT LIFE CYCLES

The term *cycle* probably became popular because most projects follow a very general pattern of investigation, approval, definition, resource assignment, implementation, and termination. It's almost certain that the term will continue to be used, although

I. Details of the project sponsor

    A. Name, title, authority

    B. Authorization signature(s) (may be at beginning or end of project)

II. Introduction

    A. Background required to understand why the project is being undertaken

    B. Purpose of charter document (generally provides authority to begin project work)

III. Overview of Project (in smaller projects, this section may be prepared in narrative form in one or a few paragraphs)

    A. Purpose of project

    B. Scope encompassed

    C. Objectives to be achieved and project deliverables

    D. Project manager and project team members

    E. Dependencies outside the project manager's control

    F. Method for determining when project is complete

    G. Unsettled issues

IV. Project timeframe

    A. Expected start date

    B. Expected final deliverable date

V. Expected cost of the project

    A. Materials

    B. Personnel

    C. Subcontract work

FIGURE 2.1   Essential Charter Elements

we believe that *life span* technically would be a more appropriate description. Your organization either may have a standardized life cycle or may allow each project team to select the life cycle their project will follow.

There have been many approaches to defining a generally accepted project life span. They all attempt to provide some standardization to the very difficult process of including all necessary elements of a successful project. Sometimes generally accepted life cycles emerge for a particular industry. For example, several industry groups have established accepted standards that provide a structure for the processes of the software development life cycle from conception through termination.

The International Organization for Standardization (ISO)/ International Engineering Consortium (IEC) 12207, created by committees of national representatives, and IEEE/EIA 12207, created by the Institute of Electrical and Electronics Engineers (IEEE) and the Electronics Alliance Industry (EIA), were developed with some of the same leadership and share the same life cycle process. The documents are very similar, with IEEE/EIA incorporating ISO/ IEC 12207 and adding a foreword, a series of annexes, and much more extensive guidance. The ISO/IEC standard is voluntarily followed by businesses in the United States, while the IEEE/EIA standard may be required for companies doing business with the Department of Defense (DoD).

The Simple Stages

We're all familiar with the age-old argument about how much time we should spend between planning the project and doing the project. This basic debate is illustrated in Figure 2.2. The first depiction follows the thoughts "Do we waste our precious time planning?" and "We need to get started on the necessary work right away." The second depiction illustrates the idea that if your plan is thoughtful and complete, it will take less time to deliver.

We often hear the familiar exhortation, "Plan your work, and work your plan," but how much time do we actually devote to

a. Typical allocation of time between planning and doing

b. Recommended allocation of time between planning and doing

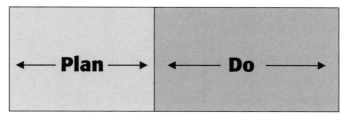

FIGURE 2.2   A Time for Planning, a Time for Doing

planning? Hoping to reduce the constant variations normally encountered in meeting customer requirements, W. Edwards Deming originated a cycle for business planning and continuous improvement that is relevant for projects and is described in some detail by Henry Neave (1990, 143). Deming's cycle is commonly called the PDCA Cycle because it contains four primary elements: Plan, Do, Check, and Act (see Figure 2.3). Attention to feedback, an essential element for all projects, is how the model is applied in projects.

A More Comprehensive Approach

One traditional pattern in software development projects is called the *waterfall* approach. The approach got its name because the activity cascades down a single line. The idea was to construct the software product with the same methodology used for hard products—a serial process (see Figure 2.4). One of the major

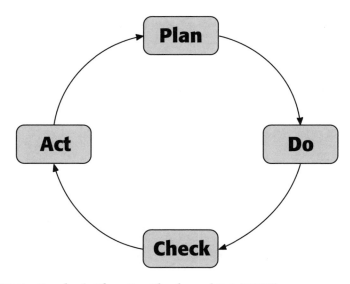

FIGURE 2.3   Deming's Plan, Do, Check, and Act (PDCA)

problems with this approach is that most projects require some iterative or review activities between stages and do not proceed continuously down the waterfall process. For many years, the software industry has been evolving the process to move from the waterfall model to a more modern, iterative development.

An alternative approach that overcomes the lack of iterations in the typical waterfall model is the *spiral* development model. Barry Boehm (1988, 64) described this concept for a software development project, but it can be applied to any project that requires iterative stages. Each iteration in this model provides increasing capability. This concept is shown in Figure 2.5.

The model is divided into four quadrants representing the major phases of the management process: *Determine Objectives, Evaluate Alternatives, Develop/Verify,* and *Plan Next Phases.* Beginning at the center of the spiral and moving clockwise, each transverse goes through each of the four management processes (resulting in the four prototypes) with increasing detail added at each loop. One caveat about the use of a spiral model is that you must limit

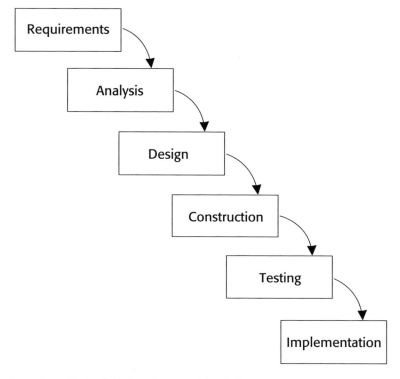

FIGURE 2.4   Waterfall Development Model

the number of cycles or the project will just keep going around in circles. As a project manager, especially if you tend to be a perfectionist, you need to learn the phrase, "it's good enough!"

There is often a conflict between those who would like to have a complete and detailed plan before any activity is started and those who would use an iterative approach, with details only for the beginning of the project. For a large project utilizing EVMS, it will be very difficult to plan using the same level of detail over the entire project's duration.

Minimum Life Cycle Requirements

Regardless of the model used, it is helpful in the planning stage to divide the project into phases. Along with a *controlling* function

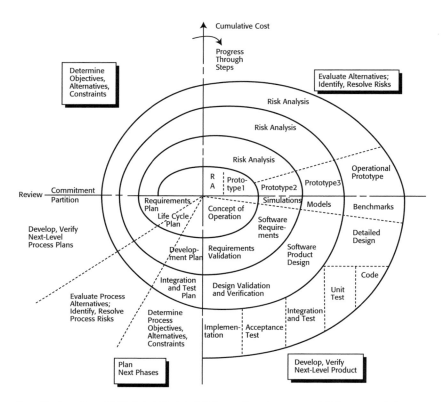

From Boehm, Barry W. "A Spiral Model of Software Development and Enhancement." *Computer* 21 (1988), no. 5: 61–72. © 1988, IEEE. Reprinted with permission.

FIGURE 2.5   Boehm's Spiral Development

that runs throughout the project, the four commonly accepted phases for the project life cycle are:

1. *Initiation:* the concept and initiation phase
2. *Planning:* the design and development phase
3. *Execution:* the implementation or construction phase
4. *Closeout:* the commissioning or termination phase.

It is important to note that each of these phases can be sub-phased using the same four phases and the deconstruction can continue until you reach a desired level of detail. Almost all discussions on project life span insist that there be checkpoints at each phase for evaluation, proposed change, and approval for continuation. For your projects, you may choose one of the models we have discussed or create one of your own; however, as our foray into the world of project life span shows, you can't just dive in and do the work—even on a small project. That is where project management tools such as EVMS enter the picture.

EVMS PROJECTS

EVMS specifically uses a work breakdown structure (described in Chapter 5) to delineate the authorized work elements of a project into identifiable pieces. A *work package* refers to a deliverable at the lowest level of the work breakdown structure and describes a *work unit* or one element of work in the project. There is an interesting example of the term *work unit* in the breakdown of the very unusual distributed computing project for the SETI program, which searches for signals of extraterrestrial life. Ksetiwatch is a monitoring tool that logs and manages all the sessions that are assigned to home computers for the project participants. They appropriately call these participant sessions work units (SETI@home 2004).

Of course, in a book on earned value that has a great deal to do with metrics, the importance of project measurements must be emphasized early in our discussion. You've certainly heard the expressions, "what gets measured gets done" or "you can't manage what you can't measure." People always find a way to deal with the way they are being measured, so it is most important to have measurements that will promote desired rather than dysfunctional behavior.

We need measurements in order to understand how well we are meeting the estimates for all projects. We need to measure—even if it is done informally—progress in *time* (schedule), *cost* (budget), *scope* (requirements), and *quality* to know where we are and how close we are following the project plan. It is necessary to rely on metrics to communicate information, from the use of a simple three-color traffic light approach to a complete EVMS. We also use measurement information to help develop corrective actions when we are off track and to predict where we will be at the end of the project.

In general, and especially with EVMS, a metric used to communicate progress may not be the best metric for developing corrective action plans. Measurements are designed to provide a basis for decisions and are reported to project owners so they can make priority and resource allocation decisions. The same measures are seldom useful in making corrective-action decisions on project work. Very often a metric will tell us where we are, but will not give us any indication of what to do.

Metrics cannot replace experience and good judgment. Poor project management will generate poor EVMS data. Just as costs cannot be reduced by focusing on the costs instead of focusing on the processes that generate the costs, EVMS metrics cannot be improved by trying to directly influence the metrics. Instead, you must focus on the project processes that generate the metrics.

THE PROJECT MANAGEMENT OFFICE

The use of project management processes for accomplishing more of the work of an organization is rapidly increasing. This concept has become know by such names as *managing by project* or *enterprise project management.* A slightly different concept, *project portfolio management,* is about managing all the projects in the organization; however, that does not mean that the organization is managed by projects. Many organizations have adopted an organizational concept called the *project management office* (PMO) to deal with the growing phenomenon of project portfolio management. The basic functions of the PMO are summarized in Figure 2.6.

If you are involved in establishing or operating a PMO, you should be aware that not everyone will appreciate the benefits of such an office. Be sure to publicize the PMO's mission as one that supports the entire organization and will not serve merely as the project police. In trying to address all concerns up front, be aware that you may be required to deal with different and sometimes

Project Management Capability	Business Process Coordination	Project Priorities	Business Metrics
• Project Management Practices • Project Management Maturity	• Strategic View • Goal Alignment • Business Collaboration	• Business Priorities • Resource Application • Leverage Skills	• Progress Reporting • Performance Feedback • Customer Satisfaction

FIGURE 2.6 Project Management Office Functions

very personal agendas. To counteract these forces, the PMO must have firm senior management commitment and support.

A team of senior level representatives from each functional area, with representation by the PMO, is the control behind *project portfolio management* (PPM). This team sets the policies that the PMO will follow. One of the biggest challenges to successful project management is that the project resources are most often owned by various functional departments and not by the project managers. It is easier to apply these resources to the most strategic projects if there is a portfolio management process in place.

An often-unrecognized challenge is managing the number of projects that the organization will have active at any given time. The prevailing management thought is that the more projects there are in the pipeline, the busier everyone will be and the more projects will be completed. Whenever an opportunity arises, it is tempting to start a project right away; once it is started, everyone involved will be pressured to keep the project active by reporting its progress.

There is a great deal of anecdotal evidence that strongly indicates that when resources are stretched, efficiency and effectiveness are drastically reduced. In general, the more projects there are in the pipeline, the longer it will take for any one project to finish because resources are rarely sufficient to complete work on one task or project without interruption.

A very important function of PPM is the selection, prioritization, and termination of projects. A balanced view from outside the project management function (including the PMO) can concentrate on potential overall value and control the number of projects in order to better accomplish resource utilization and quicker returns. An analysis from a PPM team of the strategic value of projects will eliminate most of the parochial interests that are too often used as selection criteria.

The PPM team may use a risk/benefit grid to be more selective and to ensure a balanced project selection. Figure 2.7 illustrates a simple risk/benefit decision grid with sample projects located at various points within the grid. A continuing risk/benefit analysis should be made for each project after every major phase. Early termination can be as valuable as appropriate selection and initiation.

There is a great deal of software available to help both with PPM and enterprise project management. An Internet search on either term will provide voluminous data about these vital components of project management.

	High Benefit	Low Benefit

L o w R i s k	X
	
	     X
	BEST
	
	     X
		X
		
		X

H i g h R i s k	X	X WORST

FIGURE 2.7   Simple Risk/Benefit Grid

PROJECT MANAGEMENT MATURITY

Public literature and the media abound with personal improvement schemes. We all want to be better at something—our appearance, our job performance, our relationships—something. You probably want to be a better project manager or you wouldn't be reading this book! Organizations, too, should have a plan to continuously improve their ability to gather the right measurements, construct realistic plans, and exploit their constraints.

Several tools and programs offer guidance in improving an organization's project management maturity. They are designed to improve an organization's processes from an unpredictable, sometimes chaotic, state to a disciplined process of continuous improvement. Most of the models include four basic steps:

1. An early learning phase
2. The integration of lessons learned with processes
3. A reengineering of the business processes
4. Moving to a new phase of maturity.

A detailed explanation of improvement programs is beyond the scope of this book, so we have provided the following list if you wish to investigate further:

- "Organizational Project Management Maturity Model (OPM3™)" (Project Management Institute 2003). The standard details *Knowledge, Assessment,* and *Improvement* elements and probably is the most comprehensive treatment for projects.
- "Capability Maturity Model® (SW-CMM®) for Software" (Software Engineering Institute 2004). The stages in this model are *Initial, Repeatable, Defined, Managed,* and *Optimizing.* The SW-CMM® has been incorporated into a new Software Engineering Institute model called CMMI® (Capability Maturity Model Integration).
- "Project Management Maturity Model" (Crawford 2001, 210). Strategies are presented to facilitate the implementation of efficient project management systems to increase the level of organizational improvement and maturity.

- "Getting Started with the Baldrige National Quality Program" (Baldrige National Quality Program 2003). The program presents steps for *Assessment, Action Planning,* and *Implementation* and sets out criteria for performance excellence.
- "ISO 9000 Quality Management Principles" (International Organization for Standardization 2004). This is a family of standards in which most of the standards are highly specific, but are considered generic management system standards because they can be applied across almost all sectors of business, industry, and technology.
- "Parkinson's Law and Its Implications for Project Management" (Gutierrez and Kouvelis 1991). This stochastic model using Parkinson's Law models the deadline effect on project management.

The objective of all of these models is to continually enhance the delivery processes of the organization with the goal of reaching a consistent level of success.

THE PROJECT MANAGER

Successfully managing a project has a set of very demanding requirements, including organizational ability, communication skills, leadership, persistence, consistency, hard work, and a *system* (think EVMS). Too often, we expect the best technical person in a particular area to be the most capable of managing a project in that area. It is true that technical knowledge may be required for a project, but that knowledge does not necessarily have to be possessed by the project manager, who must exhibit all the skills of a successful salesperson, a disarming negotiator, a clear communicator, and a charismatic leader. A perfect example is being able to coach a winning athletic team made up of individual stars.

The most important characteristic for a project manager is goal orientation. All human beings have an innate desire to achieve goals—even our games have goals. Numerous journal articles and books have been written on the subject. One such a book is even called *The Goal: A Process of Ongoing Improvement* (Goldratt and Cox 1992). Establishing a baseline in EVMS has very practical benefits for that project's goals. Beyond the obvious benefits, working toward a goal is a major motivational factor for the project team. Locke and Latham developed this idea in their goal setting theory (Locke et al. 1990).

For additional information, refer to *Human Resource Skills for the Project Manager* (Verma and Thamhain 1996), which provides a quick look at thumbnail descriptions of some motivation theories, or check the website established by Chun Wei Choo, a faculty member at the University of Toronto (Choo 2003).

One of the project manager's greatest challenges is dealing with many different people both inside and outside the organization. To further complicate matters, some of them will be managers of functional areas who control resources that impact the project. The project manager's degree of power and authority will depend to a great extent on the organizational structure.

Organizational structures are generally considered to be *functional, matrixed, project-oriented*, or some combination of the three. Of course, the project manager will find the most organizational power in project-oriented structures. (Organizational structures will be covered in detail in Part III when we discuss EVMS Criterion 2.)

A Personal Observation of Authority

We were coming back into port from our short cruise in the Caribbean and the captain had invited us to the bridge to watch the docking maneuvers. A local harbor captain came out to actually dock the ship because he was familiar with the nuances of the harbor and also with the tug operators who were helping with the many small and careful adjustments that had to be made to bring such a large ship into the dock. At first, when the local captain barked an order, the ship's crew did not move until the ship's captain repeated it. After a short time, the crew began responding almost immediately to the local captain even though the ship's captain continued to repeat the orders. It was interesting to observe the nuances of the shift and change in authority in a real-life situation.

THE PROJECT TEAM

When you have the authority to choose team members, you must be very careful to resist selection by reputation alone. Sometimes personal reputations are developed at the expense of others. Remember that your project will not be evaluated on the reputation or popularity of its team members, but on its results. Herb Brooks, the coach of the U.S.A. 1980 Olympic gold medal hockey team, often said that he did not want the "best" players—he wanted the "right" players.

A manager once told us that the ideal player has four traits: intelligence, professional skills, a pioneering spirit, and a hint of excellence in innovation and creativity. Having team members with diversity in both their work background and skills will foster your team's inventiveness and creativity. In today's more competitive marketplace, the old ways of working no longer ensure success.

For all team members to be on the same page, the project manager must communicate with them and not just establish some rules. The project's mission statement is a perfect example. The team must understand what it is trying to accomplish; therefore, it is necessary to hold straight-to-the-point discussions of the project's objectives and what will be required to accomplish those objectives. Some questions that need to be asked and answered are:

- Why are they on the team?
- What are they individually expected to accomplish?
- How must they operate differently?

You may find it useful to construct a team charter establishing the team's operating assumptions and rules.

In our efforts to improve team performance, we have spent a substantial amount of time looking at the problems experienced by teams. If you are interested in learning more about teams, we recommend that you look at Lencioni's *Five Dysfunctions of a Team* in which he lists absence of trust, fear of conflict, lack of commitment, avoidance of accountability, and inattention to results as the most significant problems in team effectiveness (2002,

240). Kerzner (2003) and Flannes and Levin (2001) have some interesting material in their chapters on resolving conflict for project managers that you will find very helpful. For a more positive approach, try Glickman's *Optimal Thinking* (2002).

One more term, *expectation*, must be mentioned. Although you will not usually find this term in project management journals, we think it is one of the most important aspects of team leadership. Our good friend, Harry Morgan, coached a very successful high school football team for many years. His secret was not hard-driving discipline, expert football strategy, or rigorous conditioning (although they were also part of his philosophy); his teams executed well because that was what he expected.

Joe Batten—author, speaker, trainer, one of the authors' mentors, and the person who created the U.S. Army tagline, "Be all you can be"—often said that the finest gift we can give another person is a stretching expectation of excellence. One of his numerous publications that we refer to often is an autographed copy of *Expectations and Possibilities* (Batten 1990).

> This chapter is the deliverable of the authors' own "mission impossible"—to summarize in one chapter all the basics concerning projects, project managers, and project teams. While each of these topics has been the subject of entire books, it has been our primary objective to alert you, as a project manager, to topics and sources that you might like to explore further.

In addition to the references mentioned in this chapter, we would like to recommend the following sources for your future study and development:

- Adams, J., and John R. Adams. *Principles of Project Management.* Newtown Square, PA: Project Management Institute, 1997.
- Meredith, Jack R., and Samuel J. Mantel, Jr. *Project Management: A Managerial Approach.* 5th ed. New York: John Wiley & Sons, 2003.

- Project Management Institute. 2000/2004 (3rd. ed.). *A Guide to the Project Management Body of Knowledge (PMBOK® Guide)*. Newtown Square, PA: Project Management Institute.
- Verma, Vijay K. *Organizing Projects for Success.* Newtown Square, PA: Project Management Institute, 1995.

DISCUSSION QUESTIONS

1. Discuss the following statement: "The processes of performing repetitive manufacturing processes and project management are entirely different."

2. In your experience, what is the major reason that a project succeeds in delivering on time, on budget, and with full specifications?

3. Are charters necessary for internal projects?

4. How long and detailed should a charter be?

5. Why is it important to understand project life cycles?

6. Describe your organization's project life cycle template. If none exists, how would you initiate one?

7. In general, what percentage of total project time should be consumed in planning the project?

8. Respond to the following statement: "Earned value primarily is a project management philosophy."

9. What are the major objectives of a project management office (PMO)?

10. What is the major purpose of project maturity models?

11. Discuss the following statement: "Project managers have power only through their position."

12. Describe your ideal project team.

Preparing To Use EVMS

Thus far, we have reviewed some general project management information that you may have already known. Even so, we hope you have picked up a few new ideas to store in your personal portfolio or were made aware of a few trails to investigate later.

Part II will present the basics of EVMS along with some rules and guidelines for implementation. Chapter 3 provides an overview of EVMS—what's good, what's not so good, and a big-picture view of the 32 criteria. In Chapter 4, you will find some caveats, cautions, and the nuts and bolts of a full-blown EVMS implementation that conforms to all 32 criteria.

CHAPTER 3

Earned Value Project Management: An Overview

Because of the combination of the importance of critical projects, the ever-increasing speed required for completion, and the notorious failures in project management, there is a genuine need for dependable, objective information. Top management depends on project progress reports and projections of end-of-project results to make vital decisions. EVMS arose from these needs and is a valuable, objective process. This chapter focuses on the system's origins, benefits, and deficiencies.

REQUIREMENTS

The U.S. government was instrumental in the development of EVMS and many departments require its use on federally funded projects. For example:

It is NASA policy to apply Earned Value Management (EVM) to NASA contracts to ensure that contractor management systems provide the contractor and the Government program and project managers with accurate data from which to make responsible management decisions. EVM is a commonly used performance measurement tool for program and project managers that integrates cost, schedule, and technical performance to enable effective program planning and control. (National Aeronautics and Space Administration 2002)

That quotation is the first paragraph of a directive issued by the National Aeronautics and Space Administration on its website in 2002. In the same year, the U.S. Office of the Secretary of Defense issued an interim guidebook to govern project contracts and their controls. A statement in section C2.9 states that, unless waived by the Milestone Decision Authority, the program manager[1] "shall require that the contractors' management information systems used in planning and controlling contract performance meet the Earned Value Management Systems guidelines . . . ." (Department of Defense 2002, 192). The guidelines do not require the contractor to change its systems; the contractor simply must prove that it complies with the EVMS criteria.

The Department of Defense (DoD) guidebook thoroughly defines when EVMS must be used:

> The PM shall apply EVMS guidelines on applicable contracts within acquisition, upgrade, modification, or materiel maintenance programs, including highly sensitive classified programs, major construction programs, and other transaction agreements. EVMS guidelines shall apply to contracts executed with foreign governments, project work performed in Government facilities, and contracts by specialized organizations such as the Defense Advanced Research Projects Agency. EVMS guidelines shall apply to research, development, test, and evaluation contracts, subcontracts, other transaction agreements, and intra-Government work agreements with a value of $73 million or more (in FY 2000 constant dollars), or procurement or operations and maintenance contracts, subcontracts, other transaction agreements, and intra-Government work agreements with a value of $315 million or more (in FY 2000 constant dollars).

Obviously, the U.S. government is a strong proponent of EVMS. One must not infer, however, that EVMS is useful only in a military

---

[1] The Department of Defense uses the term "program manager" to designate an individual who manages one or more contractor projects. The abbreviation "PM" can refer to either a program manager or a project manager.

or government environment. The use of this internal control system has equal merit in the commercial world and it is highly valuable in successfully managing an entire portfolio of projects.

EVMS WAS *REALLY* NEEDED

To succeed in our current accelerating environment, projects must be completed in record time to take advantage of marketing and other windows of opportunity. However, public reports of project results are not encouraging. Too frequently we read about projects that are dismal failures—they are over their budget by a large amount, the time overrun is measured in months or even years, and the final product of the project (if it emerges at all) lacks some of the planned features or has unexpected performance failures.

In light of these failings, you might ask the same question as Schulte (2004) asks in the title of her white paper, "Is Poor Management a Crime?" Her answer was the same as ours, "Yes, it could be." The Sarbanes-Oxley Act of 2002 (SOX) has some very stringent requirements for internal controls and current reporting of any material changes in the internal control of an organization's financial operations. To fully comply with the intent of SOX, organizations must have detailed cost and schedule measurements and senior management must have complete, accurate, and timely information on major projects. EVMS can help in providing these controls and fulfilling those reporting requirements.

Companies that claim that their projects are never late are probably referring to the latest baseline due date (which may be considerably later than the original date) or are allowing such long task times in their original project plans that the project takes far longer than it should. Thankfully, there are project successes that inspire us to continue examining our processes and searching for better methodologies. EVMS is one methodology that instills confidence that project managers are providing valid information on in-process projects.

As we mentioned in Chapter 1, the U.S. government in the 1960s commissioned a predecessor system composed of 35 requirements that was modified into today's 32 criteria. The objective of the first system, Cost/Schedule Control Systems Criteria (C/SCSC), was to provide a common basis for reporting and decision making by both the project initiator and the project contractor. The project initiators were seeking current and reliable information on project progress; a valid relationship between cost, schedule, and technical requirements; and information provided in a summarized, but meaningful, format.

EARNED VALUE DEFINED

The term *earned value* has been used and applied in many different ways, but the term *Earned Value Management System* has been universally accepted as being a management system that, at a minimum, complies with the 32 criteria as set forth in the American National Standards Institute Guidelines, ANSI/EIA-748-1998. Compliance with the EVMS criteria has historically been required by the Department of Defense, such as in DoD Instruction 5000.2 (Department of Defense 2003, 28), and has been mandated in many cases by agencies such as the Department of Energy (DOE), the National Aeronautics and Space Administration (NASA), and the Office of Management and Budget (OMB).

It is fairly obvious that the metrics in EVMS were developed from the traditional standard cost system measurements. EVMS compares cost, budget, and schedule components to produce cost and schedule variances in dollar-denominated metrics. It is a way to express performance measures and variances in comparable financial terms. Of the 32 EVMS criteria, approximately 40 percent establish organizational structure, project planning, and change control requirements; approximately 60 percent involve accounting for costs by way of budgeting, reporting, and forecasting. There are four primary measurements: the first launches the expectations of the project's performance and the other three report periodic progress and forecast end results.

EVMS METRICS

EVMS metrics play an increasingly important role because project management is now recognized as a desirable professional skill. Many organizations require project management applicants to be certified by a recognized professional organization. To acquire any professional project proficiency designation, such as the Project Management Institute's Project Management Professional certification, you will have to master certain metrics. To understand the EVMS criteria, you must understand these metrics.

Four Primary Metrics

There are four primary EVMS metrics.

Measure 1: Budget at Completion or Total Value

The first EVMS measure, *budget at completion* (BAC) or *total value* (TV), is prepared in the planning stage before the project is begun. (See Chapter 8 for a detailed discussion on the preparation of this important metric.) BAC is developed by examining all the work to be accomplished on the project and the estimated cost of each portion of work. The budget and the project schedule then become the baseline against which the project progress is measured. Remember that this metric is established before work is begun.

As work on the project progresses, EVMS requires periodic status reports. At the status point, the three periodic measures used to report the project status and to derive other report metrics include (1) the original cost estimate for the work scheduled to have been completed, (2) the original cost estimate for the work actually completed, and (3) the actual cost of the completed work.

Measure 2: Budgeted Cost of Work Scheduled

At each status reporting date, the portion of the project's total value or BAC corresponding to the elapsed time from the beginning of the project to the status date details both the work that should have been completed and the costs that should have been incurred. The U.S. Department of Defense calls this subset of BAC the *budgeted cost of work scheduled* (BCWS); others refer to it as *planned value* (PV). BCWS or PV is the dollar value of the work that was scheduled for completion by this point in the project's schedule.

Measure 3: Budgeted Cost of Work Performed or Earned Value

The second periodic measurement shows the original estimated costs for work actually completed. Its formal name is *budgeted cost of work performed* (BCWP), but it is commonly referred to as *earned value* (EV). This can be the most confusing of the basic measures because it uses both an actual measurement and a budget measurement. It is a measure of the work actually performed during the status period, but at its planned (budgeted) amount— not its actual cost. Both EV and PV represent cumulative values, but this additional label is seldom used.

Measure 4: Actual Cost of Work Performed or Actual Cost

The actual costs incurred from the beginning of the project represent the third periodic measure. Note that costs incurred (direct or indirect costs used on the project) are not the same as costs paid in cash. The formal name still used in government circles is *actual cost of work performed* (ACWP), but industry people generally refer to it as *actual cost* (AC)[2]. Like the other two basic periodic status measures, this is a cumulative amount.

To summarize, the four basic measurements are BAC (or TV), BCWS (or PV), BCWP (or EV), and ACWP (AC). Two other major reporting metrics that are derived from these basic measures are cost and schedule variances. The *cost variance* (CV) is the difference between the budgeted cost of work actually performed (EV) and the actual cost of that work (AC). The *schedule variance* (SV) is the difference between the budgeted cost of work scheduled for completion by the status date (the planned value) and the

---

[2]For consistent terminology, we could call this Actual Value (AV); it is equivalent to Actual Cost.

budgeted cost of the work that was actually completed by the status date (the earned value). In addition, an *estimate to complete* (ETC) and *estimate at completion* (EAC) can be calculated; those will be more easily explained after a look at the standard cost system and the calculation of ratios.

Analogy to the Standard Cost System

A perfect analogy to earned value analysis is found in a standard cost system. If you have ever had a management accounting class, you probably were exposed to the bar or triangle approach to calculating variances in a standard cost system. This triangle approach can be applied to compute earned value variances as shown in Figure 3.1.

Calculation of Ratios

The cost and schedule variances are absolute amounts that are influenced by the size of the project and thus are difficult to compare with performance on other projects. Converting the variances into schedule and cost ratios standardizes them.

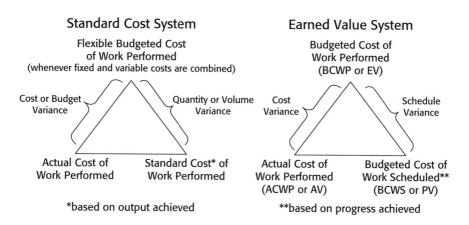

FIGURE 3.1   Standard Cost System and EVMS Triangles

The *schedule performance index* (SPI) is the result of dividing the earned value (at the top of the earned value triangle illustrated in Figure 3.1) by the planned value (bottom right of the earned value portion of Figure 3.1); the *cost performance index* (CPI) is the result of dividing the earned value by actual costs. SPI and CPI enable comparisons across projects. Further, these two indices, or ratios, are included in formulas used to produce a host of other metrics that provide estimates of total cost at completion and also are used in an index ratio that measures additional effort required to complete the project that can also be used to compare performance on many different projects.

The SPI, therefore, shows schedule completion on the measurement date (the earned value) relative to planned completion by that date. A ratio result of 1 would indicate that EV and PV are identical. Any amount greater than 1 indicates a favorable performance.

The CPI indicates the cost that should have been incurred for the project portion completed—the earned value relative to the costs actually incurred as of the status date. A ratio producing a number greater than 1 would indicate favorable performance (compared to the baseline budget), while a ratio less than 1 would mean that actual costs are higher than were expected for the work completed.

In an EVMS, we never make any comparisons across the bottom of the triangle: ACWP and BCWS (actual cost or value and planned value). Although this variance makes sense in certain environments, such as in standard cost systems where the standard costs applied during the period are computed for work actually completed, it is uninformative and can be misleading for projects. This *total variance* merely indicates that actual costs do not equal the amounts budgeted as of the time elapsed since the project started and is meaningless without knowing how much of the project's work has been completed.

Two pair-wise comparisons of the three basic performance measurements provide the variances that are used to compute important status metrics as the project progresses. Formulas for the most important of these metrics are shown below.

$$\textbf{\textit{Schedule Performance Index (SPI)}} = \frac{Earned\ Value}{Planned\ Value} \text{ or } \frac{EV}{PV}$$

$$\textbf{\textit{Cost Performance Index (CPI)}} = \frac{Earned\ Value}{Actual\ Value} \text{ or } \frac{EV}{AC\ (or\ AV)}$$

Estimate to Complete (ETC) =

$$\frac{Budget\ at\ Completion - Earned\ Value}{Cost\ Performance\ Index} \text{ or } \frac{BAC - EV}{CPI},$$

sometimes modified to show the impact of SPI as well:

$$\frac{BAC - EV}{CPI * SPI}$$

Estimate at Completion (EAC) (revised total final cost)= *Actual Cost + Estimate to Complete or AC + ETC*

$$\textbf{\textit{To Complete Performance Index (TCI)}} = \frac{Budget\ for\ Remaining\ Work}{Estimated\ Cost\ of\ Remaining\ Work} \text{ or } \frac{BAC - EV}{EAC - AV}$$

Calculations Example

The Project: A status is taken at the end of week 2 for a 12-week project. The total planned budget for the project is $120,000 for work that is evenly spread over 12 weeks. The project staff has completed work that was scheduled to have been completed by half-way through the middle of week 2. Actual costs incurred to date on this project total $16,000.

BAC or TV = $120,000

AC = $16,000

$$EV = \frac{\$120,000}{12} \ (budget \ per \ week) * 1.5 \ \ (1\frac{1}{2} \ weeks) = \$15,000$$

$$PV = \frac{\$120,000}{12} * 2 \ \ = \$20,000$$

$CV = 15,000 - 16,000 = (\$1,000)$ (Unfavorable)

$$CPI = \frac{\$15,000}{\$16,000} = 0.9375$$
$$\text{(Less than 1, less than planned performance)}$$

$SV = \$15,000 - \$20,000 = (\$5,000)$
$$\text{(Unfavorable—schedule is slipping)}$$

$$SPI = \frac{\$15,000}{\$20,000} = 0.75 \text{ (Unfavorable)}$$

To Complete: Calculations that consider only the CPI provide the most optimistic estimates:

$$ETC = \frac{\$120,000 - \$15,000}{0.9375} = \$112,000$$

$EAC = \$16,000 + 112,000 = \$128,000$ ($8,000 more than the original estimate)

$$TCI = \frac{\$120,000 - \$15,000}{\$128,000 - \$16,000} = 0.9375 \text{ (Less than 1, = unfavorable)}$$

Alternative to Complete: Calculations that take into account both the CPI and the SPI provide the most pessimistic estimates:

$$ETC = \frac{\$120,000 - \$15,000}{0.9375 * 0.75} = \$149,333$$

$EAC = \$16,000 + \$149,333 = \$165,333$ ($45,333 more than the original estimate)

$$TCI = \frac{\$120,000 - \$15,000}{\$165,333 - \$16,000} = 0.703 \text{ (much more unfavorable than}$$

the optimistic estimates that considered only the CPI)

USING THE MEASUREMENTS

Calculating the metrics is only a small part of managing an EVMS project. Calculations and measurements can be used in many different ways and accomplish a variety of objectives.

The Challenge of Meeting All Targets

Wanting to be successful, project managers simultaneously want to look good on both cost and schedule metrics. Textbooks and earned value implementation research usually warn that a cost variance and a schedule variance should never be "netted" together. One source specifically cautions that, "A poor cost variance combined with a good schedule variance does not mean that everything is all right" (Humphreys 2002, 675).

Since meeting the schedule may be critical to the customer—meaning we must meet SPI targets—project teams may be encouraged to spend as much time as necessary to meet SPI targets. At the same time, meeting cost targets is probably critical to the company responsible for completing the project. Therefore, project teams also are pressured to spend as few hours as necessary to meet CPI targets. Project managers are expected to expend the necessary resources to meet SPI targets while at the same time feeling strong pressure to use as few resources as necessary to meet CPI targets.

This conflict between the two metrics typically leads to alternating compromises, as shown in the abbreviated cause-effect diagram of an earned value system (see Figure 3.2).

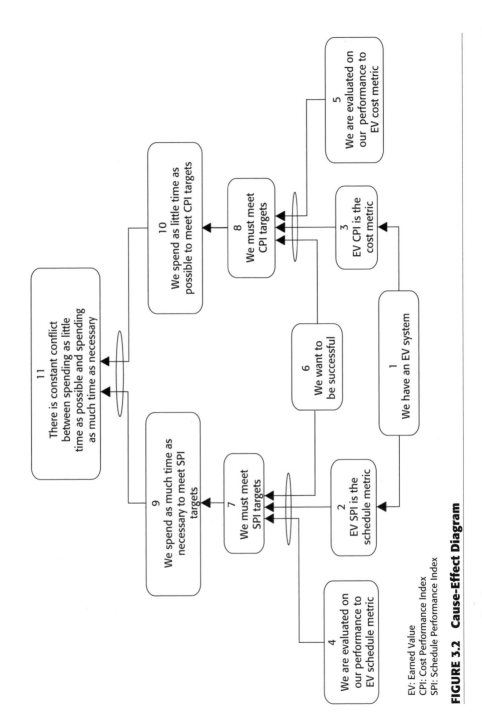

FIGURE 3.2 Cause-Effect Diagram

EV: Earned Value
CPI: Cost Performance Index
SPI: Schedule Performance Index

W. Edwards Deming emphasized the importance of distinguishing between two kinds of variation: *common cause variation* (variation within the capability of a system to repeatedly produce results—a system in control) and *special cause variation* (variation beyond the capability of a system to repeatedly produce results, usually variation with causes outside the system—an out-of-control situation). Attempting to "fix" common cause variation worsens the results by overcorrecting an in-control process to an out-of-control state. The same concept applies to projects. That is, responding to small variances by making project changes very likely will result in decreased project performance.

Obviously, there are possible tradeoffs between CPI and SPI. For example, to improve a poor schedule performance, additional costs might be incurred (overtime, acquisition of additional resources, etc.). Another scenario is that the schedule might be put on hold until prior resource commitments have been fulfilled, thereby reducing the need for additional costs but resulting in schedule slippage. The attempt to keep both measures on track instead of making appropriate decisions to complete the project frequently results in conflicted behavior.

Attempting to keep on schedule, as reflected in SPI, and stay within budget, as reflected in CPI, means that project managers will try to make both metrics look better by constantly adjusting behavior to garner better performance on each metric. Because of a tradeoff effect, focus on an unfavorable SPI (or CPI) naturally makes the CPI (or SPI) metric worse. The conflict between spending as few hours as possible and spending as many resources as necessary means that attempting to improve both SPI and CPI simultaneously ensures that neither metric will improve.

Neither metric improves because the actions intended to make each metric look better means that shortcuts and temporary patches will quickly cause other problems. These activities make remaining project tasks even more difficult and the spiraling situation ultimately and inevitably results in failure to meet any of the targets.

Information and Motivation

We must have measurements to communicate progress, but an ideal indicator of performance may be especially difficult to find. Arrow (1971, 278) showed that all measures of performance are not equally easy to measure. Thus, performance metrics adopted by organizations are constrained by practicality and cost. It should not be surprising that all critical dimensions of project performance do not get measured and reported.

One Size Does Not Fit All

Robert Austin (1996, 216) partitions measurement into two categories: *motivational measurements*, which are explicitly intended to affect behavior, and *informational measurements*, which are used primarily for the information they convey. He maintains that informational measurements should be used to improve decisions and should not be used to affect behavioral changes.

Earned value metrics provide information to project owners but they may inadvertently affect the behavior of project team members attempting to perform to those metrics. In fact, it is as true today as when described by Flamholtz (1979, 71–84) that accounting measurements are simultaneously intended to facilitate multiple functions, including accountability, performance evaluation, and motivation, as well as provide information for decision making. This "one size fits all" objective of internal managerial accounting information must be questioned just as many analysts recently have questioned the appropriateness of one financial report for external users.

Managers who make decisions determined by their impact on the next quarter's results or annual report rather than the long-term health of the organization for all stakeholders have been severely criticized and punished by the market. Analogously, making project decisions based on an imperfect measurement system that does not measure all critical dimensions of project performance is detrimental to ongoing project process improvement, possibly to project completion, and certainly to project success.

Decision Metrics

In any event, there are some clear implications for any organization that implements EVMS. First, the earned value metrics that are a source of information to stakeholders must not be used to make project decisions. That means that the EV metrics must not be used to determine how work should proceed. Project decisions must be based on sound project management practices. Project team members must be motivated to complete a project as quickly as possible and at the lowest cost. Decisions must be made using real-time data and not based on historical data or the impact of the decision on data to be reported in the future.

A 1990 study by Beach illustrated that as early as 15 percent into a project, EV metrics can predict the ultimate completion date and project cost (Fleming and Koppelman 2000, 39). However, EV measures may not track closely with project performance early in the project. Therefore, management may have to be careful not to be too hasty in demanding corrective action if initial reports show unfavorable earned value variances. Management must avoid forcing project people into the destructive spiral of chasing improvement on one EV metric at the expense of another.

At the same time, some projects, for any number of reasons, will not deliver intended results. These projects should be killed early in order to release resources for more valuable work. Rarely are these failures the fault of the project teams and cancellation should not reflect unfavorably on individual performance.

Response to Measurements

Finally, organizations must be very aware of the behavioral responses to measurements and be extremely careful in designing performance evaluation systems. If Austin is correct, motivation and information metrics must be separated in order to minimize dysfunctional worker behavior. Establishing appropriate organization measurements is hard work and may require that management not be allowed access to all the information measures that the project staff needs in order to do its best work. There are no easy answers where performance evaluation is involved.

Management's not having access to all information possessed by workers might mean that management must place more reliance on the subjective judgment of supervisors and fellow employees.

WHY ALL THE INTEREST IN EVMS?

You should be getting a general feeling now for the mechanics of EVMS. At this point you probably are more interested in learning if EVMS really helps an organization. In the following sections you will find some published opinions along with a detailed illustration that demonstrates the value of EVMS.

Support for the Value of EVMS

Christensen (1998, 380) has published extensively in the area of earned value and cites 10 benefits of EVMS:

1. It is a single management control system that provides reliable data.
2. It integrates work, schedule, and cost into a work breakdown structure.
3. The associated database of completed projects is useful for comparative analysis.
4. The cumulative *cost performance index* (CPI) provides an early warning signal.
5. The schedule performance index provides an early warning signal.
6. The CPI is a predictor of the final cost of the project.
7. It uses an index-based method to forecast the final cost of the project.
8. The "to-complete" performance index allows evaluation of the forecasted final cost.
9. The periodic (e.g., weekly or monthly) CPI is a benchmark.
10. The management by exception principle can reduce information overload.

Schulte states, "EVMS is a set of best business practices, processes, and tools for enterprise project planning and control." She adds that, ". . . it provides an excellent means to establish and maintain internal processes and controls" (Schulte 2004, 1). Stephen Wake, Chair of the Earned Value SIG for the Association for Project Management in the United Kingdom, may be a bit biased, but in his EV booklet (2003) he implies that EVMS might solve a multitude of thorny problems. Besides the ones listed by Christensen above, Wake includes the ability to cancel an over-budget project with confidence when it is only 20 percent complete, quickly locate problems in reams of data, and standardize reports across budget programs. He believes that all these things taken together might allow competition in markets from which your organization is currently excluded.

With promises such as these, is it any wonder that organizations are seriously considering implementing earned value even if they aren't required to do so? Let's take a closer look.

Discussion of the Evidence

Companies are adopting EVMS for good reasons. The system requires a *work breakdown structure*, recognition of task dependencies and organizational responsibilities, a time-phased budget, and other formal planning and reporting procedures that constitute excellent elements of today's best practices in project management. Project status reporting has historically been overly optimistic and very subjective.

Subjective Project Reporting

Without some objective measure of performance, stakeholders (principals who cannot directly monitor the project progress) must rely on the subjective judgment of the project manager (agent of the principal who knows the details of the project's progress) who may be encouraged by optimism to report that everything is progressing as planned (on time, on budget) even if difficulties are requiring more time and money than planned. The manager may truly believe that a time and/or cost overrun can be made up later and does not want project work to be questioned or stopped. Therefore, it is not uncommon to report after one month of a three-month project that the project is "on time" and "on budget" if one-third of the total budget has been spent, regardless of how much project effort remains. In this way, the bad news may be delayed until it becomes obvious that the project has no possibility of successful completion.

The traditional accounting now used on many projects compares costs incurred to date with expected budgeted expenditures for the period since the project began (sometimes using cash flows but with no accrual accounting). With no connection to schedule completion, information content and predictive ability of the resulting variance are extremely low or nonexistent. That is, there are no answers to questions such as, "Are we ahead or behind schedule?" and "Will the project finish on time, within cost, and to specification?" For example, assuming a $208,000 project for a one-year time period, the cost/funding plan might look something like the one illustrated in Figure 3.3. The project should require $69,000 by the end of the first quarter, $108,000 by the end of the second quarter, $148,000 by the end of the third quarter, and $208,000 by the end of the project.

The executive management committee fully expects the project manager to stay within the limits of the $208,000 commitment and to continuously monitor performance during the life of the year-long project. At the end of the first quarter, when the plan called for an expenditure of $69,000, the actual expenditure was only $65,000. When asked if the project is behind schedule, the project manager quickly responds that the project is right on course (meaning that one-quarter of the one-year project has elapsed) and under budget by $4,000.

Another approach sometimes used is to compare actual costs incurred with the project's estimated total completion costs and thereby estimate the percentage completed. This is the standard accounting *percentage of completion* approach. Of course, the estimated cost of the project may change from period to period, but anecdotal evidence suggests that estimated total project cost is sticky and not readily adjusted. Also, a bottom-up approach to estimating the total cost of work yet to be completed is very time-consuming. It should be noted that using this percentage-of-

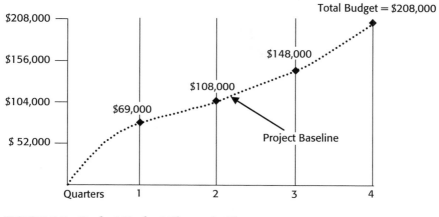

FIGURE 3.3   Project Budget Shown in Phases

completion approach and not adjusting the total cost would result in the assumption that the project is over 30 percent complete at the end of the first quarter.

A Better Way

To obtain more relevant information, costs incurred must be tied to schedule completion. Earned value management requires a time-phased budget baseline against which contract performance can be measured. Thus, earned value looks at not only planned and actual spending, but also scheduled work. To provide this detail, the project plan must include detailed tasks to be accomplished, estimated durations of the tasks, and a sequencing of the tasks.

A Gantt project network for the previous example is shown in Figure 3.4. The thick black line represents the critical path—the longest series of sequential tasks—requiring a total of 52 weeks to complete the project.

By the end of the first quarter, Tasks 1 and 3 should be completed, Task 2 should be about 14 percent complete, and Task 4 should be about 57 percent complete. Therefore, the anticipated

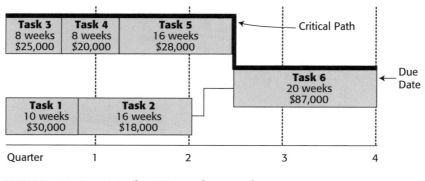

FIGURE 3.4   Gantt Project Network Example

expended budget by this point is approximately $69,000 [$25,000 + $30,000 + (.57 x $20,000) + (.14 x $18,000)]. The project manager reports, however, that while Tasks 1 and 3 have been completed, Task 2 has not been started, and only 20 percent of Task 4 has been completed. Assuming costs for each task after Tasks 1 and Task 3 are incurred uniformly over time, the project's earned value is $59,000 ($30,000 + $25,000 + .2*$20,000). Therefore, the project has earned $59,000, not the $65,000 actually spent. This situation is graphically illustrated in Figure 3.5.

It is clear that this project is *not* on course and under budget. The schedule variance is $10,000 unfavorable ($59,000 - $69,000); the cost variance is $6,000 unfavorable ($59,000 - $65,000); SPI is .86, meaning this project is running about 14 percent behind schedule; and CPI is .91, showing that the project is almost 10 percent over budget at the end of the first quarter. Further, based on progress to date, the estimate at completion is not $208,000 but somewhere between $228,571 and $265,781.

An earned value system provides objective measures of progress and enables some meaningful projections of future costs. Thus, project owners have access to performance data other than verbal assurances of managers intimately involved with the project. In addition, the planning, reporting, and control requirements of EVMS reflect good project management techniques.

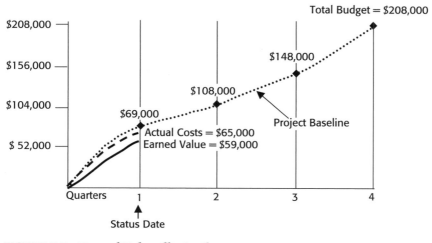

FIGURE 3.5   Earned Value Illustration

THE DARK SIDE

Like standard costs from which EV was developed, earned value metrics summarize past performance, compare actual results to those planned, and signal developing problems. However, earned value metrics do not unambiguously indicate appropriate actions that should be taken. EVMS variances, even more so than standard cost variances, do not report information that is sufficiently timely and transparent to all interested parties.

Some Missing Information

Consider the two projects illustrated in Figure 3.6. The projects have identical baselines and each task (block) requires the same time to complete and has the same planned value. The darkened blocks are those tasks that have been completed.

Both projects have the same earned value, the same SPI, and the same CPI, but which project is likely to be completed first? Other things being equal, the project plans in Figure 3.6 indicate that Project B will complete before Project A, which has seven

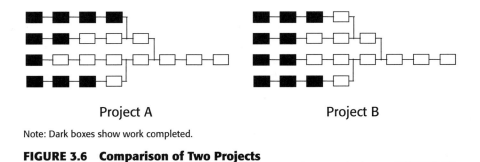

Project A   Project B

Note: Dark boxes show work completed.

FIGURE 3.6   Comparison of Two Projects

incomplete tasks on one path. EVMS metrics would not signal this situation. Earned value metrics must be related to a project's time-phased baseline.

The fact that the SPI must be compared to the project schedule to obtain an accurate picture of the project's true schedule position has been well known at least since the Department of Defense commissioned an Arthur D. Little Company study in the 1980s (Fleming and Koppelman 2000, 113–120). However, stakeholders receiving the earned value measures rarely have access to the detailed project plans. Most commonly, comparison of EV measures to the project plan is not a formal part of earned value metrics. Even if stakeholders have access to all project plans, they do not have the same information as the project manager and the proper corrective action is not obvious to either the stakeholders or the project manager.

None of the EVMS metrics that purport to reflect progress and remaining work actually correlate directly with completion of the project plan itself. While SPI and CPI are designed to measure cost and schedule deviations from the planned baseline, both indices incorporate the earned value metrics and both have components that are denominated in dollars. Therefore, SPI and CPI have the appearance of measuring progress on the project baseline. However, as pointed out by the Arthur D. Little Company's analysis and illustrated in Figure 3.6, the measures are susceptible to manipulation.

Resource managers control assignment of resources to projects. Once a project has begun, the resource manager can expect that the project manager will demand his or her share of the resources. A resource manager typically has to show weekly progress on all projects. Because EV metrics are not perfectly linked to the project's plan of work, when managers use EV to manage their projects, priorities between tasks on different paths and/or between projects are not always clear to either the resource manager or the project manager. A project easily may suffer delays due to the assignment of limited resources to noncritical tasks.

Although EV can provide some objective measures of performance, the dollar-aggregated project measurements can point neither to specific areas of good or poor performance nor to their causes. Without knowledge of the area of concern, remedial tactics cannot be undertaken or directed. If corrective action must be taken, other project management tools must be employed to identify problem areas and potential solutions.

Dysfunctional Behavior

Because of a basic disconnect between EVMS metrics and project operations and/or completion, and because project funding often is tied to EVMS performance, some project managers have developed certain EV coping mechanisms. These coping behaviors are an example of the impact of dysfunctional measures that Robert Austin (1996, 10) defines as "consequences of organizational actions that interfere with attainment of the spirit of stated intentions of the organization." He maintains that an incentive system becomes dysfunctional when it encourages people to take actions that reduce value to the customer below what it would have been without the incentive system. Further, Austin maintains that the main problem for most incentive plans is not measurement error but bias intentionally introduced by the people being measured. However, this bias need not be designed to deceive and may result merely from the conscious effort of people to do what they are being asked to do.

A HIGH LEVEL VIEW OF THE EVMS CRITERIA

The EVMS criteria are usually divided into five sections:

1. Organization
2. Planning and budgeting
3. Accounting considerations
4. Analysis and management reports
5. Revisions and data maintenance.

This division was intended to address basic management concepts; however, many management concepts will overlap this division of the criteria. The criteria are presented fully in Appendix A, but let's take an introductory look at them now by selecting a few key words from each criterion.

Organization

1. Define the work with a work breakdown structure.
2. Identify organizational structures.
3. Provide for integration of company processes and the program structure.
4. Identify the function for controlling overhead.
5. Provide integration that permits performance measurement from the work breakdown structure and the organizational structure.

Planning and Budgeting

6. Schedule the work with task sequence and interdependence.
7. Identify indicators of measurable progress.
8. Establish and maintain a time-phased budget baseline at the control account level.
9. Establish budgets with identification of significant cost elements.
10. Identify and establish budgets in discrete work packages within control accounts and identify far-term work in larger planning packages.
11. Ensure that the sum of the work package budgets and planning package budgets within a control account equals the control account budget.

12. Identify and control any work defined as level-of-effort.
13. Establish overhead budgets.
14. Identify management reserves and undistributed budget.
15. Ensure that the project's target cost equals the sum of all budgets and reserves.

Accounting Considerations

16. Record direct costs in a formal system.
17. Summarize direct costs from control accounts to the work breakdown elements.
18. Summarize direct costs from control accounts into the contractor's organizational elements.
19. Record all indirect costs.
20. Identify unit costs.
21. Provide accountability for a material accounting system.

Analysis and Management Reports

22. Generate management control information at the control account level.
23. Identify and explain differences between actual and planned schedule and cost performance.
24. Identify budgeted and applied indirect costs.
25. Summarize data and variances through program organization or work breakdown structures.
26. Implement managerial actions.
27. Revise estimates of cost at completion based on performance to date.

Revisions and Data Maintenance

28. Incorporate authorized changes.
29. Reconcile current budgets to prior budgets.
30. Control retroactive changes to records.
31. Prevent unauthorized revisions to the program budget.
32. Document changes to the performance measurement baseline.

Now that you have completed this chapter, you are well on your way to understanding EVMS. You will have the opportunity to practice your knowledge and ability with the sample problems in the Discussion Questions and Practice Calculations section.

Chapter 1 discussed how EVMS started, covering in detail its definition, evolution, and requirements. Many government agencies are strong proponents of EVMS and have defined the requirements for its use on their contracted projects. But the benefits of an objective status and reporting system go well beyond the contractual requirements.

The metrics of EVMS are based on a standard accounting system, but have their own nomenclature. The primary measures are:

1. *Budget at Completion (BAC) or Total Value (TV) of the project*—the original budget prepared at the initiation of the project.

2. *Budgeted Cost of Work Scheduled (BCWS) or Planned Value (PV)*—the dollar amount of the work that was planned to be completed by the date of the status report.

3. *Budgeted Cost of Work Performed (BCWP) or Earned Value (EV)*—the budgeted dollar amount of the work that has been completed by the date of the status report.

4. *Actual Cost of Work Performed (ACWP) or Actual Value (AV)*—the dollar amount incurred (charged to the project) by the date of the status report.

From these basic metrics, cost and schedule variances can be calculated to indicate project progress. The variances can be converted to ratios and indices to facilitate comparisons across projects. Further calculations then can be used to predict the final cost of the project. There are many challenges in preparing and using measurements and the project manager must be aware of their informational and motivational aspects, as well as the potential consequences.

No discussion of EVMS would be complete without presenting the positive and the negative. The system has a long list of benefits—notably the integration of work, schedule, and cost into a work breakdown structure and its predictive ability. EVMS "is a set of best business practices, processes, and tools for enterprise project planning and control" (Schulte 2004, 1). The dark side is that the metrics can be misleading without the employment of other good project management techniques. The chapter finishes with an overview of the 32 EVMS criteria.

DISCUSSION QUESTIONS AND PRACTICE CALCULATIONS

1. Is EVMS required on all government projects? Why or why not?

2. Name and describe the three points of the EVMS standard cost triangle.

3. Discuss the strengths and weaknesses of using the EVMS metrics.

Practice Calculations

Use Figure 3.7 to calculate EVMS metrics for the following test problems:

Plan at End of 2nd Quarter: Tasks 1, 3, 5 and 6 should be completed, Tasks 2 and 4 should be 96 percent complete, and Task 7 should be 51 percent complete.

Results at End of 2nd Quarter: Tasks 1, 3, 5, and 6 have been completed, Task 2 is 50 percent complete, Task 4 has not been started, and Task 7 is 10 percent complete. $137,500 has been charged to the project.

Calculate the following values (assume that all tasks incur costs uniformly over time):

1. At project initiation, what was the total projected cost of this project (BAC or TV)?

2. On the status date, what is the budgeted cost of work scheduled (BCWS or PV)?

3. What is the actual cost (AC or AV) on the status date?

4. What is the earned value (BCWP or EV) of this project on the status date?

5. Calculate the cost variance (CV) and the cost performance index (CPI).

6. Calculate the schedule variance (SV) and the schedule performance index (SPI)

7. Compute the "optimistic" and "pessimistic" estimate at completion (EAC)

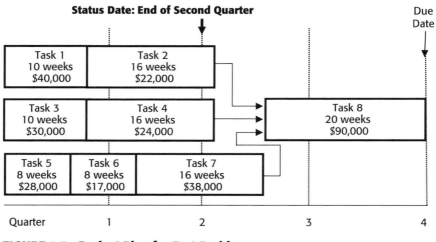

FIGURE 3.7   Project Plan for Test Problems

CHAPTER 4

Implementing EVMS

Toward the end of their very late project, we overheard a member of another project team say, *"We need to find that plan we made when the project was authorized."*

There are many great plans in file folders that have never been used. Projects often have difficulty not in their conception or planning, but in their implementation. This chapter presents information about EVMS implementations in general and government implementations in particular. The discussions will cover some basic considerations, detail some requirements, and provide a few hints, caveats, and helpful suggestions.

There are several reasons to implement an EVMS. Often, an organization must use EVMS because of contractual requirements with entities such as the Department of Defense (DoD) or other federal agencies. Other times, internal management would like the control and reporting mechanisms of an EV system. Your organization's requirements for implementation may differ significantly from those of other organizations. Depending on technology, processes, and procedures currently in place, some management systems will necessitate a great deal of change while others may satisfy the EV criteria well in their existing state.

In fact, many federal agencies analyze the extent of modification that must be made to an organization's system when EVMS is adopted. Their analysis indicates the maturity of the organization's management process. A mature system that conforms to the spirit of EVMS already captures cost and schedule performance data that satisfy the following five criteria:

1. Relates time-phased budgets to specific contract tasks and/or statements of work
2. Indicates work progress
3. Properly relates cost, schedule, and technical accomplishment
4. Captures and processes valid data in a timely and auditable manner
5. Supplies managers with information at a practical level of summarization. (Department of Defense, FAA, and NASA 1997, section 1-2.)

If an organization has a system in place that provides all of the above basic capabilities, an EVMS implementation flows fairly smoothly. Otherwise, the organizational changes and investment in time and dollars may be significant.

Just as in any change initiative, knowing where you want to go (i.e., meet the EVMS criteria) is a required but insufficient first step. Of course, all the members of the project team must know the EVMS criteria thoroughly, but that still will not ensure successful implementation. While EVMS metrics proclaim the project's progress, metrics alone cannot manage the project. As always, it is the project manager who must possess strong project management skills and direct the project's progress. In addition, EVMS implementation must have strong top management support and cooperation from all functional departments.

PREPARING FOR IMPLEMENTATION

It would be highly unusual for a new management system to integrate seamlessly with existing systems and to perform successfully from the outset without considerable advance planning.

The project manager should approach any new EVMS implementation with careful first steps.

Organizational Support

A project team cannot implement an EVMS; the entire organization must be involved. As you undoubtedly are aware, the first principle of any new system implementation is to have unequivocal top management commitment. Every organization has been through several of the latest and greatest management tools; some were successfully implemented, but many were not. Without strong management commitment, team members may view EVMS as another improvement process that safely can be ignored and eventually will fade away. Senior management's commitment must be written and well-publicized and the project manager must have the support of several departments as well as methods to encourage positive reactions and behavior.

Resource Managers

In a functionally designed organization, where project teams include members from various functional areas, project work performance generally is considered only incidentally and informally (if at all) in evaluations by functional heads, often referred to as resource managers. Selection of individuals for project assignments also falls under the resource manager's purview. When functional duties collide with project requirements, the project team member is placed in a difficult dilemma. Part of the implementation process may include the formal incorporation of performance evaluations by the project manager.

Functional heads, especially if they do not have a clear understanding of project priorities, may not be in the best position to assign resources to individual project work packages. Functional heads either must be far more involved in project work or must share responsibility for work assignments with someone familiar with the organization's project portfolio. The project manager should nurture relationships with department managers and promote the establishment of a Project Management Office.

Because accounting personnel will have the responsibility of gathering, aggregating, and reporting EVMS data, their role requires the project manager's special attention.

The All-Important Accounting and Finance Team

Possibly the most important team that the project manager must deal with is the accounting and finance team. In many organizations the accounting and finance roles are intertwined and overlapping. In others, accounting reports to the chief financial officer. On the other hand, accounting and finance may be independent functional areas. In any event, accounting personnel will be charged with accumulating project data and preparing reports. It is extremely important for project managers to understand the accounting position, the positions to which they report, and then work with them to ensure the speedy capture and reporting of all relevant data.

We are not suggesting that project managers learn accounting. However, it is vital to cooperate with the accountants and appreciate the work they do. EVMS evolved from a standard cost system and accountants are able to readily master the intricacies of both systems, as well as understand the systems' deficiencies. In addition, they are willing and able to answer questions and help project managers master the requirements for their inputs. The vast majority of accountants do not relish their perceived role of "enforcer."

Everyone wants up-to-date information. As a project manager, you have the ability to either help or hinder the work performed by accountants. EVMS reports provide valuable information. Therefore, we urge you to make friends in the accounting department and forgo attempts to "game" the system. Accountants can explain the importance of acknowledging project commitments prior to receipt of transaction documentation and the need to keep up-to-date records.

Education and Training

In order to effectively apply the concepts of EVMS and to generate and report all the information that a compliant system should produce, training is highly recommended. Education and training of everyone charged with providing input for EV metrics should be included as part of the comprehensive implementation plan. Besides those intimately connected with responsibilities impacting EVMS reports, entire project teams should be informed as to why the new system is being adopted and how the teams will be impacted. In addition, their individual contributions to its successful implementation must be explicitly addressed.

On-the-job training, self-learning, and internal training are opportunities for acquiring EVMS knowledge that have an advantage in convenience and cost, but they may not provide the necessary level of rigor and acceptance outside the organization. Many companies and several universities offer formal EVMS training, including U.S. government departments and agencies. Also, the majority of government contractors with approved EVMS systems offer in-house training that in some cases may be attended by outsiders.

Most of the federal government's training courses are specific to their staff needs such as an Internet-based course designed to provide knowledge and comprehension of applying EVMS to evaluate contractor cost and schedule performance. Most of the government classes are restricted to their personnel or staff of active government contractors; however, if you qualify, the training opportunities are excellent. The Defense Acquisition University (http://www.dau.mil/) maintains an Earned Value Management Department and provides a list of member organizations as well as other recognized educational institutions. The Air Force Institute of Technology (http://www.afit.edu/) has a course that is required for all their personnel that will be involved in reviewing EVMS systems.

Eliciting Desired Behavior

> *"Any change, even a change for the better, is always accompanied by drawbacks and discomforts."*
> —Arnold Bennett

Most of us underestimate the level of overt and covert resistance to change. It may be necessary to spend what might seem to be an extraordinary effort on the change management process. Introducing change is a complex subject involving many disciplines, including psychology, and is beyond the scope of this book. There are voluminous sources (books, articles, and white papers) on the subject of change. While many of the issues that must be addressed are common across all organizations, successful change generally requires an atmosphere of trust, respect, openness, and learning. Support for learning can be enhanced by sharing problem-solving techniques and lessons-learned documentation across the organization through a formal information sharing process. The closing process for a project, as presented in Chapter 12, supports this type of learning.

When new processes or procedures are put in place to support a change initiative, new performance metrics designed to support the change also must be in place. EVMS metrics are designed to evaluate a project, not the people working on the project. The organization must expend the effort developing a personnel evaluation system that encourages the desired behavior and minimizes or eliminates dysfunctional actions. We know of no simple solutions to this issue; however, the organizations that recognize the problem and apply their best efforts to find a solution will find themselves in a better long-term competitive position. It is important for the project manager to recognize who controls and administers staff evaluations. In many organizations this duty falls to functional or resource managers.

DO YOUR OWN THING, BUT CAREFULLY

No organization produces its project deliverables in exactly the same way as another organization. The many differences in an organization's objectives and projects will not produce identical systems. Working relationships are different and depend a great deal on the organization's culture. Cultural differences and difficulties in combining or changing them have been substantiated repeatedly during attempts to bring together organizational units in mergers and acquisitions. No universal EVMS could satisfy the great diversity of management needs.

In fact, there is no universal EVMS. A reasonable or acceptable EVMS system is one that adheres to the 32 stated criteria.

The earned value criteria provide a *framework* for determining an acceptable project management system. They do not describe specific system requirements nor do they even provide all the necessary requirements of good internal control and management of project cost, schedule, and scope. However, the criteria have many years of proven value and meeting their requirements provides a basis for effective management decisions.

Certain Department of Defense contract guidelines state that the contractor must meet EVMS criteria, but they do not mandate that a specific information system be used. They allow the project manager the flexibility to utilize any project management system or tools that meet the criteria. The prospective contractor, however, must describe the system for planning, controlling, and reporting project performance in enough detail to evaluate its compliance with the EVMS criteria.

Whatever systems and processes the project manager utilizes, it is important to be certain that they integrate with existing organizational systems. It is not cost-effective, nor would it be very popular, to generate additional collection and reporting mechanisms for one project. Within that caveat, the government agencies encourage a serious effort in pursuit of the continuous improvement of organizational processes.

That means that the organization, collection, and reporting of data can be done manually if that best fits your organizational processes. Of course, EVMS projects are usually complex, so we highly recommend that you use as much automation as is economically reasonable.

SOFTWARE ASSISTANCE

Due to the size of projects that typically use EVMS, EV metrics can be difficult to gather and manage. The project manager will need as much computerized help as possible. In fact, the Department of Energy requires certain of their personnel to "demonstrate a working level knowledge of computer applications used in project management" (Department of Energy 1995, Section 1.5).

There is software that can be used to track and report EVMS data. C/S Solutions' wInsight and Welcom's Cobra® are two of the programs most well known for drill-down capability, forecasting, schedule integration, top-down planning, and customization; however, a number of companies provide such software. DoD has a website that lists software tools to assist the program manager at: http://acc.dau.mil/simplify/ev.php?ID=52966_201§ID2=DO_ TOPIC.

When evaluating software, the two major considerations should be that the software has the functions and capabilities needed for EVMS compliance and that it is compatible with current tools, systems, and processes. If you are currently using a specific project scheduling tool, the new software must work with it or you must be prepared to make sometimes significant modifications to one or both of the software programs.

Desirable software also would include certain functionality. Two primary requirements for the software are its ability to (1) differentiate between the baseline and a forecast, and (2) handle multiple forecasts, each with its own set of assumptions. Also, the software must store earned and actual data in a manner that allows the calculation of the required variances and does not compromise the historical metrics if replanning is necessary. Other favorable functionality would include the ability to make global adjustments and to provide statistical forecasts such as predicted funding and staffing.

Just as in any software acquisition, it is important to involve representation from a variety of functional units in EVMS software selection. Rather than using the software company's data for demonstration purposes, it is wise to use a sample of your own company's data to compare relative performance of the program offerings of various companies.

IMPLEMENTATION COST

It has been difficult for us to determine the cost of implementing EVMS. First, few organizations have been able to separate the incremental costs of EVMS from their historic project management operations. Second, although there were definite improvements in operations in almost every case where EVMS was implemented, the value of those improvements was almost impossible to quantify.

An example of cost saving is illustrated by several attestations to the value of an early determination to terminate the project for economic reasons. Rather than continue project expenditures until completion or until it is obvious to everyone that the project will not deliver its objectives, early termination means that valuable and scarce resources can be transferred to more profitable work.

One area where we found that increased costs are sometimes unnecessarily incurred is in gathering data and reporting at the lowest levels of the work breakdown structure. Extreme breakdown of project details not only adversely affects costs but also encourages undue micromanagement without enhancing the value of the information. Many of the earned value criteria involve the calculation and reporting of variances of actual results from those planned. This is a very time-consuming effort for relatively small (in both time and cost) pieces of work and there is the tendency to overreact and try to fix unfavorable variances that merely reflect the uncertainty involved. W. Edwards Deming described this type of overcorrection as *tampering*. Rather than improving the situation, tampering makes the situation worse more often than it makes it better.

Further, there are tradeoffs in trying to improve cost or schedule performance. If costs are excessive (i.e., significantly more than expected), remedies include eliminating overtime and deferring work. Of course, both of these remedies will result in lengthening completion times. Similarly, actions to remedy an unfavorable schedule variance, such as hiring additional personnel or outsourcing work, usually require extra expenditures. The trick is to keep costs and schedule in balance.

Earned value metrics highlight problems, but not the cause or the solution. Therefore, trying to concentrate on cost and schedule independently or alternating focus between them can result in some nasty unintended consequences. For example, an organization working on a major defense project that had serious problems was spending more than one hour every day reporting status and plans. Every correction that was attempted simply worsened their performance. When we finally convinced them to reduce the level of management detail and concentrate on using good project management practices without trying to manage EV metrics, the project recovered.

GOVERNMENT CONTRACTS

Although the various federal departments and agencies have slightly different approaches to EVMS implementation, they all follow the same basic requirements. The Defense Acquisition University (DAU), Department of Defense (2004), recently released a *Defense Acquisition Guidebook*, an interactive, Web-based application that covers many of the regulations, requirements, and best practices for members and contractors of the defense industry (http://akss.dau.mil/dag/). Chapter 11.3.1 of the *Guidebook* presents information on earned value management. DAU also maintains an earned value management section in the *Special Interest Area* on its website at http://acc.dau.mil/simplify/ev_en.php.

Compliance guidelines have not changed substantially for several years, but in November 2004, DAU published draft EVMS compliance revisions. One of the proposed revisions emphasized that earned value management, if implemented correctly, provides the required knowledge to avoid Fitzgerald's *First Law of Program Management*: "There are only two phases to a big military program: Too early to tell and too late to stop. Program advocates like to keep bad news covered up until they have spent so much money that they can advance the sunk-cost argument; that it's too late to cancel the program because we've spent too much already. (Stevenson 1993, 305)

In April 2005, DAU issued the revised *Earned Value Management Implementation Guide* incorporating most of the proposed revisions (Defense Acquisition University 2005).

The project manager is not usually the responsible party for complying with many of the federal agency contract requirements, but should have some familiarity with agency contacts, EVMS certification requirements, certain applicable federal regulations, and the general contracting process.

Councils and Agencies

In discussions of government contracts and requirements, we often hear the term *components*. A component is defined as "a service or agency with acquisition authority" (Department of Defense, FAA, and NASA 1997, Part II, Section 1.2). A government component refers to any agency that has authority to acquire goods or services. The head of the component or a designee is referred to as the *executive agent* (EA). The authority of the EA is assigned at the time of the designation, but generally the EA will be the responsible agent for conducting the terms of an acquisition contract.

Many government components will have an *Earned Value Management Support Office* (EVMSO) to ensure effective earned value management implementation. The EVMSO will usually participate in system reviews and can provide training and assistance for the contractor. Many other agencies are involved in government acquisition of goods and services. While neither contract acquisition nor implementation of EVMS is the general responsibility of the project manager, you may be expected to understand the terminology and be familiar with the various governmental components with which you must communicate.

Agency definitions in this section are referenced from the DoD *Earned Value Management Implementation Guide* or the *ACQWeb* (Department of Defense, Acquisition, Technology & Logistics 2004). These definitions are generic in the sense that they more often describe activities than specific organizational entities.

- A *focal point* is established by the DoD component to serve as the principal point of contact for coordination and exchange of information on the implementation of EVMS. Lists of appropriate contacts for component and other agency focal points are available at the Office of the Secretary of Defense (OSD) earned value website (http://www.acq.osd.mil/pm/keypers/keypers.html).

- The *procuring activity* executes the acquisition contract and is composed of the *Program Management Office* (PMO) and its integrated support. The *Performance Management Advisory Council* (PMAC) provides a forum for the procuring activity and other non-DoD agency representatives to exchange information related to EVMS. The *Contract Administration Office* (CAO) is assigned to administer contractual activities at a specific facility in support of the PMO. The Defense Contract Audit Agency (DCAA) is responsible for conducting surveillance and audit reviews.

- The *Milestone Decision Authority* (MDA) has a very basic authority in government projects. It is the MDA's responsibility to make decisions if and when a project should be started. Once a project is initiated, the MDA decides whether the project should proceed into the next phase of the acquisition life cycle. At each major decision point, the MDA determines whether the program, or a key increment of the program, should be terminated, modified, or approved to proceed.

- The *Defense Contract Management Agency* (DCMA), formerly the Defense Contract Management Command (DCMC), is the DoD contract manager. DCMA is responsible for ensuring that federal acquisition programs, supplies, and services are delivered on time, within cost, and meet performance requirements. This agency maintains the acceptance and review schedules for the contractors' EVMS. The agency is also responsible for maintaining an implementation guide and a cooperative relationship with industry.

EVMS Certification

At this time, there is no recognized industry standards-setting body that has established certification requirements for EVMS. Therefore, many EVMS implementations rely primarily on self-evaluation; after review, DoD often accepts self-certification.

When self-certification is deemed insufficient, DCMA will provide formal certification of an EVMS.

Once EVMS has been accepted on one contract, future acceptability generally follows. If EVMS was previously accepted, an *integrated baseline review* (IBR) usually will be conducted only when some condition has changed or is suspect. When the contracting organization does not have a previously accepted system, DoD attempts to involve the organization in a self-evaluation compliance review by offering cooperative assistance. The review itself may take only about one week to complete; however, with a learning process up front and a post-review evaluation, the elapsed time could be more in the range of six months.

DoD recognizes industry's EVMS standard 32 criteria and publishes implementation guidelines on its acquisition website. The Program Management Systems Committee of the National Defense Industrial Association (NDIA), in cooperation with the Aerospace Industries Association, Electronic Industries Association, American Shipbuilding Association, Shipbuilders Council of America, Performance Management Association, and Project Management Institute, also publishes information on the guidelines.

The PMSC of the NDIA published an *Intent Guide* that can be used by "a contractor who needs to demonstrate that their system complies with the standard [ANSI/EIA 748 EVMS Guidelines]" (National Defense Industrial Association 2005, 1).

Federal Acquisition Regulation System

DoD often issues Defense Federal Acquisition Regulation Supplements (DFARS) to notify organizations and agencies of contractual requirements. The governing clause for EVMS is 234.005 (Department of Defense 2004), which sets out other clauses for solicitation and contracting. DFARS 252.234-7000 and 7001 are notices about the use of EVMS. The first requires documentation of a validated EVMS or the submission of a comprehensive plan for EVMS compliance. The plan must include the following:

- A description of the system the contractor intends to use
- A delineation of modifications to the contractor's existing system in order to comply with the EVMS criteria
- A description of how the system will be applied in terms of the criteria
- A description of how the criteria will be applied to subcontractors
- Documentation of the process and results of any evaluation of the system's compliance with the criteria.

DFARS 252.234-7000 also states that the government will review the plan, requires the contractor to provide information and assistance for the review, and requires the identification and acceptance of subcontractors or subcontracted work. DFARS 252.234-7001 prescribes the use of a recognized or accepted management system that complies with the 32 EVMS criteria. The government will require an integrated baseline review to jointly assess the contractor's planning and ensure complete coverage of the statement of work, logical scheduling, adequate resourcing, and identification of risk. DFARS 252.234-7001 also requires approval of any EVMS changes, authorizes access to pertinent records and data, and dictates subcontractor requirements.

DoD encourages contractors and the entire industrial sector to assume a growing responsibility for earned value management processes. DoD will continue to review the management systems of contractors, but would prefer to see industry certification standards, such as those of the International Organization for Standardization (ISO), with third-party accreditation. There is certainly a growing source of consulting and training assistance for EVMS. One organization has developed an Earned Value Management Maturity Model.® That model and the abbreviation EVM3® are trademarks of Management Technologies (Management Technologies 2004).

Contract Solicitation and Award

The flow chart in Figure 4.1 illustrates the EVMS contract solicitation process.

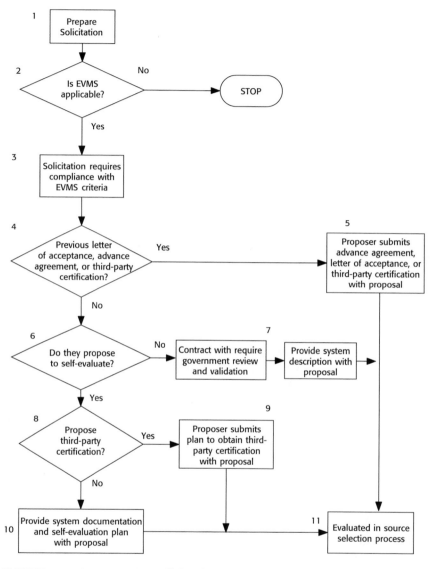

FIGURE 4.1   Government Solicitation Process

Different federal agencies provide different information and documentation for potential contractors during the contract solicitation. The contractor will be required to describe the project's EVMS. The contractor will typically use an existing system if it meets the criteria. If the government has previously accepted the system, the contractor should cite an *advance agreement* (AA), a previous *letter of acceptance* (LOA), or a third-party *certificate of validation* and indicate previous contracts on which the system was used. If the system has not been previously accepted, the contractor must submit a certification plan.

Following the award of a government contract, EVMS activities will include system surveillance, monitoring of any changes to the approved system, and reviews of the contractor's data and management processes (Department of Defense, FAA, and NASA 1997, section 3). The post award process is illustrated in Figure 4.2

System Surveillance

Several agencies may be involved in the surveillance of the contractor's EVMS implementation. These include the CAO with the primary responsibility as well as the Field Audit Activity of the Defense Contract Audit Agency (DCAA FAO), the Program Management Office, and the EVMSO. The selected grouping of participating agencies is referred to as the *integrated surveillance team* (IST) and the contractor is encouraged to participate in the surveillance process.

Surveillance begins prior to the contract award and continues throughout the duration of the contract (see Figure 4.3). The surveillance is to ensure that the contractor's EVMS adheres to the following six steps:

1. Providing timely and reliable cost, schedule, and technical performance measurement information summarized directly from the contractor's internal management system
2. Complying with the criteria
3. Providing timely indications of actual or potential problems

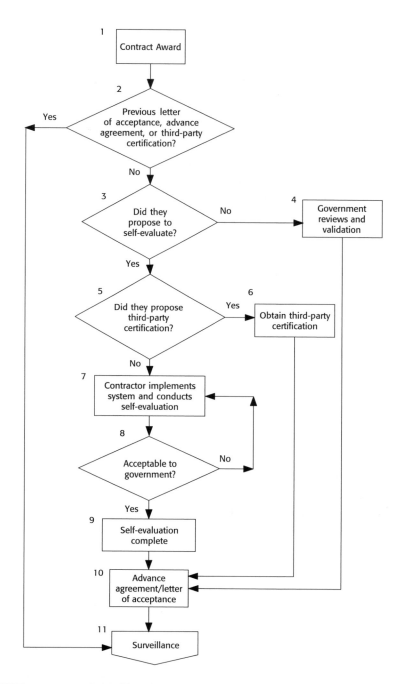

FIGURE 4.2   Post Award Process

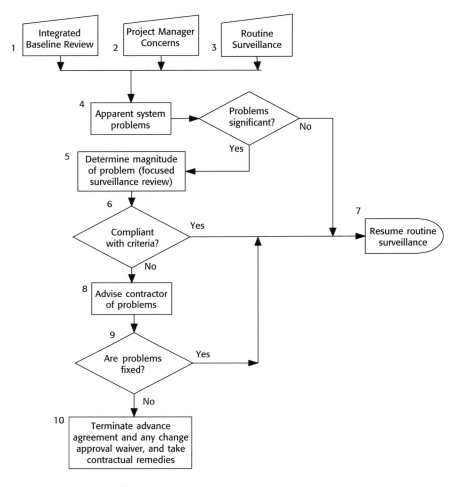

FIGURE 4.3   Surveillance Process

4. Maintaining baseline integrity
5. Providing information that depicts actual conditions and trends
6. Providing comprehensive variance analysis at the appropriate levels, including proposed corrective action in regard to cost, schedule, technical, and other problem areas (Department of Defense, FAA, and NASA 1997, section 3-2).

Quality assurance personnel of the Defense Contract Management Agency (DCMA; http://www.dcma.mil) may conduct such reviews as:

- Product examinations to ensure contract requirements are met
- Process reviews to determine the suitability, adequacy, and effectiveness to achieve product outputs
- Systematic, independent assessments and audits to determine the contractual quality management system.

Evaluations and Reviews

The primary reviews are the *initial compliance review* (ICR), the integrated baseline review (IBR), and *reviews for cause*. The EA of the contracting agency appoints a Review Director to approve and coordinate the review activities. The Review Director also approves members of the review team and they are administratively responsible to the Review Director. The project manager is not usually a principal in the contract process, but there are two areas, the ICR and the IBR, that will involve you and your team.

Initial Compliance Evaluation

For contracts requiring EVMS, the government agency requires assurance that the contractor is using the system as the principal means of project management and that the contractor is actually reporting data from the system. The compliance evaluation is performed to validate that the system meets the EVMS criteria and that the contractor's description of its system is accurate, and to ensure that the system described is being used to manage the contracted project. It should be conducted as soon as possible after the contractor implements the EVMS for the contract.

The following activities should be a part of the compliance evaluation:

- An overview briefing by the contractor
- A review of documentation "to verify that the contractor has established and is maintaining a valid, comprehensive integrated baseline plan for the contract"

- A review of the cost and schedule performance reports against the baseline plan "to verify the adequacy of the control aspects of the systems and accuracy of the resulting management information"
- Interviews with managers and work teams "to verify that the contractor's EVMS is fully implemented and being used in the management of the contract"
- An exit briefing disclosing the review team's findings along with the contractor's action plan, with established "responsibility and a time-frame for corrective action" (Department of Defense, FAA, and NASA 1997, 4-3.1).

The Review Director will prepare a compliance evaluation report within 30 working days after the completion of any required corrective actions. Upon receipt of an acceptable report, the agency's Executive Agent will certify system compliance. DoD may also recognize a third-party evaluation and certification.

Government policy encourages the contractor's self-evaluation with agency participation. The contractor's commitment to a compliant EVMS, its openness, the project team's knowledge of EVMS, and opportunities for government participation will have an influence on the government's level of involvement in evaluations and reviews. The initial compliance evaluation may concentrate on particular elements of the EVMS or may cover the entire system.

If the government performs the formal reviews and system evaluations, it may conduct a *progress assistance visit* (PAV), sometimes simply called a plant visit. Selected representatives of the review team will visit the site to carry out an initial review of the system description and establish an early dialogue between the review team and the contractor. This visit is an opportunity for the contractor to receive assistance in developing the system description, identifying potential problems, and developing the schedule and procedures for future reviews and evaluations.

Integrated Baseline Review

The IBR is conducted by the government and the contractor to assess the validity of the *performance measurement baseline*

(PMB). The review is conducted within six months of the contract award, but also occurs when a major contract change occurs or at the discretion of the program manager. The government program manager (or designee) will lead the IBR team, staffed potentially by CAO personnel, members of the PMO, and EVMS support personnel as well as the contractor's project manager and technical staff. Participation by members of the IST is also encouraged. The IBR is intended to be a continuous part of the project management process.

Five primary objectives of the IBR are listed here; the terms will be fully defined and discussed in subsequent chapters that cover the EVMS criteria. The objectives are designed to:

1. Ensure that the technical content of work packages and cost accounts is consistent with the contract scope of work, the contract work breakdown structure (CWBS), and the CWBS dictionary.
2. Ensure that there is a logical sequence of effort planned that is consistent with the contract schedule.
3. Assess the validity of allocated cost account and *summary level planning package* (SLPP) budgets, both in terms of total resources and time-phasing.
4. Conduct a technical assessment of the EV methods that will be used to measure progress to ensure that objective and meaningful performance data will be provided.
5. Establish a forum through which the government program manager and the project technical staff gain a sense of ownership of the EVMS process.

"By understanding the internal earned value management system, government and contractor technical counterparts can jointly conduct recurring reviews of Performance Measurement Baseline (PMB) planning, status, and estimates at completion to ensure that baseline integrity is maintained throughout the life of the contract" (Department of Defense, FAA, and NASA 1997, 4-2.c(5).

Working with the contractor, the government program office will determine the content and range of the IBR. That office will decide which control accounts are to be reviewed and which contractor managers will be interviewed. No formal report is required at the conclusion of the IBR, but the team should identify all concerns and establish estimated dates for resolution. If differences in opinion or interpretation of the EVMS or of the review process itself cannot be resolved within the lower levels of the PMO, the EVMSO, the CAO, and the contractor, then either a government or contractor representative can make an appeal for resolution to the DoD Executive Agent.

Implementing EVMS can be either a mandatory condition or an elective one, but every process change requires support from all parts of the organization plus education and training in the new methodology. Implementations will differ across organizations both in degree of change and in the cost. If the implementation is a change for the organization, it will need visible support from executive management, department heads, and especially the accounting team. Comprehensive training and appropriate measurement systems can encourage positive reactions from the entire organization.

A definitive management system is not specified as long as it adheres to the EVMS criteria; however, there may be some significant changes to your current system. We recommend that you investigate all sources of assistance, including relevant software. The cost of implementing EVMS will vary depending on the state of the current systems, the valuation of benefits, and the treatment of potential tradeoffs.

Governmental requirements for EVMS are constantly being reviewed and revised and differ greatly depending on the particular agency, the type, and the value of the contract. For example, DoD has its own way of grouping the 32 EVMS criteria under nine management processes rather than five. For government projects, the project manager must interact with different agencies and authorities, each having a variety of guidelines to follow. The project manager will be expected to comply with all of them in just as many different ways. The system will need to be "certified," and there are several avenues available. You should consult the Federal Acquisition Regulation (FAR) to find out more about federal requirements.

There are eligibility standards for EVMS contracts and a procedural flow for the contractual process. The process begins with the contract solicitation and the proposed EVMS, proceeds with the contract award, and includes system surveillance, evaluations, and reviews. The primary reviews are the initial compliance evaluation and the integrated baseline review.

DISCUSSION QUESTIONS

1. Select the statement that best describes a project manager's involvement in a required EVMS implementation for a major government contract:

   a. The project manager is responsible for managing the entire implementation as well as the contract.
   b. The project manager has no responsibility for implementation other than general familiarity with inputs for EVMS metrics only for the contract.
   c. The project manager is responsible for seeing that team members understand the basic requirements of implementation and take part in required reviews.
   d. The project manager and the accounting department share equal responsibility for implementation.

2. In a functionally designed organization:

   a. Accounting personnel must implement the EVMS.
   b. Department managers will usually assign resources to project work packages.
   c. The project manager will usually have control over the selection of the project team members.
   d. EVMS project work always takes priority over other duties.

3. An acceptable EVMS requires:

   a. The use of a Gantt project network.
   b. The use of prescribed management objectives.
   c. Substantial revisions to the organization's accounting procedures.
   d. None of the above.

4. The government agency with authority to make decisions if and when an EVMS project should proceed through each phase of the acquisition cycle is:

   a. The CAO.
   b. The MDA.
   c. The DCAA.
   d. The EVMSO.

5. For DoD to accept an organization's EVMS, the system may be certified by:

   a. A cooperative self-evaluation and self-certification.
   b. An accredited third-party certification.
   c. A government Initial Compliance Evaluation.
   d. Any of the above.

6. An EVMS Initial Compliance Evaluation:

   a. Begins with an overview briefing by the contractor.
   b. Must be conducted prior to the contract award.
   c. Is not concerned with the project baseline plan.
   d. Does not require a formal report.

7. What do you think will be your biggest obstacles to a successful EVMS implementation?

8. Your proposed project must use EVMS but you have heard that one of the executive management team thinks an EVMS implementation will be too difficult and expensive. What steps could you take to promote the system?

9. How much accounting knowledge or training must the project manager have for an EVMS project?

10. What are some dangers of having too much information?

It's All in the Plan

The first 15 EVMS criteria are to ensure that the project management system is correctly and adequately established. The system must provide the means to

- Define the project objective
- Assign the major deliverables to functional units (including outside contractors)
- Schedule the work
- Prepare budgets
- Facilitate the collection and reporting of management information
- Provide for accurate estimates of project completion that include both cost and schedule.

For these requirements, EVMS relies on the careful construction of a baseline plan.

Chapter 5 discusses Criterion 1 and its requirement for detailing the project plan with a work breakdown structure, but it does not deal with the subject of scheduling time. Chapter 6 covers Criteria 2 through 5 and the organizational structure and responsibilities. Then Chapter 7 outlines the requirements of the scheduling process by examining Criteria 6, 7, and 8. Chapter 8 discusses the budgeting requirements required by Criteria 9 through 15.

CHAPTER 5

The Project Plan (Criterion 1)

The first EVMS criterion really sets the tone for following the entire management system. You will need a complete understanding of the *work breakdown structure* (WBS) that includes *work packages* (WPs), a WBS dictionary, and additional project input. We will recommend some ways to develop the WBS and introduce the concept of the control account and its influence on the construction of the WBS.

EVMS CRITERION 1

Define the authorized work elements for the program. A work breakdown structure (WBS), tailored for effective internal management control, is commonly used in this process.

The very first sentence of this EVMS criterion seems quite simple, but it contains two extremely important words: *define* and *authorized*. The *earned value* of any project cannot be measured without having first *defined* all of the deliverables or effort of the project. Secondly, an effective project management system must begin with solid management *authorization*, including all of the organization's functional areas that will contribute to or be affected by the project. We firmly believe that this authorization applies not only to the specific project, but also to EVMS itself. Management commitment is extremely important in any organizational endeavor.

Even though you may not know the complete details of the total effort, EVMS requires a definition and estimation of the entire project scope. Other EVMS criteria will allow for changes and the addition of unauthorized work under specific conditions. You should also note the use of the word *tailored* in this criterion. EVMS is about project control and it is of special interest to see that the criteria recognize that control is best exercised when it is tailored to the particulars of the organization. The impact of tailoring is clearly seen throughout our examination of EVMS.

THE WORK BREAKDOWN STRUCTURE

In the 1980s (and occasionally in the present), one of the favorite disparaging phrases about the lack of project planning was, "Ready, Fire, Aim!" Too often a project plan was considered only as a quick way to keep management off the project managers' backs so they could get something accomplished. Besides, the thinking went, if they told anyone what they were going to do, then they would really have to do it. For the most part, especially within the growing ranks of professional project managers, these comments are now used in jest.

Of course, there are many serious and compelling reasons to plan carefully; however, in implementing EVMS, there is one above all others—fulfilling the very first EVMS criterion. Beyond its EVMS requirement, a WBS is a strong foundation for the management of any significant project. The EVMS criterion tells us that it is used to "define the authorized work elements" and should be "tailored for effective internal management control." A well-defined project using a WBS is designed to facilitate the collection, analysis, and reporting of the cost and schedule data.

WBS Definitions and Standards

The grandfather of references to a WBS was by the U.S. defense establishment in Military Standard (MIL-STD) 881 (1 November 1968). That standard was superseded by MIL-STD-881A (25 April 1975) and MIL-STD-881B (25 March 1993). The 1993 revision was developed through the cooperative efforts of the military services with assistance from industrial associations. The second revision (881B) talked about a work breakdown structure (WBS) as a product-oriented family tree composed of hardware, software, services, data, and facilities. The WBS defines the product(s) to be developed and relates the elements of work to be accomplished.

The standard was cancelled about five years later by MIL-STD-881B Notice 1 (2 January 1998). The cancellation notice stated that, "Information . . . for Work Breakdown Structures is now contained in MIL-HDBK-881, 'Work Breakdown Structure.'" Most of the 1993 standard was updated with little material modification and repeated in the new handbook. The WBS always has been considered to be a primary mechanism for project planning, control, and reporting. The handbook specifically states, "The work breakdown structure forms the basis for reporting structures used for contracts requiring compliance with the Earned Value Management System (EVMS) Criteria" (Department of Defense 1998, C.1.5).

There have been many other definitions and descriptions of the WBS. *A Guide to the Project Management Body of Knowledge* describes one of the outputs from the scope definition as a WBS with this comment, "A WBS is a deliverable-oriented grouping of project components that organizes and defines the total scope of the project; work not in the WBS is outside the scope of the project."(Project Management Institute 2000, S. 5.3.3.1). James Lewis said, ". . . the most important tool of project management is the work breakdown structure (WBS). The WBS lists all the tasks that must be done in the project to achieve desired results" (2000, 88).

One Department of Energy document defines the WBS as:

... a numerical, graphic representation that completely defines a project by relating elements of work in that project to each other and to the end product. The WBS is comprised of discrete WPs, called elements that describe a specific item of hardware, service, or data. Descending levels of the WBS provide elements of greater and greater detail. The number of levels of a WBS depends on the size and complexity of the project. (Department of Energy 1997, 8)

Meredith and Mantel (2003, 260) report that "... the Work Breakdown Structure (WBS) is *not one thing* [emphasis added]. It can take a wide variety of forms that, in turn, serve a wide variety of purposes."

Almost all literature on project management devotes significant exposure to some form or other of the WBS. There has been considerable discussion about whether the WBS should be oriented to "deliverables" or "activities," but in any of its many definitions and uses, the WBS offers obvious benefits for all stakeholders in the management of a project. For the implementation of EVMS, the most important aspect of the WBS is that it provides the structure for the tracking and reporting of the schedule elements of the project.

We will more generally follow the product or deliverables orientation. (Note that the DOE definition above cites work elements referencing hardware, services, or data.) Following the product orientation facilitates the comparative or analogous estimation requirements of EVMS. If the project owner or sponsor does not require a product-oriented WBS, it is perfectly acceptable to follow an activity-oriented WBS. Regardless of its form, the purpose of the WBS in EVMS is to define the scope of the project in sufficient detail to provide adequate tracking.

Two Possible WBS Structures

In many environments, especially the military environment, the WBS is usually the combination of two structures: a *program work breakdown structure* (PWBS) and a *contract work breakdown structure* (CWBS).

The PWBS provides the basic framework on which to hang logical elements of the program. Remember that the WBS definition usually describes a *product-oriented* set of elements in a hierarchical relationship. It is usually more natural for a project manager to start out thinking about a project in terms of activities and tasks. This could be very acceptable for a small nongovernment program, but the project manager may not be using the EVMS criteria in that situation. When developing the PWBS, the project manager should be oriented to the program deliverables and not the tasks required to deliver them.

Ideally, the project manager will be involved when the program objective is being defined because this begins the construction of the PWBS and is the initial step in the entire planning process. It is critical that this part of the process be comprehensive and thorough because this first step may characterize the planning for the entire project. If the program deliverables have already been defined when the project manager is appointed, the next best step is for the project manager to develop (rewrite) a PWBS to ensure that all interested participants are in complete agreement prior to further work. Each element in the PWBS is a point at which the EVMS measurements can be evaluated.

The second structure is the CWBS. Your organization may be an outside contractor for a large project (government or commercial), but we can define the project manager as the contractor for any project. The CWBS becomes the mechanism for coordinating all project resources. It includes all the elements of the PWBS, but will be further extended to enable the project manager and subcontractors to identify any detail required to meet all the objectives of the program. It is very common and completely acceptable for the CWBS to use more task-oriented language in its extensions.

The purpose of the WBS is to separate a proposed product or objective into its component parts and to clarify the relationship of the parts to each other and to the end product. The WBS is the most important planning tool for the assignment of the management and technical responsibilities. Together, the PWBS and the CWBS will be the tools for tracking resource allocations, actual effort, cost estimates, expenditures, and project performance. All project deliverables must be identified in the WBS and all involved organizational units must work within those parameters.

Steps in Constructing a WBS

The following 11 steps are involved in constructing a WBS:

1. The first level of the WBS is the name for the project deliverable, the project objective, or product. This product identification must be one that is widely recognized throughout the organization. This first level is numbered as 1.0 or numbered with the assigned project number and .0, such as 242.0.
2. The next level is a listing of all the major components. Everything that is a part of the project product must fit somewhere under one of these major components. These components for project 242 would be numbered as 242.1, 242.2, etc., out to the number of components at this second level.
3. If at all possible, you should try to construct *all* the elements of the second level before performing the work breakdown to the next lower level. It is very tempting to begin thinking about all the products of the first entry in level 2, but it can be very distracting. The objective is first to get agreement on all the major components of the project. Some elements may be moved into lower levels as the WBS construction progresses.
4. Next determine which of the elements require more information and begin that definition on a subordinate level. Continue breaking down each element at each level into further levels until a level of detail has been reached that will provide the organization with the required reporting data and the project manager with sufficient management information without over-controlling the project team. Each successive level will add another decimal place to the numbering scheme. Level 3 elements in project 242 for element 242.1 will be numbered as 242.1.1 through 242.1.n. Level 3 elements for element 242.2 will be numbered as 242.2.1 through 242.2.n.

5. It may be necessary to vary the defining scope of the products on each level depending on how many levels the WBS will contain. An element on the second level may be defined very broadly if it is going to be broken down through many levels. Fewer levels may require more elements across each level, but even in very complex projects, 99 elements on a level would be extreme—group some of them into a more broadly defined element and break it down through more levels.

6. Since most reporting is generated from the top levels, the decision about how many elements will reside in upper levels and how many can be delegated to lower levels (or left under the control of team members) will depend greatly on the reporting requirements of the contracting organization. If detailed reporting is not required, you may wish to have fewer elements in each level. Fewer elements in each level will usually generate additional lower levels, but you will not generate executive reporting at those levels.

7. Break down the WBS elements into only as many subcomponents as you need for the cost/schedule reporting and effective management. You cannot think of everything nor will a list of thousands of project elements provide for more effective control. Remember that the project *team* will achieve the project objective, not the *system*! A breakdown into objectives that can be met in periods of from one week to eight weeks (depending on project complexity) is a good general rule.

8. The lowest level will be the *work package* (WP). This is the formal designation to a responsible team member for the delivery of a product of the WBS. A *statement of work* (SOW) should include enough information to ensure the clarity of the contract between the project manager and the team member.

9. The number of breakdown levels under each element need not be the same. For example, a particular element may be on an upper level for reporting purposes, but will not require as many levels of breakdown as others. You should attempt to make each final deliverable of about the same

scope as other final deliverables regardless of on what level they exist.

10. Do not be overly concerned about the sequence in which the major project objectives will be met. Sequencing can be done later when the project schedule is completed. Again, the objective in the construction of the WBS is to ensure the inclusion of all the control points for management and reporting.

11. Construct a WBS dictionary to describe all components.

DEFINING THE PROJECT

The project's major objective is the global or highest single element of the WBS. The project should have only one objective. If there is more than one project objective, there is almost certainly more than one project. The objective must state not only what the project will include, but also what is *not* expected from the project. If the exclusions are carefully documented, it will help preclude assumptions that later will lead to possible conflict concerning additions and project changes.

It is not difficult to generate the second level of objectives for the project—often they will be a part of the project charter. What may be difficult is to generate all the intermediate and minor objectives that must be part of the successful project. We were first introduced to a basic process to accomplish this in our study of the Theory of Constraints. Since then we have expanded our work with this process, used it successfully in several situations, and written software to automate the association and sequencing of its elements.

We call our version *Obstacles and Required Conditions.* The idea is to generate the entire project's intermediate objectives by first imagining all possible obstacles. It is much easier to address the negatives if they are recognized early in the planning stages. Listing obstacles first also overcomes the tendency to jump to what will be partial solutions if potential problems are not identified.

The next step is to visualize the conditions that must exist if the obstacles are to be overcome. These "required conditions" lead to the project's intermediate objectives. Then "for each intermediate objective, resources and time required are necessary to establish a *work breakdown structure* [emphasis added] that can be entered into project management software, such as Microsoft Project©" (Budd 2003, 20–23).

The project's *scope* encompasses all of the objectives and the work required to accomplish them. As a project manager, one of the biggest problems you will encounter is *scope creep*. An example goes something like this: The project manager has met numerous times with the project sponsor and the implementation staff and they have carefully documented all the project's requirements—its scope. Now the project is nearing completion and someone needs just one *minor* change and then another and soon it has changed from minor to major. Effective project control can be achieved only with careful project planning, a tightly defined deliverable, and a rigorous change control system.

Thus, the initial and most critical activity for a project is to define its scope. The purpose of scope definition is to divide the project's objective into reportable and manageable units. The scope must be defined in just enough detail that the project stakeholders, especially the project team members, understand what must be done. Four important elements of definition during planning are:

1. Technical definition of the product or result
2. Schedule—a clear understanding of available time and required time
3. Cost—an important element of the earned value management system
4. Resources required and available to accomplish the objective.

Many project managers believe that the more detail they put into the project plan, the more control they will have. The opposite is more generally true. Breaking the project down into an almost endless series of short tasks makes project tracking much more complicated and difficult to control. It may, in fact, increase the risk of late delivery. When everyone—especially the project manager—has a huge list of tasks, no one will be able to accurately track and report progress or the project manager may be so busy with data that there may not be any progress to report. Focusing on a list of tasks can cause you to lose sight of the project's objective. Base your project on the achievement of objectives, not on the multitudinous achievement of a long list of tasks.

Ralph Porter, a longtime friend who works with Marines at 29 Palms in California, told us about a "five paragraph order" that the Marine Corps uses to explain all aspects of a mission. The basic acronym is SMEAC, which stands for:

1. Situation
2. Mission
3. Execution
4. Administration and logistics
5. Command and signal.

We think it's a good idea to keep SMEAC in mind when planning your project!

THE MECHANICS OF A WBS

The definition of a project (see Chapter 2) includes its being temporary and *unique*; however, many projects in an organization will have some common features. Project managers should make note of commonalities that can be used to construct project templates, which can provide a head start in constructing a new project WBS.

There are several ways to represent the data when constructing a WBS for the current project. There are software products available to assist in creating the WBS and converting it from one format to another. An Internet search on "WBS chart" will produce several hits.

WBS Charts

Although one example of the WBS looks similar to an organizational chart (the Organization Breakdown Structure—OBS)
with connected boxes of lower level detail, the WBS must not be
thought of in terms of people, but as a project scope chart. The
box at the very top of the chart is the project itself. The next level
is a set of boxes connected to the top box (but not to each other)
and represents the project's major deliverables. Each major deliverable can then be further described by its subcomponents in a
lower level. A partial breakdown of one of the major components
of our sample project on the Customer Relations Management
(CRM) system is illustrated in Figure 5.1.

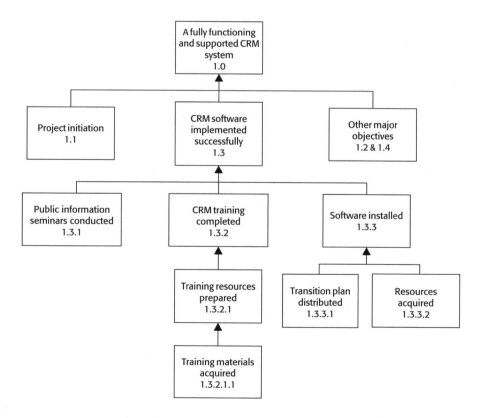

FIGURE 5.1   WBS Project Chart

Those who are familiar with a Bill of Materials might compare this form of the WBS to what is commonly called a *Gozinto* chart.[1] That chart describes a breakdown of parts that make up (or go into) more complex parts. The WBS has the same form, but not as much detail. In whatever form the WBS is constructed, it represents a hierarchical plan of the project elements.

Another common format, including the one recommended by the military, illustrates a line-indented format. It is a vertical listing of project elements with each indentation being an expanded level of detail (a *breakdown*) of the product in the higher indentation. Each line is numbered for easy reference. The first line, representing the entire project, is labeled 1.0. It is quite common for organizations to number their projects and they will often use the project number as the first digits of the line numbering scheme. For example, the first line in the WBS for project number 242 would be 242.0.

For project number 242, the second level of indentation will be labeled 242.1 to 242.n, depending on the number of major deliverables in the project. It would be quite unusual to have more than seven major deliverables in the project. If there are more than seven, it might be wise to attempt a consolidation in order to simplify the tracking and reporting function. The indentation continues for each element until a level is reached where the elements of that deliverable are easily understood by all stakeholders in the project and satisfy the reporting requirements. Figure 5.2 illustrates part of our sample project in the line-indented format.

WBS Levels

There have been as many disagreements about the required number of levels for a WBS as there have been about its orienta-

---

[1]The fictional mathematician, Zepartzatt Gozinto was invented around 1956 by Professor Andrew Vazsonyi, professor emeritus at the McLaren School of Business, University of San Francisco. Vazsonyi is a very interesting person and it's worth a side trip to read about him at: http://reallifemath.com/informs_pr.htm.

DESCRIPTION	WBS REF
Customer Relationship Management system fully functioning and supported	242.0
Project Initiation	242.1
Objectives established	242.1.1
Sublevel detail	242.1.1.1
Plans Completed	242.2
Training plan completed	242.2.1
Training objectives defined	242.2.1.1
Resources located	242.2.1.2
Training schedule completed	242.2.1.3
Training times estimated	242.2.1.3.1
Facilities arranged	242.2.1.3.2
Training schedule developed	242.2.1.3.3
Training budget established	242.2.1.4

FIGURE 5.2   Line-Indented WBS

tion. Many have advocated a standard number of levels such as six or seven. These proponents argue that, with a fixed number of levels, the project manager would be more inclined to include all the elements of the project—a forced thinking process. There have also been attempts to name the levels in a fixed hierarchy, but no standard has emerged. Lewis and others call the first six levels: (1) Program, (2) Project, (3) Task, (4) Subtask, (5) Work Package, and (6) Level of Effort or Activity (Lewis 2000, 91).

The military WBS handbook also defines the levels in a WBS. Level 1 is the entire *material item*, such as an electronic warfare system. Level 2 elements are the *major elements* of the material item, such as an automatic flight control system. Level 3 elements are *subordinate elements* to level 2 major elements, such as a radar mechanism. The handbook goes on to state:

A WBS can be expressed down to any level of interest. However the top three levels are as far as any program or contract need go unless the items identified are high cost or high risk. Then, and only then, is it important to take the work breakdown structure to a lower level of definition. (Department of Defense 1998, 1.6.3)

The preponderance of current project management theory tends to agree that there is no pre-set number of levels for a properly constructed WBS. Smaller projects may require only a few levels while a complex one can have 20 or more if all of the levels in a CWBS are counted. One leg of the WBS may have a different number of levels than another part. The WBS should be extended only to the number of levels that makes it practical to plan, budget, collect costs, track performance, and satisfy the reporting requirements. Distant deliverables that cannot be planned in detail until earlier work has been completed may be shown only at the highest levels until detailed planning is practical.

A WBS Dictionary

Although the military WBS handbook requires a WBS dictionary, we highly recommend that you prepare one even for projects where it is not required. It is used to describe each WBS element and the resources and processes to produce it. "The work breakdown structure dictionary should be routinely revised to incorporate changes and should reflect the current status of the program throughout the program's life" (Department of Defense 1998, 2.2.4).

A WBS dictionary can be invaluable in cases where the WBS is very large or the elements are not self-explanatory. The dictionary is a more detailed description of each element in the WBS. It clarifies what makes up the element and, in many cases, what is not a part of the element. The description should start with the element's number and its name. The definition should give sufficient information so that all stakeholders understand the nature of the element and how it will be produced. As the dictionary is developed, it may even provide indications of required changes in the WBS. A dictionary entry for an element of our sample project is illustrated in Figure 5.3.

WBS # **1.3.3.3** Workstation software downloaded from server. Each organization member who interfaces with the Customer Relationship Management system must download the appropriate software from the CRM file server and send an acknowledgment to the installation team. The installation project team will provide detailed instructions, an on-line manual, answers to frequently asked questions, and a download schedule. Installation team members will be available for assistance. Training will have been completed through intermediate objective number 1.3.2.

FIGURE 5.3   WBS Dictionary Entry

CONTROL ACCOUNTS

Although the *control account* or cost account (CA) (synonymous terms) is not mentioned specifically until Criterion 8, there are implicit references in the organization criteria and many explicit references later. The CA has a definite interface with the WBS.

At some point, as the project objective is subdivided into smaller elements at lower WBS levels, the required effort can be allocated to a specific organizational unit. The project manager should have a CA established at the point where the WBS and the organizational structure coincide. A CA is an accounting feature set up to organize and manage the project at juncture points of the WBS and the organizational structure.

The CA is the point where the schedule and cost numbers for both budgets and actual charges are accumulated and where the earned value comparisons begin. The CAs should be set at the levels where reporting is required. Reporting below the first few levels of the WBS usually does not add significant value; however, it will adversely affect the preparation time and difficulty of accumulating the data.

A member of the functional area that is responsible for the delivery of this element of the WBS can manage the CA. The accounting department (with input from the CA manager) will make the actual accounting entries. The CAs are subdivided into WPs and planning packages. This WBS element may be made up of several WPs as long as all the WPs are assigned within this organizational area.

There will be much more detail about CAs in discussions of later EVMS criteria. For now, it is sufficient to note that you will need to arrange with the accounting department to establish CAs at certain points in your WBS. As you set up WBS elements, consider the reporting requirements, schedule formats, and potential manager assignments. Figure 5.4 illustrates a CA for our sample project WBS and a generic organization.

A *planning package* is a part of the CA that is reserved for work that has not yet been fully defined, but may be assigned to an or-

Control Account ID: WBS # 242.3.2.3.

Project Name: Customer Relationship Management: The Final Step.

Control Account Title: Customer Relationship Management User Training.

Control Account Manager: Training Manager, Human Resources Department.

Planned Duration: February 22 through March 28

Applicable Charges: The Control Account Manager will voucher all expenses for Customer Relationship Management user training including time, materials, and location rentals for publishing the training schedule, distributing training manuals, and conducting user training.

Notable Exclusions: Preparing trainers, purchasing and preparing training material, and identifying training locations are not charged to this control account.

FIGURE 5.4   Sample Control Account

ganizational unit. Sometimes there is a portion of the WBS that, during the initial planning stage, cannot be allocated to a CA. One reason may be that a specific organizational unit has not yet been identified. This type of effort is one that is defined and for which a schedule and budget will be prepared. This part of the plan can be allocated to what is called a *summary level planning package* (SLPP). WPs are the basic building blocks of the WBS.

WORK PACKAGES

A WP describes a discrete unit of effort and is assigned for planning and control to one organizational unit; it can vary in size depending on its WBS level and the complexity of the project. In a moderately sized project there are often WPs that describe an objective that will take about 10 days to accomplish. Responsible project team members can write the details of the WP for approval by the project manager.

The U.S. Navy work package technical manual defines the WP as:

> 3.2.90 Work packages (WPs). Presentation of information functionally divided into individual task packages in the logical order of work sequence. These WPs should be stand-alone general information, descriptive, theory, operating, maintenance, troubleshooting, parts, and supporting information units containing all information required for directing task performance (Department of the Navy 2001, 12).

A WP is the deliverable unit at the lowest level of a branch of the WBS. This WBS element must have scheduling and accountability because it is assigned to one responsible party, such as an individual team member or a contractor. The WP is the mechanism for passing responsibility for a deliverable to a team member. Even when a product-oriented WBS is used, the language at the level of the WP can usually be stated in measurable *tasks* or *activities*.

"A WP shall consist of an individual unit of information containing all data necessary for a technician to perform a specific task" (Department of the Navy 1997, 10). The WP does not have to be at the same level in every leg of the WBS and the team member responsible for that WP may further break it down into more detailed activities. In some complex projects, the WP even becomes a subproject of its own; however, the project manager will only be concerned with management down to the WP level. At this level, the project manager can schedule work, measure performance, monitor changes, and collect cost/schedule data.

As will be described more fully later, the WP must be linked to an organizational (functional) CA. A WP is a subdivision of a CA that constitutes the basis for planning, controlling, and reporting on project performance. It must be assigned to only one specific performing unit of the organization. The WP is the level where costs are estimated and all reporting data are initiated. For EVMS reporting, it is important that cost data for all elements of the WBS add up through each level to form the total cost for the entire project. In addition to cost information, the WP statement should include a technical description and the standards of the deliverable, along with reporting and completion requirements.

The *statement of work* (SOW), preferably written as a performance-based statement, describes the effort to produce the specific deliverables of a WP. The SOW outlines what, where, and when (schedule and milestones) required work will be performed. The statement will not generally describe how the work will be done, but will include standards, requirements, and the acceptance criteria. Although Figure 5.5 illustrates a simplified SOW (for a WP in our sample project), you must consider the following items for a complete statement:

- A product description for all required products
- Defined work standards
- Location of work
- Delineation of all necessary interfaces
- Specified dates coordinated with the overall project
- Measurable checkpoints
- List of required logs and reports
- A provision for exception reporting
- A discussion of possible constraints

Work package number and title: Customer Relationship Management (CRM) Information Seminar: WBS Ref# 1.3.1

Type of activity: Conference

Timetable: 1 day (three 2-hour sessions). Start date = 02/21/yyyy.

Preparations: Completed in advance.

Objectives: The objective of the package is to inform team members of our organization about the advantages of the CRM system and introduce the basic concepts.

Description of the contents, the work plan, the steps, the approach, or the methodology: One representative from the software company and one internal trainer will coordinate three 2-hour seminars to introduce the advantages and basic concepts of the CRM system. The CRM company representative will introduce another client who has successfully implemented the product. The other client will make a brief presentation of about their experience. The CRM company will distribute product brochures. The seminar leader will discuss the decisions and steps already taken, including their rationale, and present the tentative installation schedule. The CRM representative and our company partner will present the basic concepts of the system, its advantages, and the expected benefits.

Event publicity will be performed upon commencement of this work package.

Presentations will be made with prepared slides.

The rooms with necessary equipment will be rented.

Partners involved: Charlene Budd, HR trainer (external: Supplier Representative).

Deliverables, expected results, milestone for the overall package: We expect to encourage involvement in the new system, elicit suggestions for smooth implementation, answer questions, and overcome possible objections.

FIGURE 5.5   Simplified Statement of Work

- Special requirements (security clearances, travel, specific training, etc.)
- Clearly defined quality criteria
- Formal acceptance requirements.

The SOW differs from a WBS dictionary entry in that the former is written only for the WPs (the lowest level element of the WBS), while the dictionary entries will describe each WBS element and are not written with nearly as much detail as the SOW. Another form of the SOW is a general one that is sometimes provided by the project sponsor as part of the project charter and will have the same characteristics as those described for the WP, but will cover the overall project. This general form is often called a *statement of objectives* (SOO) and will provide only the basic top-level objectives of the project. It is similar to a *request for proposals* (RFP) and specifies the operational and technical requirements of the project. It can be used to develop the WBS, WP, and SOW.

In Chapter 4, the importance of management support and authorization was emphasized. Authorization comes up again in Chapter 5 as an important part of defining the work of the project. The first EVMS criterion requires that all the work elements of the project be authorized and defined, even if all the future details are not yet known. The extent of the work in a project is known as the project's scope.

A work breakdown structure (WBS) is most commonly used for the definition and can be represented as a diagram, chart, or indented list. The level of detail in the WBS representation will vary depending on the complexity of the project. Each element of the WBS should be described in detail as a WBS dictionary entry.

Control (cost) accounts (CAs) are closely tied with the WBS primarily through their subparts, the work packages (WPs). Control accounts are the major element of the accounting system set up at juncture points of the WBS and elements of the OBS. They constitute the basis for performance measurement and should be established at a work level where management reporting is meaningful. A WP describes a discrete unit of work at the lowest level of the WBS and is performed by a specific individual or department of the organization. The statement of work (SOW) describes the full extent of each work package.

DISCUSSION QUESTIONS

1. What are the advantages and/or disadvantages of constructing a WBS using objectives or deliverables rather than activities?

2. A project is planned to produce some desired result. Should the project planners be concerned with any results that are not to be produced and why or why not?

3. Define *project scope* and discuss the ramifications of *scope creep*.

4. What are the four primary elements of consideration in any project plan?

5. Discuss your preference for constructing the WBS in chart or list format.

6. What is an appropriate level of detail in the WBS? Why?

7. What is the primary reason for establishing control accounts?

8. Where are WPs depicted and what do they describe?

9. What would you include in a SOW that describes a WP?

10. Do you think you could use the "Obstacles and Required Conditions" technique to effectively solicit the intermediate and minor objectives of the project? Why or why not?

CHAPTER 6

The Organization (Criteria 2–5)

The breakdown of the project's objectives has been covered and there is still a substantial amount of work to do on the breakdown scheduling, but first we need to look at the structure of the organization. The EVMS Criteria 2 through 5 require both an analysis of the organizational structure and integration along several lines of the project's work components and the components of the organization.

We will examine how organizations are structured and the challenges you will encounter with each type. The project manager must scrutinize the organization to identify all the processes with which he or she must work and understand. Then it is possible to isolate all the integration points between the project's components and the organization's structure.

ORGANIZATIONAL CONFIGURATIONS

Every organization has some managerial structure that is either expressed in a formal organization chart or informally followed. These structures are usually classified in three general types by the way the reporting levels of the organization's members are arranged. These three classifications are identified by many different names, but they are generally referred to as:

- Functional style
- Matrix style
- Project-oriented style.

There are many subdivisions, variations, and combinations of these styles and the style may vary across different segments of the same organization.

Functional Style

Most organizations use the *functional* style, which divides the organization into operational units according to their functions—marketing, sales, operations, research and development, recruiting and training, financial accounting and reporting, and production. All members of each functional area report directly or indirectly through middle managers to the senior management of their respective functional areas. Each member usually has only one direct supervisor. Large projects are often separated into functional pieces and their management is then maintained within the various departments.

When a project crosses functional boundaries, the functional structure usually gives the project manager little control over the project team members because they are managed and evaluated more directly by their functional managers. The functional organization is also not adept at providing administrative assistance to the project manager because he or she has no functional role.

To be successful in this environment, a project manager must be a skilled negotiator and motivator. The project manager must convince both the functional head that assisting in completion of the project is in the department's best interest and also the potential team members of the project's challenges and opportunities. The establishment of a Project Management Office can often help overcome many of the difficulties encountered by the project manager in a functional organization.

Matrix Style

The *matrix* style is generally more responsive than the functional style for the project manager. The word *matrix*, as used for a style of organizational management, is taken from its definition as an array of mathematical elements that can be combined to form sums and products with similar arrays. A member of an organization with a matrix style generally reports to the functional manager, but also is expected to have a dotted line or part-time relationship to other managers. The project team is a new array of members formed from the functional arrays. The strength (weak, balanced, or strong) of the matrix style depends on the amount of supervision that is shared between the managers. Part of a project team formed from the organization's functional areas is illustrated in Figure 6.1.

The project manager is given a more direct authority in the matrixed organization because the staff members are usually assigned for part of their time to the project and the project manager. However, the project manager should be aware of potential

Group Function \ Project Task	Training	Software Distribution	Policies and Procedures
Human Resources	Member of the Project Team		
Technical Writers			Member of the Project Team
Information Systems		Member of the Project Team	

FIGURE 6.1   Project Team Member Matrix

problems similar to those in the functional organization. Since the team member's time is often divided between the project and the functional area, the project manager must be diligently aware of the amount of time that team members spend on the project. In some extreme cases, the functional manager may wish to charge as much time to projects as possible to reduce the department's expense; therefore, it is imperative that the project manager be aware of any potential problems.

Project-Oriented Style

The project manager has the most authority in the organizational structure with a *project-oriented* style. Some organizations, such as contractors of various types, consulting companies, law firms, and public accounting firms are particularly suited to the project-oriented style. Others may have instituted a management structure based upon a process of treating all work as projects. In a fully project-oriented (project-organized) environment, each project group has its own functional operations, support, and team members reporting to the equivalent of a project manager. This structure is similar to a *cell structure* design in a manufacturing firm.

Because a project is a temporary construct, the personnel and team relationships are also usually temporary. The interrelations with functional structures both inside and outside the organization will be very intricate. Complex projects require effective communication paths between team members of varying technical skills and abilities. Because of these issues, the project manager must use a simple and consistent communication system, such as the EVMS reporting mechanisms.

EVMS CRITERION 2

Identify the program organizational structure, including the major subcontractors, responsible for accomplishing the authorized work, and define the organizational elements in which work will be planned and controlled.

This criterion requires the identification and definition of two primary elements of the performing organizational structure: those *accomplishing* the work of the project and those *planning and controlling* the project. These two functional elements will almost assuredly cross the organization's normal functional boundaries and include entities totally outside the organization, as will be the case for subcontracting portions of the project. This will entail the creation of an *organization breakdown structure* (OBS) that will be similar in appearance to the *work breakdown structure* (WBS).

Organization Breakdown Structure

The OBS is a graphical representation of the hierarchical management structure of the organization or organizations responsible for completing the project. It designates the areas responsible for the various components of the project. Like the WBS, it is broken down in detail to the lowest levels of management necessary to control the project, and identifies the accountability and authority of each project team member and his or her functional area.

Like the WBS, the OBS can be graphically displayed in a variety of formats (see Figure 6.2 for an illustration of part of an OBS in a chart format).

A project's OBS can be constructed in the same way as one for the entire organization and portrays only the organizational units or individuals directly responsible for completing some element of the WBS.

Project Staffing

The project manager will need a comprehensive knowledge of the organization to identify and assign project roles. Constructing the OBS is an excellent way for the project manager to gain an understanding of responsibilities, authority, relationships, and staffing opportunities. The first step in getting staff resources is

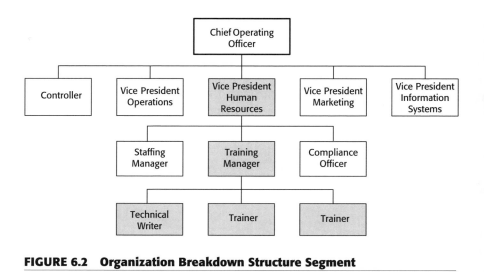

FIGURE 6.2   Organization Breakdown Structure Segment

to identify the required skills for the WBS elements and then to determine if and where the skills exist in the organization. A *timing plan* is necessary for when and how long resources will be required; however, that requirement falls under the criteria for scheduling and is covered in Chapter 7. For now, although we are concerned with *who will do what*, we are not necessarily concerned with *when*.

There are many interfaces and existing relationships within the organization that must be considered as the project plan is developed. Formal reporting relationships should be obvious in the OBS, but the project manager must look at the informal relationships that exist in every organization. Because components of a complex project certainly will cross the technical boundaries within the organization, sensitivity to these technical relationships will increase project success. Although interpersonal relationships may enhance assignment opportunities, they may also create boundaries similar to technical ones.

The project manager must also be aware of any constraints that may limit the assignment of project elements. The constraints may include legal determinations such as collective bargaining agreements, but the project manager should not overlook possible problems among the project team members, who may have preferences and preconceived expectations for certain assignments.

Criterion 2 requires the identification of organizational structures that will be involved in the project. Remember that the requirement only extends a few levels into the WBS. It will be the responsibility of the subcontractors or structural management units to provide resources for the delivery of assigned project objectives. When there is a subcontracted component of the project, a member of the primary organization must be designated to manage the outside effort. This manager should have the same authority and responsibility of other control account managers and have the ability to ensure the proper performance of the subcontractor (Department of Defense, FAA, and NASA 1997, S.3-9.a).

OBS Limitations

Cleland and Ireland list several limitations of the organizational chart:

- It fails to show the nature and limits of the activities required to attain the objectives.
- It does not reflect the myriad reciprocal relationships between peers, associates and many others. . . .
- It is a static, formal portrayal of the organizational structure. . . .
- It . . . neglects the informal, dynamic relationships that are constantly at play in the environment.
- It may confuse organizational position with status and prestige. (Cleland and Ireland 2002, 270)

They are absolutely right when they say, "it . . . tells little about how individuals function or relate to others in their environment" (2002, 270).

The OBS is necessary to depict the framework and hierarchy of the organization. Of course, more detail will be required when work packages (WPs) are described and particularly when the schedule time line is generated. Also, the project manager must be able to relate the elements of the WBS and the OBS. For that we look to the third criterion.

EVMS CRITERION 3

Provide for the integration of the company's planning, scheduling, budgeting, work authorization, and cost accumulation processes with each other, and as appropriate, the program work breakdown structure and the program organizational structure.

Now the criteria begin to address the issue of integration. The first criterion to do so is a tough one. The first part of the criterion requires tying together the organization's major functions; that can be a very difficult requirement for most establishments, especially those that are functionally organized.

One way to satisfy this criterion is to have a management control system and integrated data store such as commonly associated with *enterprise resource planning* (ERP) systems. A formal ERP system is certainly not the only way, but there must be a mechanism where all project elements can be readily visible to all the planning, scheduling, authorizing, and accounting functions of the organization.

To meet the requirements of this criterion, it is helpful to use at least two organizational constructs: a *linear responsibility chart* (LRC) and a *control account plan* (CAP).

Linear Responsibility Chart

Once we have constructed the WBS and the OBS, we can relate the elements of each. The LRC is a matrix view of the intersection of the elements of the WBS and the OBS. The LRC is known by several names such as the *responsibility assignment matrix* (Humphreys 2002, 100) and "has been called the *linear organization chart,* the *responsibility interface matrix,* the *matrix responsibility chart,* the *linear chart,* and the *functional chart*" (Cleland and Ireland 2002, 271).

An LRC illustrates which elements of the WBS are performed or managed by the elements of the OBS and to what degree. It details the responsibility of each member of the project team. In the matrix view, there are rows, columns, and cells as you would see in an ordinary spreadsheet showing project data—the WBS elements, the responsible organizational units, and the extent to which the units are responsible for each WBS element. The data may be laid out using the rows, columns, and cells for whichever of the three LRC elements is preferred in each, but the data are usually located in the manner illustrated in Figure 6.3. The innermost cells depict the level of responsibility for the organizational unit (three columns) that is responsible for the management of a work package (four rows). Other graphical representations of the LRC use the standard symbols of a flow type diagram (see Figure 6.2).

WBS Elements / OBS Elements			Implementation WBS 1.3					Other 1.n
			CRM Training WBS 1.3.2				Other 1.3.n	
			User Training WBS 1.3.2.3			Other 1.3.2.n		
			Publish WBS 1.3.2.3.1	Distribute WBS 1.3.2.3.2	Conduct WBS 1.3.2.3.3			
Department of Human Resources		V.P.					A	P
		Assistant				N		
		Clerk	N		N			
	Training Area	Manager	S	S	S			
		Technical Writer	P					
		Trainer A			P			
		Trainer B		P				
	Other H.R.				N	C		
Other Departments			N		N	N		

P = Primary Responsibility; S = General Supervision; C = Consultant; N = Notification; A = Approval

FIGURE 6.3   Portion of a Linear Responsibility Chart

Regardless of the type of LRC representation, several components and steps will ensure its accuracy, ease of comprehension, and completeness:

1. Determine the WBS components that will be delivered by each functional area. Enlist cooperation and assistance from the members of the functional areas.
2. Identify organizational units (most often individual team members) for different kinds of activity:
   • Primary performance
   • Cross-training
   • Supervising
   • Consulting
   • Notification
   • Review
   • Approval.
3. Analyze the LRC with all stakeholders to determine where activities should be restructured and for other possible improvements.

The LRC provides an excellent point for a review of the planning that went into the construction of the WBS and the OBS. A review at this time presents an opportunity to check for controls in the project plan and potential for risks to the project. System components to verify include:

• Internal controls such as verification requirements and segregation of duties
• Compensating factors where traditional internal controls are not feasible
• Cross-training or other types of backup
• Review and approval systems
• Potential risks (legal, financial, technical) and costs to minimize
• Corrective action plans.

The LRC can also be a useful place to look for the grouping of work packages that can be summarized to formulate control accounts.

Control Account Plan

Any system, automated or manual, to satisfy EVMS criteria must incorporate a control account plan (CAP). This plan is the establishment, control, and reporting from control accounts or cost accounts. The control account data should be maintained in a common database in order to provide the project information that will be accessed by all the organization's functional areas. CAPs must be defined narrowly enough that they do not cross any structural boundaries in the organization so that they can be summarized within the OBS as well as within the WBS. As the WBS product is subdivided at lower WBS levels, the effort required by each subproduct is assigned to a functional organization unit.

"The assignment of lower level work segments to responsible lower-level managers provides a key control point for management purposes and cost collection. This is called the control account (CA)" (Department of Defense, FAA, and NASA 1997, S.3-1.b). The concept of the control account was introduced in Chapter 5, but Criterion 3 implicitly requires its establishment. Figure 6.4 illustrates the location and makeup of CAs. They are the heart of EVMS and will be referenced more frequently as we proceed through the discussion of the EVMS criteria.

The CA is the pivotal point for planning, controlling, and reporting the project's activity. These accounts are the focus of budgeting, scheduling, assignments, data collection, progress assessment, and status determination. The difficulty of the activity and the ability of the management at each level should determine the levels at which CAs are established. The CA is the lowest level of planning and control necessary for management reporting. At this level, management should be able to identify any factors that might cause significant cost and/or schedule variances.

The subdivision of the WBS will often result in separate elements that will be produced by the same functional area of the organization. For example, software development may be a part of several WBS subproducts. Some care must be exercised so that the WBS is not subdivided so extensively that existing management structures are compromised.

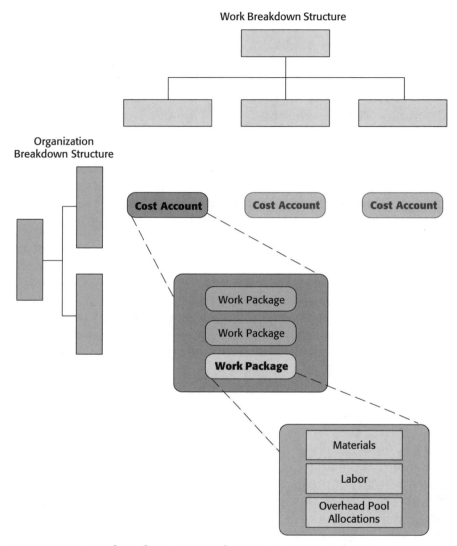

FIGURE 6.4   Work Packages, Control Accounts, WBS, and OBS

The responsible organizational level is a function of the company's management span of control and upper management's desire to delegate the responsibility for WBS elements to lower management levels. In identifying control accounts, the contractor is expected to establish organizational responsibilities at meaningful and appropriate levels. Otherwise the contractor's existing management control systems and responsibility assignments may be affected adversely (Department of Defense 1998, S. 3.1.4).

EVMS CRITERION 4

Identify the company organization or function responsible for controlling overhead (indirect costs).

One of the elements of the OBS is to clearly identify the managerial positions responsible for establishing and controlling indirect costs. This position must be clearly identified in the OBS. The management entity should have the "authority to approve or to avoid the expenditure of resources" (Department of Defense, FAA, and NASA 1997, S. 3-5.a).

In addition, EVMS requires a clear definition of the overhead costing system and the policies and procedures (P&P) set up to control indirect costs. In the P&P there must be a formal assignment of the required duties and a prescription of the limits of responsibility.

There is usually little argument about the direct costs of a project. The amount of time spent by a team member can be tracked by each project on which he or she works, but who decides how much of vacation time and employee benefit programs or the accounting department's time (overhead and indirect costs) is to be allocated to a variety of project and nonproject work? Criterion 4 requires the identification of those responsible for overhead allocation and implies that they should be *responsible* for an equitable and consistent allocation.

Overhead/indirect costs are identified as all costs not originating from direct material purchases and direct labor. They may also include costs that are part of delivering the product, but not usually or historically charged to the product. The key identifier for indirect costs is that they must be allocated on an *arbitrary* basis; that is, units of production cannot directly measure them. Indirect costs and their allocation will be detailed in Chapter 8 on budgeting. For now, Criterion 4 requires the identification of the functional unit responsible for controlling such expenses.

An interesting point about indirect costs and project costs in general is that the type of contract into which the parties entered for the project may influence their control and reporting. Contract types can vary from cost types such as *cost plus fixed fee, cost plus incentive,* and *cost plus percentage* to fixed types such as *firm fixed, fixed plus incentive,* and *unit price.* In a *cost type* project, the provider is interested in allocating as much expense to the project as possible while the recipient is interested in checking expenses very closely. In a *fixed type* contract, the provider would attempt to increase the project profit by minimizing expenses. The EVMS criteria attempt to provide controls that will restrict "gaming" the system.

EVMS CRITERION 5

Provide for integration of the program work breakdown structure and the program organizational structure in a manner that permits cost and schedule performance measurement by elements of either or both structures as needed.

The control account (CA) is the key to fulfilling the requirements of this criterion. CAs are established at juncture points of the WBS and the OBS and therefore will reflect measurement from elements of either or both structures. When building the OBS, there are points where CAs are assigned. Those same points exist in a well-constructed WBS. The organizational elements can report from their CAs or reporting can be done from the project's breakdown of the deliverables, the WBS. The reporting should be the same from either angle and, as a matter of fact, *must be* in order to satisfy Criterion 5.

There are many project management reports that are helpful to all project stakeholders. One of the important points of the fifth criterion is that the reporting will be integrated because there is a common point for performance measurement of cost, schedule, and technical perspectives. EVMS also requires the expression of these standard measurements in a standard measuring unit, usually the dollar. It does not matter how the organization is structured; it can be in any of the styles discussed at the beginning of this chapter. The information available to senior management is the same as the information used by the functional manager when looking at team work assignments and the same as the information seen by the project manager when looking at the project structure.

The *Cost Performance Report* (CPR) is most often used for EVMS projects and is covered in detail in Chapter 10 where Criterion 27 requires the generation of management information. The CPR and other reports can vary in format depending on the contracting agency's requirements, but they are used to provide comparisons of EVMS measurements. In general, reports will contain information about cumulative cost, cost/schedule performance, current budgeted value of the project, estimates at completion, cost and schedule variances, and narrative descriptions of status and problems.

Keep in mind that these reports should be kept to higher levels of the WBS/OBS, almost always at the CA level. That is sufficient for management reporting; however, the project manager may need more detailed information, particularly about the status of specific work packages.

Criteria 2 through 5 separate the first criterion for defining the project's work from those that delineate the scheduling of that work. This interruption enables the organization to mandate its definition so that project work requirements and organizational responses can be integrated.

The definition of the organization originates with its organizational style. Organizations are configured in some form of three general classes: functional, matrix, or project-oriented. The functional style is most common and is organized by groups that provide departmentalized services such as marketing or accounting. A project manager in the functional organization must have special skills because the project team members will have primary responsibilities to their functional departments.

The project manager has more authority in the matrix style because the team members are assigned directly to the project for at least part of their time. However, it is in the project style that the project manager has the most authority. The project teams in organizations such as consulting companies will have at least some of the functional services within the team.

Criterion 2 requires the identification and definition of the elements of the organization(s) that will plan, control, and accomplish the project's work. An organization breakdown structure (OBS) is best used for satisfying this criterion; similar to the work breakdown structure (WBS) the OBS can be represented in different formats. The OBS has several limitations in its portrayal of the organizational relationships.

Criterion 3 can be quite difficult to satisfy, as many organizations do not have well integrated functionality. A linear responsibility chart (LRC) is helpful with some aspects of the integration effort and a control account plan (CAP) is absolutely necessary. The control account (CA) is the pivotal point for planning, controlling, and reporting the project activity.

It is obvious that EVMS considers *overhead* or indirect costs a vulnerable aspect of project management; Criterion 4 is devoted exclusively to its control. The control of overhead is addressed further in the criteria concerning budgeting, recording, and controlling costs. Criterion 5 requires integration of the project's work breakdown and the project's organizational structure so that measurements are permitted from either or both structures. The Cost Performance Report is the primary method for reporting these integrated EVMS measurements.

DISCUSSION EXERCISES

1. Identify the organizational style of your organization. List the advantages and disadvantages of the style for your organization.

2. List your organization's major functional processes.

3. Identify the normal interactions between departments in the organization.

4. Identify the primary staff members and any external influences in each of the functional processes.

5. Identify some informal working relationships or reciprocal arrangements within the organization.

6. Identify any current cross-training practices or other types of personnel backup.

CHAPTER 7

The Schedule (Criteria 6–8)

"The first 90 percent of a project takes 90 percent of the time; the last 10 percent takes the other 90 percent of the time."
—Unknown

A comprehensive project schedule, done properly, is the basic tool for EVMS. It helps determine activity and total project duration, shows the sequence of work, identifies task and resource dependency, provides the ability to measure progress, and shows time periods when funding is required.

Criteria 6, 7, and 8 are the criteria that deal with project schedules. Criterion 6 requires a sequencing of work that identifies task interdependencies, while Criterion 7 requires schedule indicators for measuring progress. Criterion 8 mandates a time-phased budget baseline, which introduces the criteria on project budgeting (see Chapter 8).

There are two important considerations about preparing a project schedule: management support and schedule uncertainty.

SCHEDULE UNCERTAINTY

The one major project problem that occurs over and over again is that projects overrun their completion dates. There are many reasons for project overruns, for example, not working closely with the end user, inadequate planning, incomplete information, and lack of commitment. It is usually not because there was some calamity or a crucial failure, but the accumulation of day-after-day small task duration overruns.

As you have no doubt experienced, a project's greatest uncertainty is its completion date (which also affects cost). When the project plan is laid out in black and white with activities and times, it becomes a very deterministic view. The project manager must understand the effects of probability and educate the stakeholders concerning the challenges of accurate estimating and its effect on a predetermined schedule.

Challenges in Constructing a Realistic Schedule

One of the major deterrents to achieving a reasonable project schedule is having a completion date forced by some other requirements of the organization. Such a situation is difficult to reconcile and the best solution is to request and acquire adequate resources. A more prevalent problem results from the fact that the completion date is based on the accumulation of the multitudes of individual task duration estimates.

Estimating Task Times

We believe the most important aspect of duration estimates is to have an open and honest relationship with those who supply the estimates. Very often the people providing the estimates are members of the staff responsible for completing the task. It does not take very long to learn how to play the game. For example, if estimates are always reduced, the staff quickly learns to make them longer. If they are multitasking on several projects, they will pad completion dates to allow for the uncertainties of moving from one task to another. If the staff have regular responsibilities in the organization as well as being assigned to one or more special projects, they must bias the project task estimates to protect their jobs.

Although professional estimators are more often used for cost estimating, they also may be used effectively to determine the expected duration of crucial activities. Whether using outside professionals or project staff, it is vital that they understand which estimating methods are to be used and the reasoning behind the selection.

Even with the best of estimates, individual tasks often take longer. It is easy to see that *days* of missed task completions easily add up to *months* of delays for the entire project and a missed completion date. This is always a mystery, especially when we know that most people give themselves plenty of padding when they estimate a task's duration. Even when management insists on reducing time estimates, the project team members are somewhat assured that they still have a margin of protection. It usually doesn't take long for employees to learn the rules of the game and make the necessary adjustments. The question remains—What happens to all their protection and what can be done about it?

Dysfunctional Behavior Traits

There are at least four traits that easily waste the protection built into individual task times. The first is the *student syndrome*—waiting until the last minute to complete the task, just as many students delay studying until the night before the big test. A project task originally estimated at three weeks actually may only take two weeks; however, it will still be a week late if it isn't started until the last week of its schedule.

What if we don't fall prey to the student syndrome and the three-week (actual two-week) task is started on time? Won't there be a plus of one week for the project when the task is finished early? Well, not usually! Our second problem—*the no early work transfer*—is that little work is transferred to the next phase when it is finished early. Of course, we are often late in passing work from a task to those dependent on it—resulting in no early passes, only late passes. Therefore, dependent tasks are late and eventually the project misses its completion date. Part of the problem is that there are incentives for not reporting the task's early completion, such as avoiding management reducing the next task estimate even more stringently. Besides, if there is some extra time, the task deliverable can be improved—and that leads to the next behavioral pattern.

The third trait is known as *Parkinson's Law*: Work expands to fill the time available. First articulated by C. Northcote Parkinson in his book *Parkinson's Law* (1957), this trait is similar to the student syndrome, but has its own rationale. Just as any size closet will soon be filled, the same phenomenon occurs with any task time. We do what we can with the amount of space and time that we have.

The last bad trait is one that seems a little counterintuitive. *Polychronicity*, the habit of multitasking, would seem to allow more tasks to be completed. However, we must distinquish between good multitasking and bad multitasking. Good multitasking happens when a task must be interrupted because of some outside reason such as an unavailable resource. In that case, it makes perfect sense to work on another task—to multitask. Bad multitasking occurs when one task is interrupted for no other reason than there are other tasks on which to work. Every time there is a change of tasks, there is set-down time on the previous task and set-up time on the new task. Even our brain has to set down the old rules and set up the new ones. Bad multitasking adds unpredicted time to all of the tasks.

Overcoming Schedule Problems

The EVMS performance measurements are needed in many ways, not the least of which is the very effective early indication if the project is going to be late or over budget. Techniques are also needed to prevent schedule problems and minimize them when they occur.

Crashing a Project

Even the best project schedules often encounter difficulties that affect the completion date. There may be resource considerations or a business decision that mandates a shortened project. When the expected duration must be reduced, we refer to the process as *crashing*. Crashing a project can be accomplished in several ways. One is to devote additional resources to certain activities; another is to reduce the project's complexity by eliminating some of its intermediate objectives or reducing its technical scope. The benefits of crashing must be weighed against the cost of additional resources or the loss of project deliverables.

When determining likely places to crash a project, be sure to select areas that will affect the completion date. There are many project activities whose durations have no immediate effect on the overall project duration. This may be attributed to the adequate availability of the necessary resources and skills or it may be due to the independence of the activity. If other downstream tasks in the project are not dependent on the completion of a particular task, that first task's duration will usually not affect the overall project completion and is not a good candidate for crashing.

Critical Chain

Too often, a schedule problem is a result of the behavior patterns described earlier and changing human behavior is not easy. It is not something that happens by talking about it or even presenting logical proofs. There must be some compelling motivation.

Eli Goldratt (1997, 246) developed a system for project management that he called *Critical Chain* (CC). One function of the system operates to remove the protection time built into the individual task duration estimates and place it strategically to protect critical points in the overall project schedule. Removing the protection time from individual tasks is the compelling behavior change from the bad traits outlined above because there is just no time for them. Each task has a smaller "closet" to fill. The time taken from each task is used to provide protection for the entire project schedule when some of the individual tasks are late.

There are other components in the system such as the buffering techniques mentioned in Chapter 10. Cultural changes are also usually required in order for CC to succeed; for example, team members should not be punished for exceeding a shortened task estimate. An atmosphere of trust must exist within the organization; we have experienced several project successes using the concepts of CC. One problem is that the EVMS metrics must be calculated differently in CC, because time is removed from task durations to create the buffers. We worked with one organization that solved this problem by using a CC schedule for project management and an unbuffered schedule for EVMS calculations. They had no objections from the auditors.

Unnecessary Fixes

In Chapter 3, we presented W. Edwards Deming's idea of two kinds of variation that occur in systems. Repeating it here underscores an important point about making adjustments when schedule variances occur. Sometimes a problem is self-inflicted when schedule and resource adjustments are made without regard for differences in variation. *Common cause variation* is the result of expected variety in the normal course of events —the system is still in control. Making adjustments when a system is in control can put it out of control. *Special cause variation* is the result of unexpected events and/or malfunctioning activities. Special cause variation is the reason for risk management and that is when the project manager must act.

A Bit of Statistics and Probability

One of the problems of scheduling a project is that the task duration times are estimates. No one knows with certainty how long a specific piece of any schedule will take—it's a future event and we don't have crystal balls. While unpredictable quantities regularly produce unpredictable results, there are ways that we can address task time uncertainty.

We can use the mathematical concept of subjective probability and some basic knowledge of human behavior to help us improve both our estimates and our control of projects. A barrier to accepting probability concepts is the reality that a task or a project, after the fact, can have only one outcome, while probabilities are based on repetition. The most familiar example is the coin toss and the number of heads that will result from a set of tosses. Because the probability of a head coming up on any one toss is 50 percent, the probability of two heads occurring in only two tosses is 25 percent (0.5 x 0.5), and so on. Unlike objective probabilities associated with coin tosses, task estimates are subjective. Nevertheless, we can use subjective probability theory to examine project estimates.

Look at a very simple set of tasks in Figure 7.1 (illustrating five different resources by shaded tasks). We'll assume that each task has been estimated, with a 90 percent degree of confidence, to be completed in 10 days. Does that mean that there is a 90 percent probability that the project can be completed in 50 days?

No. The probability of completing the project in 50 days is not 90 percent, or even 70 percent, because of task and resource dependencies on each path and the fact that both paths must be completed before the final task can be started. The degree of variation in the project's completion time increases dramatically as the number of tasks and converging paths increase.

In probability statistics, this phenomenon is sometimes referred to as the *Multiplication Rule*. This rule states that the probabilities of dependent events must be multiplied to produce the

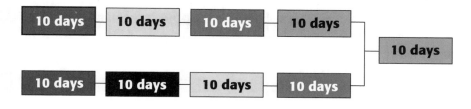

FIGURE 7.1   An Estimated 50-Day Project

probability for all the events. Of course, there is a small probability that the project will complete in 50 days or less, but there is a greater probability that the project will complete at a much later time. The point is that the degree of variation widens as the number of tasks increases. The project manager must understand and also remind project stakeholders that point estimates (a single estimated completion time of 10 days, for example) for tasks are not precise.

Notice that five different resources are required in Figure 7.1. If the project manager focuses on each task completing on time (the estimated date), the resources will do their best to complete work by the due date. However, they may well insist on having sufficient protection built into their estimates.

The probability of 90 percent was used in Figure 7.1 because that is closest to the most common probability estimate that we have experienced. When someone is asked how long it will take to complete a task, he or she will likely quote an estimate in which they have a high degree of confidence. One of the advantages of PERT (discussed in a later section of this chapter) is that it uses three estimates. The method asks for not only a safe or pessimistic estimate (the 90 percent-confidence one), but also the most likely and the shortest possible or optimistic.

Figure 7.2 illustrates the elements of a statistical distribution given three estimates with earliest possible completion setting the minimum time required, the most likely estimate (which could be the mode, median, or mean) having more heavy weight, and the pessimistic estimate (point "S") having a very high degree of confidence.

Many distributions exhibit the long right-hand tails described in Figure 7.2, such as the Beta PERT, popularly used in Monte Carlo simulations of task and project completion times, and the lognormal distribution shown in Figure 7.3, which incorporates variability as well as average values.[1]

---

[1]The ability to model spikes or jumps in expected results makes this distribution a favorite for modeling stock prices.

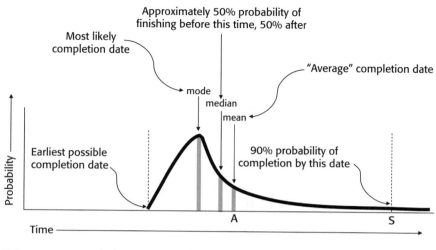

FIGURE 7.2   Statistical Distribution

EVMS CRITERION 6

Schedule the authorized work in a manner which describes the sequence of work and identifies significant task interdependencies required to meet the requirements of the program.

The two important words in this criterion about the project schedule are *sequence* and *interdependencies.* You must use a scheduling system that describes and identifies both the sequence and the interdependencies of the project activities. Although this criterion only requires the identification of these two elements, several other basic elements of a good project schedule are required in the next two criteria.

Sequence of Work

First, of course, the schedule must show all the activities that will make up this project. The *work breakdown structure* (WBS), created as a requirement of Criterion 1, identified the project objectives or deliverables (sometimes activity), but now those WBS elements must be translated into activities that will accomplish the project objectives. The activities can be decomposed until

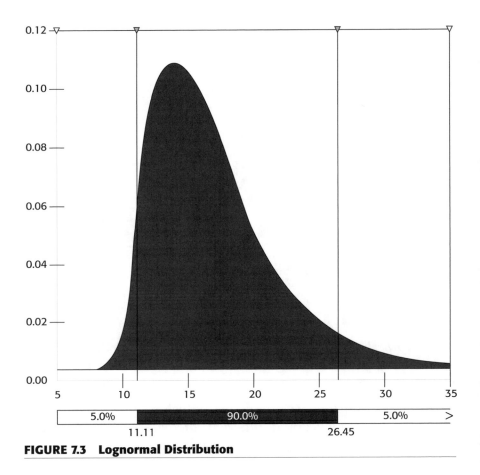

FIGURE 7.3   Lognormal Distribution

specific items of work or tasks contain enough detail to ensure adequate management and progress reporting.

The schedule should show the sequence in which the tasks must be performed according to precedence rules resulting from a variety of constraints. The order in which tasks can be performed usually arises from three causes. We refer to the cause as *technical* when a second task, the successor, simply cannot be started until another task, the predecessor, is finished. Some element of the first task contributes to the second task. Priorities may also be established where tasks are completed in a *preferred order* even without any technical or logical dependencies. A third cause for particular sequencing could be the result of a *resource constraint* where a specific resource cannot be utilized on a successor task until that resource has completed the predecessor task. The sequencing of the work should identify any significant task interdependencies.

Task Dependencies

First let's define the various forms of project task dependence. Tasks are *independent* if they have no effect on each other. They are *mutually exclusive* if one cannot occur in the presence of the other. They are *collectively exhaustive* if one of a set must occur and they are *dependent* (interdependent) if they have some effect on each other.

Task interdependencies can exist in four different ways (the first part of the relationship is the *predecessor* task and the second part is the *successor*):

1. The *Finish-to-Start relationship* is the most common and means that a predecessor task (or tasks) must be finished before the successor task can start. To construct a small concrete slab, a frame must be built and concrete must be mixed before the concrete can be poured into the frame. A subroutine of a computer program must be written before testing can begin on the subroutine. Although many tasks must be scheduled as Finish-to-Start, all tasks cannot be scheduled in this way or the project will take far too long. Many tasks can be overlapped in time.

2. The *Start-to-Start relationship* means that a predecessor task must at least be started before the successor task can be started. Priming the walls of a room must be started before putting up the wallpaper can be started. The design for a program subroutine must be started before any coding can be started.

3. The *Finish-to-Finish relationship* means that the successor task may start without regard to the start of the predecessor task, but cannot finish until its predecessor task is finished. The design of a computer subroutine may begin as soon

as some client specifications are received, but the design cannot be completed until all client specifications are complete.

4. The *Start-to-Finish relationship* is rare and can usually be represented in one of the first three relationships. We have even heard the argument that this option is not necessary at all. When used, it means that the predecessor task must at least be started before the successor task can be completed or it might be said that the start of the predecessor task causes the finish of the successor task. The terms *predecessor* and *successor* get fuzzy in this relationship. In the coding of computer subroutines, the programmer may continue to tinker with the code until testing starts. The start of testing must end any coding or the testing will be invalid. A very similar example is expressed in the Finish-to-Start relationship, but in the latter case there is a presumption that the finishing of the predecessor (coding) would not necessarily begin the successor (testing). In this case the coding might continue indefinitely unless the start of testing ends it.

In order to schedule the sequence and dependency of project activities, we highly recommend an automated scheduling system that uses techniques similar to the *critical path method* (CPM) of network scheduling. The effect of CPM is to identify the longest path of dependent tasks through the entire project schedule, called the *critical path* (CP), and thereby provide the estimated project duration. Critical chain is a similar method. Most automated project management systems utilize CPM or a similar network and we believe that *manual* charting of task sequence and interdependency can be done successfully only on very simple projects.

SCHEDULE REPRESENTATION AND EVALUATION

The many elements of a complete project schedule should be illustrated in a graphical representation. The elements include descriptions of the activities, sequence of events, task durations, start and end times, task interdependencies, milestones, and resources.

There are many ways to represent and articulate the project schedule and they each have been developed for different reasons or because of particular issues. Some of the most common are lists, bar charts, arrow diagrams, and more sophisticated network diagrams. Some of these representations, such as PERT, utilize statistical formulas to estimate the most likely project schedule.

Lists

The easiest to develop and maintain is a simple list of activities or deliverables. A list may show grouping of tasks by using indentation similar to the levels of the WBS. A list also can show the sequence of the schedule elements by their order, but it cannot convey the required information on interdependency without a great deal of creativity and manipulation; nor will it graphically display any time conditions as a bar chart can.

Bar Charts

The bar chart is more visually oriented by showing activities in bars with their length depicting time requirements and it can indicate some sequence, but again the bar chart is limited in its ability to show interdependency without some further relational mechanism. Several enhancements have been developed for the simple bar chart.

The Gantt chart is a form of bar chart and there are a host of references to it, starting almost 100 years ago. We'll quote one definition from TechTarget (Rouse 2004):

> A Gantt chart is a horizontal bar chart developed as a production control tool in 1917 by Henry L. Gantt, an American engineer and social scientist .... Frequently used in project management, a Gantt chart provides a graphical illustration of a schedule that helps to plan, coordinate, and track specific tasks in a project. Gantt charts may be simple versions created on graph paper or more complex automated versions created using applications such as Microsoft Project or Excel.

Figure 7.4 illustrates a portion of a Gantt chart for the CRM sample project. In a typical Gantt chart, the activities are listed down the left side and dates are shown across the top. Task start times and durations are indicated by the placement and length of a horizontal bar. Shading a portion of the bar can show work progress. It is an excellent way to show planned and actual work progress, but some Gantt charts do not illustrate necessary information for task dependencies. There is not a good way to determine what effect a late task will have on another task (see Figure 7.4 for an example of a chart that shows task connections).

There are usually several other vertical columns between the list of activities and the date portion of the chart. These columns are used to provide other information about each task such as duration, staff member assigned, predecessor tasks, and priority information. The time periods can be in any time denomination, such as hours or days.

Networks

A well-constructed *network* has an advantage over the standard bar chart in depicting task interdependencies and independencies. A disadvantage in the early network portrayals was a poor graphical representation of the time scale, but computer-generated networks have generally overcome this problem. There have been several variations of the networks method.

Activity on Arrow and Activity on Node

These network designs are excellent for depicting the task sequence or precedence relationships of project activities. They are often called *arrow diagramming* or *precedence diagramming* methods. This type of network is constructed with lines (arrows) showing the flow of activity and connected at points (nodes). The activities are shown either on the arrows themselves (AOA) or on the nodes (AON). The latter is also called *Activity in Box* (AIB). Historically in AOA, the length of the arrow did not indicate the duration of the activity. In AON, the expected task duration is often

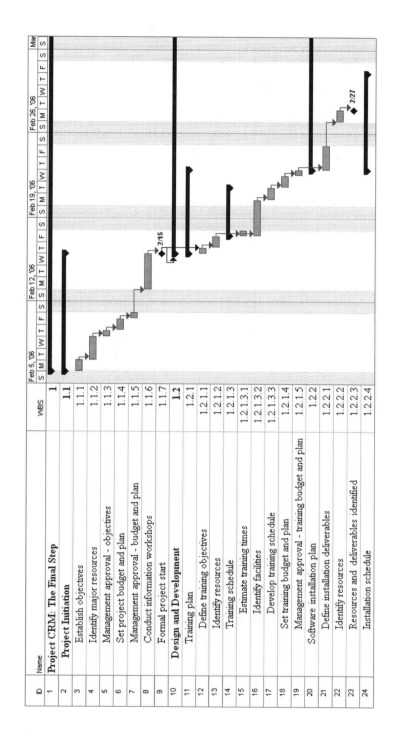

FIGURE 7.4   Portion of a Gantt Chart

listed along with the description of the activity. The PERT diagram shown in Figure 7.5 is a type of activity on node.

Program Evaluation and Review Technique (PERT)

PERT was developed in the late 1950s by the U.S. Navy with the cooperation of Booz-Allen Hamilton and the Lockheed Corporation for the Polaris submarine missile program (Archibald 1987, 29). It was created as a method to expedite project completion and appears to have some descendancy from the line of balance method. PERT uses statistical probabilities to estimate task durations and the project completion date. It has been closely associated with the CPM.

PERT can be represented as an AOA or AON network. In the AOA style, the tasks are depicted on the arrows (lines) and the nodes represent events or milestones. The network begins with a start node from which the first task or set of tasks propagates. The first task line (or lines) is then connected to its successor task through a node and all tasks are thus connected, forming the network. Sometimes a task will not be immediately succeeded in time by another task. This wait time is called *slack* and is usually represented by a dotted line connecting the ending node of the predecessor task with the start node of the successor task.

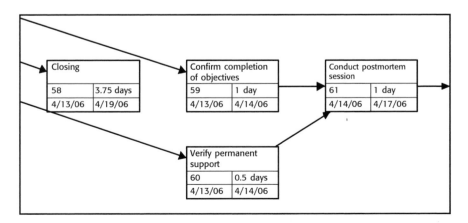

FIGURE 7.5   Portion of a PERT Diagram in AON Format

The task identification, its duration, and assigned resource (resources) are stated on the task line and the length of the line can depict the expected duration. The nodes do not represent any passage of time; therefore, events such as reviews or authorizations that will take time should not be shown as nodes. Instead, they should be shown as tasks with estimates of their duration. In EVMS, some nodes of the PERT chart will often represent a measurement control or funding point. A major project can produce a complex PERT chart of many interconnecting lines and nodes and it is much more convenient to construct the network in logical pieces of the total project.

PERT is most often used in an attempt to produce a realistic project schedule. Undertaking that effort requires three duration estimates for each activity that represent a *pessimistic time* (p), a *most likely time* (m), and an *optimistic time* (o). The PERT process then calculates:

the activity's mean time as t = (p + 4m + o) / 6
and a standard deviation as s = (o − p) / 6.

Using the estimated mean times, the probability of completing the project in a given time can be calculated.

PERT is sometimes considered a probabilistic model because of the task estimation process. However, its one drawback is that it uses the mean task times to determine a single critical path (there may be several and they often change as the project progresses). This feature tends to reduce the PERT model to a deterministic one. Projects progress more realistically in a stochastic manner and, as a result, the PERT project completion date projections are often short of the projects' actual completions. A Monte Carlo simulation can be performed on the network to ameliorate this built-in bias. A. R. Klingel has published calculations for a real network (1966; 476–489).

Graphical Evaluation and Review Technique (GERT)

Pritsker and Happ (1966, 267-274) published their fundamentals of GERT (the first of a series) in the *Journal of Industrial Engineering*. GERT was a modification of PERT that simulated the uncertain nature of project activity by allowing loops through certain parts of the schedule and skipping other parts altogether. In reality, some activities are repeated and some are partially or never performed. This methodology computed activity distributions through Monte Carlo simulation.

Despite the advantages of GERT's probabilistic simulation techniques, very complex projects could result in networks that were difficult, even impossible, to interpret. In response, Pritsker and his associates developed an extension to GERT (Q-GERT) that provided greater flexibility in simulating multiteam and multiproject environments.

Critical Path Method

CPM was developed by DuPont, Inc., in about the same timeframe as PERT (Peterson 1965, 70). Some representations of a CPM network are similar to PERT charts and they are often referred to as PERT/CPM. The critical path in a project is the longest series in time of dependent activities (each task on a particular path of the project network is dependent on its predecessor). As the project progresses, the critical path may change (and very often does) as tasks are completed either behind or ahead of schedule.

There are several calculations in the CPM and they are easily performed in automated project management software. Basically, the method first determines the dependent relationships and durations for each activity in the project. A network using the relationships and durations is then constructed usually as an AOA, but automated systems can identify the critical path in most network representations. The next step is to calculate both the earliest start and completion time and the latest start and completion time for each activity and use the results to calculate slack (the amount of time an activity may be delayed without delaying the project) for each activity. The critical path is the line of activities with zero slack.

As mentioned earlier, one variation on CPM is the Critical Chain (Goldratt 1997). The CC identifies the critical path of both dependent tasks *and* dependent resources. The CPM usually resolves resource conflicts (resource leveling) after identifying the critical path and based on the resource requirements of the critical path. The CC first levels the resources and then identifies the critical chain of dependent tasks.

EVMS CRITERION 7

Identify physical products, milestones, technical performance goals, or other indicators that will be used to measure progress.

Now we come to a primary element of EVMS—identifying the indicators on which the earned value will be calculated. We cannot enumerate all the ways to measure project progress and this criterion does not specify a particular measurement. It does require identifying *some* measurement techniques. They can be product deliveries, activity completion points, stated performance goals, or other indicators, but they must allow for a measurement of project progress.

In the Gantt chart illustrated in Figure 7.4, you may have noticed some milestone activities. These were placed in convenient measuring points in the schedule at approximately two-week intervals. This is a method of establishing measurement points that coincide with completed deliverables. For example, a contract WBS is often constructed entirely of deliverables, but they are almost always converted to activities for a project schedule. To be effective measurement indicators, milestones must be set frequently enough that their attainment can coincide closely with EVMS status requirements. Estimates of completion must be made if a status is taken and there are few coincidental milestone achievements.

Another measurement indicator can be simply the completion of *work packages* (WPs) (activities). WPs should be established with a short duration so that performance measurements for status reporting will be more accurate. It is much easier to make an accurate estimate of the percentage complete when the activity covers only a short time span. This method is one example of realizing technical performance goals as expressed in Criterion 7.

EVMS CRITERION 8

Establish and maintain a time-phased budget baseline, at the control account level, against which program performance can be measured. Budget for far-term efforts may be held in higher level accounts until an appropriate time for allocation at the control account level. Initial budgets established for performance measurement will be based on either internal management goals or the external customer negotiated target cost, including estimates for authorized but undefinitized work. On government contracts, if an over target baseline is used for performance measurement reporting purposes, prior notification must be provided to the customer.

The *cost accounts* (CA) in the control account plan (CAP) identified in the discussion of Criterion 5 now come into more direct use as a requirement of Criterion 8. CAs were required at low-level control points during the construction of the WBS. As the work schedule is created from the WBS, the CAs will be assigned to specific elements of the schedule. The dollar estimates established for each cost account and now related to the project schedule will produce a budget baseline against which performance can be measured as the project progresses.

The Target Baseline

It is very important to understand the need for and use of a project *baseline*. In sporting events, a baseline is usually a boundary line for some part of the field of play so that progress can be measured and out-of-bounds play can be determined. We use a very similar meaning in project management: the project baseline is our boundary marker from which we can measure progress and determine what is included and excluded from our project. It is called the *performance measurement baseline* (PMB).

Most industry sources define the PMB in a manner similar to the definition by the Electronic Industries Alliance:

> The total time-phased budget plan against which program performance is measured. It is the schedule for expenditure of the

resources allocated to accomplish program scope and schedule objectives, and is formed by the budgets assigned to control accounts and applicable indirect budgets. The Performance Measurement Baseline also includes budget for future effort assigned to higher Work Breakdown Structure levels (summary level planning packages) plus any undistributed budget. Management Reserve is not included in the baseline as it is not yet designated for specific work scope (Electronic Industries Alliance 2002, 7).

By this point, you should have expressed the goals for the project in the planning phase and a method is required to assess progress toward achieving those goals. The PMB is basically a performance contract. Measurements are needed to judge whether the organization's investments are producing the anticipated benefits. If they are not, decisions can be made to alter the investment or to understand changes for future investments.

Regular performance measurement promotes the effective use of resources and provides valuable information for improving other project efforts. Often the progress measurement is the basis for progress payments and project incentives. Measurement is also an obvious tool for identifying trends in the organization's performance.

All the work authorized for this project, whether performed internally or contracted externally, must be included in the PMB. Some of this work may not yet be defined in detail, but an estimate must be built into the budget. There is no need to construct CAs for an effort that is too far in the future to accurately break down the total budget cost. These estimates can be held at a higher level called *summary-level planning packages* (SLPP).

Summary-Level Planning Packages

Even though some specific work has been authorized, it may not be practical to assign it to CAs. When necessary, this work may be held at a higher level of the WBS or OBS in planning packages. The work and its related budget must be time-phased and evaluated periodically. The budget for the SLLP must be tightly controlled to ensure that it is not used for some of the other areas of the project.

The SLPP is not to be used to postpone difficult and more detailed planning. It must be subdivided into the appropriate CAs as soon as possible and always before the actual work begins.

Controls and Reporting

There must be a baseline plan with time-phased budgets that coincide with the work schedules. The schedule must indicate milestones that clearly delineate specific quantities of work and are related directly to control accounts. This quantity of work (it may be a WP) must also have an assigned budget amount. All the assigned budget values should summarize the total of the CA.

Funding from the CA plan should coincide with the schedule of the work. If work can begin earlier than the scheduled start date or must start later than that date, it must be authorized as an exception. Shifting of schedules and budget components can seriously impact the performance measurements of EVMS. It is very important for accurate performance reporting to include any authorized schedule changes.

Over-Target Baseline

For EVMS, the project performance should be measured against the current authorized plan baseline. As a project progresses, it may be discovered that the remaining budget in the target baseline is grossly insufficient and will not produce progress measurements that are meaningful. In order to bring the project in line with reasonable control and measurement, it may become necessary to replan the remainder of the project and perhaps even to adjust some past measurements. This new plan is called an *over-target baseline* (OTB). Criterion 8 requires prior notification if the OTB is going to be used for performance reporting.

This is an unusual procedure and every alternative must be examined before implementing an OTB. An OTB should be considered only if it is necessary for valid performance management. If the project stakeholders agree that the proposed OTB is reasonable and sufficient, the OTB becomes the approved base-line for the remaining progress measurements. All adjustments, both to the remaining portion of the project and to any existing variances, must be carefully documented and allow for audit pro-cedures. The causes of the unsatisfactory baseline must also be investigated and documented so as to prevent future occurrences. The military has published a 37-page document called the *Over Target Baseline and Over Target Schedule Handbook* to provide guidance on formal rescheduling (Bembers et al. 2003).

This chapter discusses the three criteria for the project sched-ule—one of the three basic constraints of project management. The project manager must have an awareness and understand-ing of the challenges in building a realistic and attainable project schedule. Too often, one of the first challenges is dealing with a compulsory completion date that is rapidly followed by the dif-ficulties of accurately estimating task duration times and success-fully meeting the project schedule. The problem often is a result of the four dysfunctional behavior traits known as the student syndrome, no early work transfers, Parkinson's Law, and poly-chronicity.

EVMS is a good early warning system for schedule problems and a management system such as Critical Chain (CC) can help address the human behavior encumbrances—just don't try to fix a system that is in control. Understanding a little of statistics and probability can help the project manager in dealing with task time estimates.

Criterion 6 requires a project schedule that describes the se-quence and interdependencies of the activities. The sequence of the tasks can be affected by technical or resource constraints or simply be the result of some preferred order. Task dependencies are expressed in four relationships: Finish-to-Start, Start-to-Start, Finish-to-Finish, and Start-to-Finish, although the last one is rarely used.

It is virtually impossible to manually handle all the challenges of scheduling a project, but fortunately there are powerful automated systems. Project schedules are often depicted in such forms as activity lists, bar charts, and networks. The critical path method (CPM) is a way of estimating the project completion date identifying time-critical activities.

Criterion 7 requires the identification of project indicators for progress measurement. If used, milestones should be set frequently so that fewer estimates of completion are required at the EVMS status points. Work packages (WPs) should be small enough also to eliminate as much estimation as possible.

Criterion 8 mandates a time-phased budget baseline at the control account (CA) level. The baseline, called the performance measurement baseline (PMB), is created by associating control accounts with dollar estimates to components of the work schedule. The PMB has a variety of uses, including: measuring performance to contract, judging the value of investments, improving resource usage, providing a basis for progress payments and incentives, and identifying performance trends. Work that is too far in the future to define for cost accounts (CAs) can be held in summary-level planning packages (SLLPs). If for uncontrollable reasons, the PMB becomes so obsolete that meaningful reporting is no longer possible, a reconstruction of the plan may be necessary. The new plan is called an over target baseline (OTB) and must be done only in very unusual circumstances and only after every other alternative has been considered.

In addition to the reference material provided in this chapter, we also recommend the following sources for further study.

1. Anderson, D., D. Sweeney, and T. Williams. *Essentials of Statistics for Business and Economics*. 3rd ed. Cincinnati, OH: South-Western, 2003.
2. Badiru, A.B. "A simulation approach to network analysis." *Simulation* 57, no. 4 (1991): 245–255.
3. Keefer, D.L., and W.A.Verdini. "Better Estimation of PERT Activity Time Parameters." *Management Science* (September 1993): 1086–1091.

4. Rumsey, D. *Statistics for Dummies.* New York: John Wiley & Sons, 2003.

DISCUSSION QUESTIONS

1. Why is it so difficult to obtain accurate and realistic estimates for task durations?

2. Discuss the four dysfunctional behavior traits that waste time in the completion of project activities.

3. What are the pros and cons of project crashing and how is it accomplished?

4. What effect should probability theory have on our thinking about the project schedule?

5. What factors might control the sequence in which project tasks are performed?

6. Name the four task dependencies and discuss their meaning and relative frequency of use.

7. What is the most common form of project bar chart and what does it depict?

8. Describe the elements of the AON and AOA project network diagrams.

9. Discuss the most important benefits of PERT. Are there any weaknesses?

10. Why does EVMS require a PMB and what is it?

11. When can project replanning be performed and what is the new plan called?

CHAPTER 8

The Budget
(Criteria 9–15)

This chapter on budgeting concludes Part III on project planning—probably the most important and most neglected part of any project. Saving budgeting until the final phase of planning must be saving the best for last (doesn't everyone love preparing budgets?). Regardless of your previous experience with budgeting, we intend to make project budgeting as painless as possible. The budgeting process for projects is very similar to budgeting in general and the basic concepts discussed here can be applied in any situation requiring fiscal control.

Budgeting is the third step in an iterative three-step planning process where the first step involves defining the work (*work breakdown structure* [WBS]), and the second step is scheduling the work (a time-phased baseline showing task dependencies). Budgeting completes the planning phase and is the basic foundation on which EVMS is built, setting a standard against which future progress is measured. Therefore, using estimates that are as realistic as possible—given the uncertainty and limited time to accumulate information—will minimize unexpected and unfavorable variances as work progresses.

Criteria 9 through 15 cover the establishment of budgets, how they are prepared and controlled, what they include, how they are stated, and to whom they are assigned. Previously, we pointed out that the project plan cost estimate should include the basis for estimates and formal acknowledgment of assumptions made in deriving the estimates. Clearly stating assumptions is a good practice in preparing any budget, but it is especially necessary in the uncertain project world. We also discuss the importance of including provisions for *contingency* in the project budget and include some techniques for estimating costs.

EVMS CRITERION 9

Establish budgets for authorized work with identification of significant cost elements (labor, material, etc.) as needed for internal management and for control of subcontractors.

Criterion 8 (see Chapter 7) required the establishment of a time-phased baseline that shows the sequence of tasks and the time period in which the tasks are to be accomplished. Criterion 9 requires that budget values representing the total resource effort, as determined in the baseline of work to be accomplished, be assigned to the responsible organizational units. All significant direct costs must be identified. Such costs would normally include direct labor, materials, subcontractor costs, and other costs directly attributable to the *work package* (WP). (Overhead or indirect cost is covered later in Criterion 13.)

To comply with Criterion 9, a management process must exist or be created within the performing organization that is capable of determining the effort to be completed, identifying the responsible organizational units, and authorizing effort and expenditures by those units. If the organization currently does not use work authorization documents, we highly recommend that such a system be implemented to properly assign the budgeted effort of each task in terms of time and cost, minimize miscommunication, and also prevent unauthorized work.

In many cases, the work authorization document should specify a "start no earlier than" start time to discourage *frontloading.* Accelerating a schedule by passing on early finishes of time and resource-dependent tasks is desirable because the work value is earned appropriately. Frontloading involves performing work out of sequence to either keep workers busy or to obtain credit for work in a period earlier than it was scheduled for completion. This practice causes problems in earned value measurements and incurs costs at unscheduled points in the project or results in other variations that inevitably lead to preventable rework. Unauthorized completion of work that is scheduled for a later time period will distort the earned values of both periods and must be strenuously discouraged.

Most projects will use physical materials for which costs must be planned, controlled, and reported. A simple project bill of materials document can be used to support material acquisition requirements. There are several good automated software products that include the capability of generating a bill of materials in their project management modules. Several can be found by searching the Internet with search terms like *project accounting* and *bill of materials.* Material requisitions for projects are handled in much the same way as a manufacturing materials requisition, except that the uniqueness of the project environment probably will increase the requisition staff's work.

Much of the work of many projects involves subcontracting work to other organizations or entities. This outsourced work must be budgeted and controlled as strictly as the work performed in-house. Whether or not project work is outsourced, every project can be envisioned as a type of contract. Figure 8.1 illustrates the elements of a contract budget base that shows the relationships of some of the topics covered in this chapter. For projects intended for internal use and authorized by a charter rather than a contract, there would, of course, be no profit component to the project budget.

Figure 8.2 illustrates an organization project control structure where several WPs fold into one general ledger *control account* (CA) that tracks budgeted and actual costs. Authorization and

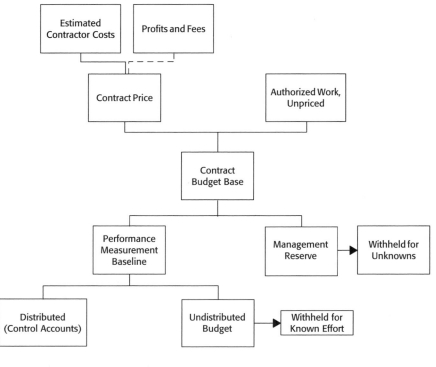

FIGURE 8.1   Contract Budget Base

broad guidelines for the work are embedded in the contract or project charter. Work budgeted and accomplished, along with cost details, is accumulated in the work packages and control accounts.

EVMS CRITERION 10

To the extent it is practical to identify the authorized work in discrete work packages, establish budgets for this work in terms of dollars, hours, or other measurable units. Where the entire control account is not subdivided into work packages, identify the far-term effort in larger planning packages for budget and scheduling purposes.

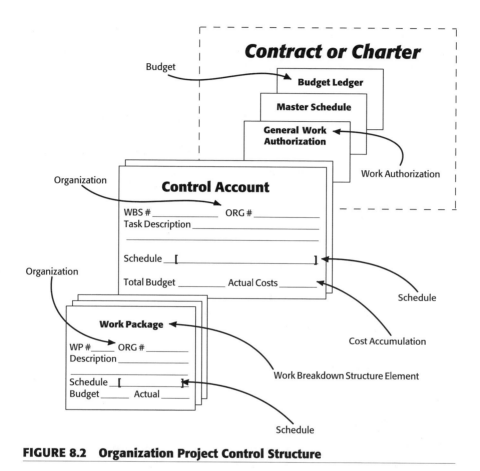

FIGURE 8.2   Organization Project Control Structure

This criterion requires that budgets be established in measurable units. Earned value is usually tracked by work accomplishment expressed in the cost of expended hours, but may be in any measurable unit. The performance indicators, such as package milestones or discrete deliverables, must be scheduled to relate directly to a CA and reflect a specific quantity of that control account. That is, the sum of all expended hours (cost) of a control account's WPs and planning packages must reflect the total expended hours (cost) shown in the control account. Sometimes progress on a certain portion of the project cannot be concluded from the direct reporting of expended hours of effort. In those cases, "an apportionment may be made based on the progress of related discrete efforts" (Department of Defense, FAA, and NASA 1997).

During the breakdown of the project, all the project effort must be included in the *control account plan* (CAP). The CAP consists of control accounts that are set up at the intersection of elements of the WBS and the *organization breakdown structure* (OBS) (see Chapters 5 and 6). The control accounts are subdivided into WPs (both internal and external) or planning packages.

Work Packages and Planning Packages

A WP is a subdivision of the control account and is an assignment of project control to a specific organizational unit at a lower level of the WBS. It defines a discrete deliverable (or activity) and should be of short duration so that work-in-progress does not need to be assessed. Typically, a WP would require 10 to 14 days of work. This generally ensures that WPs in process at the end of an accounting period are minimal.

Sometimes, however, the WP may require enough time that it will not be completed in its entirety at a point when earned value measurements are requested. In those cases, the detailed description of the WP should contain intermediate objective milestones so that an accurate assessment of progress can be made. The idea is to minimize subjective estimates of completion of the WP such as "percent complete." (A common saying in project management circles is, "There are lies, darn lies, and percent complete!")

A *planning package* (PP) is also a subdivision of a control account. It is a holding account with an estimate of effort for which WPs cannot be fully determined when the project is initiated. The PP must be subdivided into WPs as soon as feasible. The description of the PP must contain as much detail as possible so that task and cost integrity can be maintained when the PP is restructured into WPs.

Special Packages

WPs also should be established for materials that will be used during the project. These may also be PPs if any required design effort has not yet established a complete requirements definition. The packages may be a part of the same CA that holds the packages for the activities that will use the material. As with all budgets, there should be controls to ensure that material budgets are not used for other elements and in most cases they should be charged at the same rate as the activity progress.

CAs are required for outside activities such as subcontracts; the activity for those CAs may also be distributed to WPs. An internal control account manager should be assigned to monitor the efforts of the subcontractor and ensure the integration of the subcontractor's schedule with the project schedule. It would be best to require earned value measurements from the subcontractor, but where that is not feasible, the control account manager should be responsible for accurate progress reports that may include the estimation of progress when the subcontractor is not able to provide timely information.

The relationship between WPs, CAs, the WBS, and the OBS (discussed in Chapter 6) is repeated in Figure 8.3.

EVMS CRITERION 11

Provide that the sum of all work package budgets plus planning package budgets within a control account equals the control account budget.

The CA must have an approved budget, schedule, and organizational unit assignment. As discussed in Criterion 10, CAs can be subdivided in several ways including WPs, PPs, and particular items for material usage and subcontracting. Criterion 11 requires that the sum of these subdivisions always equals the approved and assigned budget for the CA. The control account manager should use the performance measurement and budget documents to verify the reconciliation.

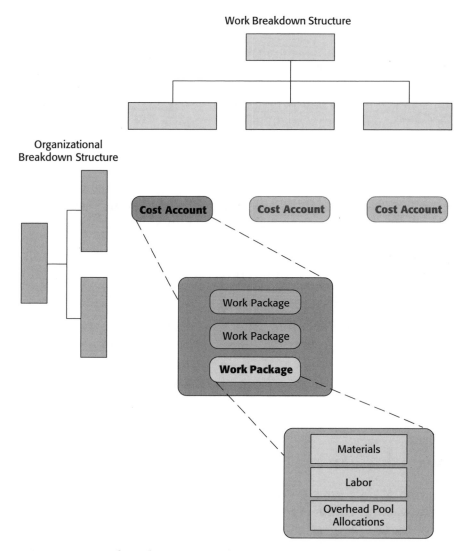

FIGURE 8.3   Work Packages, Control Accounts, WBS, and OBS

EVMS CRITERION 12

Identify and control level of effort activity by time-phased budgets established for this purpose. Only that effort which is unmeasurable or for which measurement is impractical may be classified as level of effort.

We have found few activities or services that can be justified as *level of effort* (LOE) and thankfully so. LOE is that part of the project scope that is general or supportive and for which progress measurement is impractical or for which there is no intermediate objective or deliverable. Of course, there can be many activities for which specific assignment to the project is difficult to measure, but most of those activities are a part of the indirect or overhead costs that will be covered under Criterion 13.

Some examples of LOE might be the project manager, some project staff, and some elements of security. They can be LOE if they are assigned only to this one project. In that case, the cost would not be classified as overhead because none of their cost is apportioned to any other organizational activity. Even though the cost is attributable only to one project, it still might be difficult to assess their earned value with any criterion other than elapsed time. In any event, LOE should be budgeted only when absolutely necessary and then segregated and strictly controlled.

Since there is no actual progress measurement for LOE, its earned value is calculated only by the passage of time. For LOE work, the earned value (budgeted cost of work performed) will always equal the planned value (budgeted cost of work scheduled) because it is impossible to measure what was accomplished. Thus LOE earned value presents the possibility for corruption in the measurements if LOE costs are not actually incurred over the measured amount of time. Again, LOE should be budgeted only when absolutely necessary and then segregated and strictly controlled.

EVMS CRITERION 13

Establish overhead budgets for each significant organizational component of the company for expenses which will become indirect costs. Reflect in the program budgets, at the appropriate level, the amounts in overhead pools that are planned to be allocated to the program as indirect costs.

Every organization with which we have worked has a category of expenses that consists of overhead or indirect costs. These are costs that are not directly attributable to specific project deliverables. They are costs incurred to generally maintain the organization such as senior management, organizational units that support the entire organization (accounting, information systems, human resources), and the physical site and its infrastructure (power, water, environmental controls). Overhead is generally allocated to various organizational units by an arbitrary scheme. The allocation process must be considered arbitrary because the costs are *indirect*; by their nature, there is no direct way to attribute such costs.

Criterion 13 recognizes the potential problems with the allocation of overhead costs and the accompanying project management risk. To partially counteract this risk and expose all potential project costs, the criterion first requires that *all* of the organization's indirect costs be accounted for in overhead budgets. The costs should be collected in pools of similar costs. This grouping helps in the allocation process. The portion of each pool that is allocated to the project must then be budgeted at appropriate levels of the baseline. The methods for the allocation of indirect costs will be covered in detail in the Chapter 9 on EVMS accounting requirements.

EVMS CRITERION 14

Identify management reserves and undistributed budget.

EVMS requires a careful control and accounting of all project costs. Two of the costs most vulnerable to manipulation are *management reserves* (MR) and *undistributed budget* (UB). These terms sometimes are confused with summary-level planning packages. A *summary-level planning package* (SLPP) differs from an MR and a UB in that the SLPP is identified with a specific work element that has not yet been allocated to a control account (CA) because it is a far-term effort without sufficient detail for a complete definition.

An MR is included in the total project budget, but not initially as part of the project measurement baseline. Because projects are unique events, there is considerable uncertainty about unplanned costs and an MR provides a way to deal with this type of uncertainty. This reserve is not to be used for authorized but undefined work or for authorized project modifications, both of which will have approved budgets. Nor should the MR be used for known conditions with uncertainties that can be reasonably estimated, such as a percentage of rework. Budgeted amounts for those uncertainties should be included in the measurement baseline.

The MR is a contingency budget and the state of the project's uniqueness and other special conditions will affect the contingency rate. When estimating the project cost and especially the contingency, the estimator should be aware of the availability and productivity level of the organization's staff and the anticipated working conditions. Special working conditions include security requirements, weather conditions, and hazardous circumstances. The estimator should also consider market conditions and how market fluctuations may affect costs. While an MR of 10 percent of the total project cost is fairly common, almost all sponsors of EVMS projects will carefully examine contingency estimates and will be especially concerned if the MR exceeds 15 percent in the final budget.

The U.S. Department of Energy (DOE) defines *contingency costs* as

> ...costs that may result from incomplete design, unforeseen and unpredictable conditions, or uncertainties within the defined project scope. The amount of the contingency will depend on the status of design, procurement, and construction; and the complexity and uncertainties of the component parts of the project. Contingency is not to be used to avoid making an accurate assessment of expected cost (1997, Ch. 11.2.A).

DOE has a mandatory requirement for a written contingency analysis and estimate for all contingency costs.

An MR should be maintained and accounted for at the total project level (Federal Acquisition Regulation 2004, Subchapter E, section 31.205.7). That is, the MR is part of the total project cost. When it becomes necessary, some portion of the MR can be allocated to the performance baseline for a specific control account and removed from the MR. Therefore, it will do exactly what it is designed to do and the total project cost will remain unchanged.

There is abundant useful information available on the MR, such as *An Analysis of Management Reserve Budget on Defense Acquisition Contracts* (Christensen and Templin 2000).

The MR is maintained separately from the UB, which is included in the performance baseline for effort related to a specific and planned work scope, but not yet identified in a WP. It would not yet be part of a CA, but is maintained as a separate budget item until it can be allocated appropriately. Typically, items included in this category would not be scheduled for completion in the near term.

An allocation of UB should be made as soon as possible to an element of the WBS and organizational unit. As with MR, the undistributed budget is maintained and accounted for at the total project level.

EVMS CRITERION 15

Provide that the program target cost goal is reconciled with the sum of all internal program budgets and management reserves.

The program (project) target cost goal is the negotiated or estimated contract cost. The contract may be a legal and formal document with another organization, such as a government contract, or an internal agreement made between the project sponsors and the project management. The two basic elements in the total cost are the *performance measurement baseline* (PMB) and the MR.

The PMB is the total of all the WPs and PPs in all cost accounts and the overhead or indirect budgets. In the discussion of Criterion 10, PPs were described basically as undistributed costs. The MR is not included in the PMB because that account is not assigned to any authorized work. It is added to most project budgets (frequently about 10 percent of the project cost) and becomes a part of the total project target goal, but it is not measured in the PMB.

Criterion 15 requires that the sum of all the items in the PMB and the MR must always be equal to the original total project target (authorized changes will be discussed as parts of other criteria). Earned value will be calculated using progress in completion of baseline tasks and the budgeted costs reflected in the PMB. (For a simple example of a project with task budgets, see Figure 8.4.)

Assuming a 10 percent MR and no undistributed budget, the 52-week project (as illustrated in Figure 8.4) would have a total project cost of $228,800 ($208,000 budgeted for the tasks plus $20,800 MR).

PROJECT COST ESTIMATION

The seven EVMS criteria on budgeting give project managers many rules, but no real assistance in how to estimate the cost of a project. Cost estimation is a very difficult task that comes on the heels of project scheduling. Many organizations have professional estimators and for large EVMS projects, the help of professionals may be indispensable. Project managers should find the subsequent discussion of various cost estimating methods and

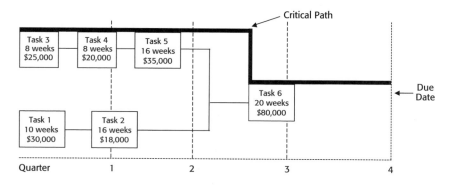

FIGURE 8.4   Activity in Box Budget Baseline

common estimating terminology beneficial. The Department of Energy's Directive G 430.1-1 is very helpful, but it is a complex document. A description and full list of its chapters can be found at http://www.directives.doe.gov/pdfs/doe/doetext/neword/430/g4301-1toc.html.

You also might be interested in using cost estimation software. Vendors easily can be located using a Web search engine. A brief discussion of cost estimation software can be found at http://www.p2pays.org/ref/01/00047/00047c.htm#3.1.

Cost Data

In forming the project cost estimate, data may be compiled from many sources. These may include costs from similar projects, cost reports, databases of historical and current product costs, the organization's purchasing department, etc. Adjustments must be made to the collected cost data based on its source and time. Some differences may be fairly apparent, such as inflationary factors, different quantities, and varying quality, but geographical differences and possible regulatory changes must also be considered.

Some adjustments may be facilitated by the use of a cost index such as an inflation index. There may be several indices available that can help the estimator determine current project costs by applying an index to the known costs from another time, project, or location.

Project Controls

Project controls are all the systems that are used to plan, schedule, budget, and measure the performance of a project. A few applicable components of project controls are discussed in the following sections. The cost estimation package sets the baseline for EVMS project controls. A spreadsheet profiling the funding schedule over the life of the project should be a part of that package; one can be constructed as the cost estimation package is developed.

Cost Estimation Package

The U.S. Department of Energy states that a cost estimation package consists "of the estimate, the technical scope, and the schedule" (1997, Ch. 2.1). This means that the estimator must begin with the WBS (and the imbedded control accounts) and the time-phased schedule. The cost estimation package establishes the project budget, provides the cost baseline, and becomes a major document for performance measurement.

As the estimate is developed, the package should contain all the documentation to support not only the costs, but also an analysis of how they were developed. This information will discuss what is included in indirect costs, a justification for the overhead rate, and the consideration of project contingencies.

Basis of Cost Estimate

Good documentation will provide reliability for the project's cost estimate and also will contribute to the success of future estimation efforts. That documentation should include all supporting data, the assumptions used, and the environment that is assumed to exist. Not all projects require the same level of detail in their cost estimates; even within a project, the detail may not be the same for different legs of the WBS.

The Federal Aviation Administration suggests four factors that should be considered to determine an appropriate level of detail (Federal Aviation Administration 2003, 1).

1. *Dollar value of the project.* High-value programs will require more extensive detail in cost estimates.
2. *Purpose of the estimate.* Early planning estimates require less accuracy than a final approved budget estimate.
3. *Nature of the project.* Regardless of dollar value, the cost estimate for a project with few intermediate objectives (less activity) can usually be prepared at a more cumulative level.
4. *Data availability.* If the technical details of a project are not completely available, an aggregate estimate may need to be prepared with budgeted uncertainty.

Estimating Methods

Several techniques can be used to estimate the cost of a project deliverable or the cost of the entire project. The estimator can choose one or a combination of these techniques based on the size and nature of the project, the estimator's experience, the time available to prepare the estimate, and the availability of information and other resources.

Different types of estimates may be required at different points in the contract process. Some estimates must be very detailed and others may be considered order-of-magnitude (ball park) estimates that are prepared using only very basic decision factors.

Bottom-Up Method

The *bottom-up method* can be used effectively when all activity to be estimated is clearly detailed. It is especially useful if the bottom-up scheduling technique was used to schedule the project. Estimates are made at the lowest level of detail and summarized as the estimator works up the levels of the work breakdown structure until a total is accumulated for the entire project or the unit to be estimated.

These low-level estimates can be very accurate, but be aware that duplication is possible:

1. Work that is performed in one organizational unit may satisfy the requirements of deliverables that might have been assumed by more than one organizational unit during the estimation process.
2. Cost estimators at lower levels of the organization may not be aware of efforts in other parts of the organization.
3. Assumptions are often used during a roll-up of costs that may not account for possible duplications at lower levels of the estimation.

Rolling Wave Method

Sometimes there is not enough detail in the initial planning stage to completely break down the project, which can undermine the ability to estimate cost in the far term. If the project sponsors agree to a certain level of uncertainty, the *rolling wave method* can be used. This technique shortens the initial planning effort while producing more accurate plans. As we are all aware, there are many cases where weeks are spent to produce a very careful and complex plan that quickly becomes obsolete because of unforeseen circumstances.

The rolling wave technique means doing the detailed planning in cycles (waves). The cycles can vary from two to nine months depending on the certainty of events and the amount of time necessary for advance support requisition. The plans for the short term (current cycle) are produced in great detail and an overall plan is estimated for the rest of the project. Near the end of the first cycle, the next cycle is estimated and planned in detail. The current cycle estimates are expected to have a very tight margin of error while the remaining project estimate may be expected to vary to a wider degree.

Parametric Method

If none of the available information is very detailed, the *parametric method* may be the only way to arrive at reasonable estimates. One would not expect such estimates to be in the same range of accuracy as a more direct estimate, but the method has been increasingly used in the aerospace industry with great success. Parametric estimating relies on historical data from similar endeavors or the ability to model the current objective. Statistical analyses are performed on the historical data to discover correlations between the cost drivers and the system parameters. The technique focuses on the cost drivers and not on the details of the project.

NASA's *Parametric Cost Estimating Handbook* defines a parametric cost estimate as:

> ... one that uses Cost Estimating Relationships (CERs) and associated mathematical algorithms (or logic) to establish cost estimates. For example, detailed cost estimates for manufacturing and test of an end item (for instance, a hardware assembly) can be developed

using very precise Industrial Engineering standards and analysis. (National Aeronautics and Space Administration 1996, Chapter 1)

The method is complex and multifaceted; the NASA handbook and others give a very complete explanation.

Analogy Method

For a specific analogy to work at all, the cost of items in a similar project must be known. The estimate starts with the cost of a similar element for a different project and adjustments are made for known differences in the projects. In using the *analogy method*, the estimator must look for differences in the characteristics of the design and expected performance of the projects or project elements. This method is a top-down method that estimates the overall cost of a project based on the known properties of similar completed project.

Expert Opinion Method

The *expert opinion method* in this estimation process consults with several experts or specialists and establishes a consensus. Many view the expert opinion technique as one of last resort, but within the domains of their expertise such estimates can be reliably substituted for ones from more empirical methods. The estimates can be viewed with an even higher degree of dependability if the expert opinions have been verified previously with empirical evidence.

Criterion 9 requires the establishment of budgets that identify all significant cost elements for the work established in the time-phased baseline. Criterion 10 covers the budgeting for work packages (WPs) and planning packages (PPs), which are the subdivisions of control accounts, and Criterion 11 requires that sum of the subaccount budgets equals the total control account budget. Criterion 12 states that any level-of-effort activity must be identified and controlled.

Criterion 13 establishes the guidelines for controlling overhead costs—a very vulnerable component of the project budget. Criterion 14 requires the identification of management reserves (MR) and undistributed budget (UB). Management reserves are held outside the project measurement baseline as a way to deal with project uncertainty. Undistributed budget is part of the baseline and represents planned work that has not yet been detailed in WPs. Criterion 15 states that all the elementary project budgets plus the amount budgeted for management reserves must equal the total project budget.

All of the criteria concerning project budgeting establish many rules and requirements, but they don't provide very much help in arriving at a budget for the project. Estimators must consider all the available cost data and should provide project control information, such as a cost estimation package, appropriate control accounts, and a basis of cost estimate. Cost estimating methods include bottom-up, rolling wave, parametric, analogy, and expert opinion.

For further study, you may check such sources as:

1. Slemaker, C.M. *The Principles and Practice of Cost/Schedule Control Systems*. New York: McGraw-Hill, 1985.
2. Stewart, R.D., R.M.Wyskida, and M.Richard. *Cost Estimator's Reference Manual*. New York: John Wiley & Sons, 1995.

DISCUSSION QUESTIONS

1. How does your organization authorize work? What would you recommend?
2. How should outsourced work be budgeted and controlled?
3. How could frontloading distort EVMS measurements?
4. Discuss why you might or might not have an LOE component in a project budget.
5. Describe the difference between direct and indirect costs and list some examples of each.

6. Describe an overhead pool and give examples of the contents of a pool.

7. In what circumstances can actual project expenses be charged against the budget for MR?

8. What data sources would you use in estimating the project budget?

9. How would you determine an appropriate level of detail for a project budget?

10. Defend one of the five cost estimating techniques.

Project Status

"Unless the PM understands the organizational accounting system, there is no way to exercise budgetary control over the project" (Meredith and Mantel 2003, 338).

As previously noted, EVMS was developed from a standard cost model. Because of this close association, many if not most of the deficiencies of traditional standard cost systems also attach to EVMS. Nonetheless, accounting metrics play a large role in EVMS and the formal 32 criteria requirements. Our intent is to make the material clear and understandable by managers with little or no accounting training or background.

The first 15 criteria discussed in earlier chapters specify planning requirements for detailing elements of the project objectives, the organization, the work schedule, and the budgeting process. The next 12 criteria cover management and accounting requirements, including those for identifying, summarizing, recording, and reporting actual project expenses and their variances from the project plan.

Chapter 9—Criteria 16 through 19—discusses estimation, recording, tracking, and allocation of project costs. The chapter includes a discussion of some special circumstances for projects with manufacturing components and an analysis of the requirements of a formal material accounting system as required in Criteria 20 and 21. Chapter 10 deals with the specific requirements of Criteria 22 through 27 concerning project variances.

CHAPTER 9

Tracking Performance (Criteria 16–21)

> *"There are three kinds of people—those who can count and those who can't."*
>
> —Unknown

Criteria 16 through 19 are concerned with recording project costs and, although they seem simple enough, are critical in maintaining an EVMS-compliant system. These four criteria, along with Criteria 20 and 21, however, usually are assumed to be difficult to understand and implement. The detail required in accounting for projects, and not the concepts themselves, cause this misunderstanding. The most important aspect of the accounting criteria is the requirement for accurate progress measurement—knowing how to account reliably and accurately.

All the criteria concerned with accounting for ongoing project work are designed to establish minimum standards and do not require use of a particular accounting system. While accountants will do the actual recording and processing of data, the project manager is charged with reporting the input data and establishing communication links between parties. Becoming familiar with these criteria will enable you to funnel appropriate and timely information into the system and assist the organization in capturing required information and following established procedures. In addition, the accounting department will be able to provide feedback that will alert you to problems or opportunities.

EVMS ACCOUNTING

The great value of EVMS is that with the required accounting reports, those interested in the project are not dependent upon subjective feelings or vague assurances. EVMS also relieves the project manager from time-consuming explanations of his or her current positions so they can concentrate on running the project. We pointed out earlier that reliable estimates of a project's total time and cost are essential for the organization to make appropriate and successful project decisions. Sometimes projects require additional resources; however, there are projects, through no fault of the project manager or the project team, that need to be put out of their misery. Accounting information aids in making these difficult decisions as well as in numerous other tradeoffs.

Specialized documents required for EVMS include a detailed *control (or cost) account* (CA) structure (the project's chart of accounts) and the data requirements stipulated by the contract or charter. In addition, an accounting manual containing the organization's accounting policies and procedures, including allocation methodologies, should be maintained and available. Project managers will find that even vague familiarity with these policies and procedures can avoid many missteps and communication problems.

For federal government projects, a formal *Cost Accounting Standards Disclosure Statement* must be submitted that details the procedures that will be followed. The purpose of the statement is to provide assurance that costs are properly recorded and there is a timely and accurate transfer of actual cost information from the general accounting system into the EVMS. While this document is not required for nonfederal earned value implementations, similar care should be taken to ensure that accounting best practices are observed.

An acceptable accounting system should be capable of accounting for all resource expenditures as the resources are consumed. As discussed in the section on Criterion 21, there is considerable variation in accounting for material usage and consistency in treatment becomes quite important.

One of the biggest complaints we hear from project managers is that their accounting systems seldom reflect up-to-date (real time) performance. It is in the project manager's best interests to form a good working relationship with the accountant(s) handling his or her project so that the project manager can assist in timely recording of transactions, which, in an earned value system, translates into project performance metrics.

EVMS CRITERION 16

Record direct costs in a manner consistent with the budgets in a formal system controlled by the general books of account.

The organization's accounting procedures must follow *Generally Accepted Accounting Procedures* (GAAP). A very real concern is that the accounting system is able to transfer accurate information into the EVMS with appropriate timing. By adhering to standard accounting procedures and following consistent planning procedures, the system will be EVMS-compliant and facilitate the audit of all the project's direct costs.

Direct Costs

Criterion 16 requires that the accounting methods used to collect direct costs and post them to the CAs are the same as those used when the baseline budget was established. (You may find a quick review of Chapter 8 helpful at this point.) Criterion 16 relies heavily on appropriate establishment of CAs and specific budget allocations during the early phases of project planning. As discussed earlier, even with direct costs, there may be some activity apportionment. The actual costs of apportioned effort must be collected in the same manner as budgeted in order to ensure accurate EVMS measurements (see Figure 9.1).

Chapter 7 of a Department of Energy (DOE) directive, DOE G 430.1-1, defines direct costs as "any costs that can be specifically identified with a particular project or activity, including salaries, travel, equipment and supplies directly benefiting the project or activity." The directive further explains that *activity* should be interpreted as being the same as a CA (Department of Energy 1997, 7.2.A). (You may want to refresh your recollection of CAs by reviewing the discussion of control accounts in Chapter 5.)

Imagine direct costs as having invisible strings that are tied to the place where the direct costs are consumed. These costs do not have to be allocated, just traced to their users. For example, materials used in one *work breakdown structure* (WBS) would be as-

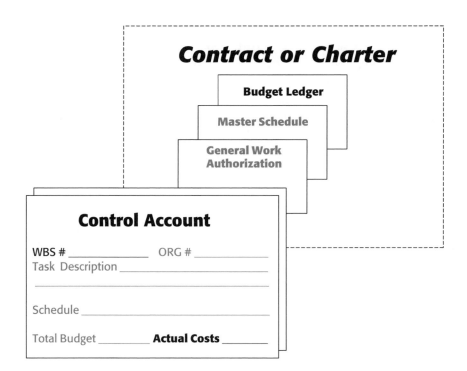

FIGURE 9.1   Actual Direct Costs Posted to Accounts Established in Budget

signed to the control account for that WBS number. Labor—other than that classified as level of effort (LOE)—is traced easily by its invisible string to the CA for the WBS benefiting from the labor.

While direct costs most commonly relate to one CA, two or more CAs may share a direct project cost. An example might be a specialized piece of equipment that is dedicated to three different WBS numbers within one project. In this case, the total cost would be allocated to the three WBS numbers on the basis of their consumption of the activity driver.

For the specialized piece of equipment, the activity driver or basis of allocation might be the ratio of equipment time used by each WBS over the total equipment productive time available. The resulting ratio multiplied by the cost of the equipment would be the amount to be charged to individual WBS CAs. Productive time available but not used would represent excess capacity that should not be allocated immediately to the WBS elements using the asset. Depending on individual situation circumstances, this excess capacity cost may or may not be allocated ultimately to the project, along with other indirect costs, but individual WBS elements should not have to bear this excess capacity cost.

Special Circumstances

Control of work performed by subcontractors is the responsibility of the prime contractor. Subcontract costs must be recorded in the same accounting period as the associated primary effort. If the subcontractor cannot supply timely information, the project manager must establish estimates of subcontractor costs to comply with period reporting requirements. Additionally, some subcontract costs must be separated into the appropriate cost elements for accurate posting to appropriate CAs. Therefore, the more detail the project manager can supply, the better.

For projects involving the Department of Defense, special rules govern material management and accounting systems. The DoD website, where you can find complete information, is http://www.acq.osd.mil/dpap/dars/dfars/index/htm. Criterion 21, discussed later in this chapter, details some of these requirements.

EVMS CRITERION 17

When a work breakdown structure is used, summarize direct costs from control accounts into the work breakdown structure without allocation of a single control account to two or more work breakdown structure elements.

This criterion exists simply to require that costs do not become duplicated as they are summarized up through the levels of the WBS. (Remember that Criterion 5, as presented in Chapter 6, required that performance measurements be the same whether from the WBS or the OBS.) This requirement depends heavily on a carefully developed WBS and CAs. It also will rely on the accounting system's ability to collect and allocate the costs in a consistent and reliable manner. For an illustration of how actual costs incurred are traced to the WBS, see Figure 9.2.

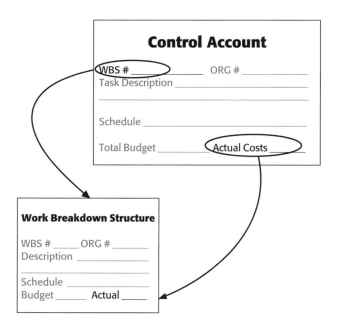

FIGURE 9.2   Control Account Distribution of Actual Costs Match Budgeted Locations

The most care will be necessary when costs need to be apportioned from one CA to another. While the organization's accountants handle the actual accounting, it is the project manager who provides a reality check on the reasonableness of accounting department distributions.

EVMS CRITERION 18

Summarize direct costs from the control accounts into the contractor's organizational elements without allocation of a single control account to two or more organizational elements.

This is the same requirement as for Criterion 17 only as it applies to the *organization breakdown structure* (OBS). Cost data integrity must be maintained as it is summarized from the CA to the highest unit level of the OBS. This requirement heavily depends on the careful assignment of project elements to organizational units. Figure 9.3 illustrates how actual costs are assigned from the CA to the OBS as well as the WBS.

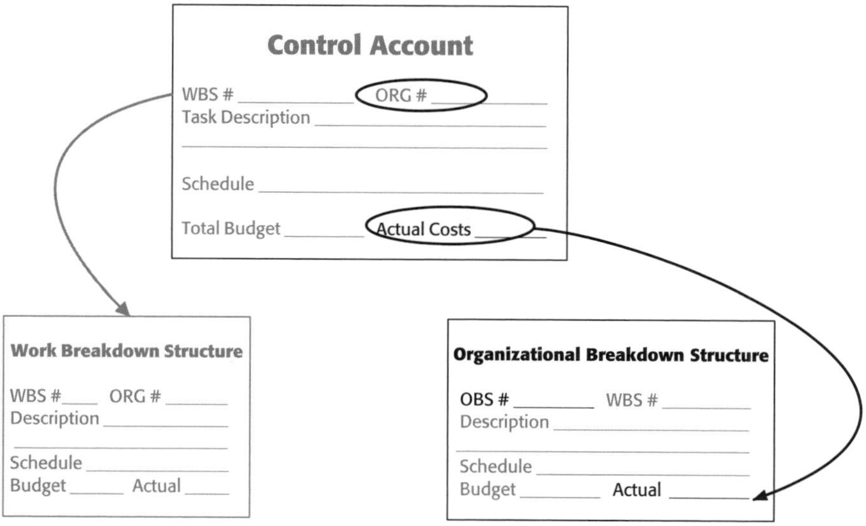

FIGURE 9.3   Control Account Costs as Summarized in the WBS and OBS

Thus far, we have addressed three criteria (16, 17, and 18) that concern direct project costs. Now we turn our attention to indirect costs.

EVMS CRITERION 19

Record all indirect costs which will be allocated to the contract.

Indirect costs (overhead) represent expenses that are attributable to more than one project or organizational entity. Criterion 4 (Chapter 6) requires identification of the organization's function responsible for controlling indirect costs, and Criterion 13 (Chapter 8) requires establishment of the budget for indirect costs. Now Criterion 19 requires the allocation of indirect costs in the same manner as they were planned in the budget. They should be allocated often (at least monthly) in order to maintain accurate EVMS measurements. Some contracts require dividing the indirect costs into recurring and nonrecurring costs. *Recurring costs,* for example, might include supervisory or administrative costs, while property taxes are an example of a *nonrecurring (one-time) cost.*

Indirect costs do not have invisible strings connecting the cost source to the user as was described for direct costs. The DOE directive defines indirect costs as those costs "incurred by an organization for common or joint objectives, and which cannot be identified specifically with a particular activity or project" (U.S. Department of Energy 1997, 8). A good example of such an indirect cost is the chief executive officer's (CEO's) salary. The CEO is charged with setting the direction of the entire organization and rarely is involved with individual projects.

Cost Pools

Rather than have all indirect costs accumulated in a single account, or pool of costs, a far better approach is to establish a cost pool for each group of related activities. Then the costs of each pool are allocated to the users of the pool according to some rational allocation basis, or driver.

If several candidate drivers exist, cause-effect criteria generally can be invoked to select the best driver. That is, the driver that is the better candidate is the one whose changes most directly cause costs in the pool to change (assuming all other things are equal). (*Caveat:* As the project manager, you should consider whether the employee behavior likely to result from using a particular driver is the behavior desired.)

For example, resource costs first might be assigned to various pools using relevant resource drivers (allocation bases) and then the pool costs would be assigned to users based on relevant cost pool drivers (allocation bases). For an illustration of how this might look for a simple three-pool environment, see Figure 9.4.

Cost Pool Drivers

Only totally variable costs have unique drivers. If the overhead pool consists of purchased travel costs, for example, most (if not

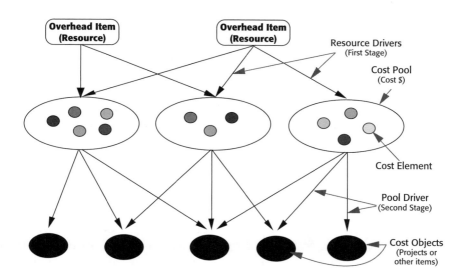

FIGURE 9.4   Overhead Cost Pools with Their Source and Allocation

all) of the costs will be variable with the number of trips taken or the number of miles traveled. That is, travel costs are variable with the number and/or type of trips.

If cost pools contain fixed costs as well as variable costs, there is no perfect driver that can be selected to allocate the costs of the pool. Therefore, if the organization has a permanent travel department, a certain amount of costs is fixed in nature; moreover, there is no absolute base or driver for the travel pool that can be defended against all other potential drivers. Therefore, the allocation of these fixed costs, to some extent, would be arbitrary.

Selection of the pool driver is important because cost allocations may change dramatically from use of one driver versus another candidate driver. The solution to the driver-selection problem is to select rational cause-and-effect drivers that have the least undesirable unintended consequences. That is, the drivers should minimize attempts to "game" the system. The project manager's expertise is invaluable in helping accounting personnel select appropriate drivers for indirect cost allocation pools.

COST ALLOCATION METHODS

One of the three basic methods known as *direct, step-down,* or *reciprocal* may be used for the allocation of indirect costs (see Figure 9.5 for example data that will be used to illustrate these three different methods). Many government agencies and private organizations highly regard a specific allocation system known as *activity-based costing* (ABC). Therefore, it too is covered briefly in this section.

Of the three basic methods, the *direct method* is simplest and is accomplished by using some rational allocation base or driver, such as number of staff involved, to allocate a pool's costs to the users of that pool. The example in Figure 9.5 reflects three overhead pools where resource costs of $80,000, $60,000, and $40,000 have been traced to the accounting, human resources, and maintenance pools. The illustration also shows drivers selected for each overhead pool, the number of hours worked, the number of

	Overhead Pools			Projects		
	Accounting	Human Resources	Maintenance	1	2	3
Costs	$80,000	$60,000	$40,000			
Driver	work hours	# employees	sq. ft.			
Quantity						
hours	1,000	5,000	500	20,000	8,000	12,000
employees	2	10	20	250	150	90
sq. feet	250	500	100	2,500	3,000	1,550

FIGURE 9.5   Example of Overhead Costs and Consumption

employees, and the number of square feet occupied by each of the overhead departments and the three projects. The three projects are the only "productive" activities of the organization.

Direct Allocation Method

With the *direct allocation method,* any possible interdepartmental services provided to other overhead pools is ignored and each overhead pool's costs are allocated only to projects and production areas. This allocation is accomplished by forming a simple ratio of the allocation base or driver consumed by a project over the total consumed by all users of the overhead pool. The resulting project costs in the direct allocation method would be as follows:

Overhead Pools			Projects		
Accounting	Human Resources	Maintenance	1	2	3
$80,000	$60,000	$40,000			
($80,000)			$40,000[1]	$16,000	$24,000
	($60,000)		30,612[2]	18,367	11,020
		($40,000)	14,184[3]	17,021	8,794
- 0 -	- 0 -	- 0 -	$84,797	$51,389	$43,815

[1]20,000/(20,000+8,000+12,000) * $80,000 = $40,000
[2]250/(250+150+90) * $60,000 = $30,612
[3]2,500/(2,500+3,000+1,550) * $40,000 = $14,184

Step-Down Allocation Method

When overhead pools provide significant services to themselves as well as to projects and production areas, such as the human resources department handling all personnel needs of the other pools, the direct method, which ignores this reciprocal service, is inappropriate. In this situation, the indirect costs of supporting activities might use a *step-down allocation method* to distribute costs to other overhead pools and projects more equitably. That is, the overhead pool providing the most service to other pools is allocated to other pools as well as to projects and other producing areas such as manufacturing (if they exist).

Assuming that accounting provides the most service to the other pools (this selection is debatable and is part of the problem of using this methodology to allocate overhead pool costs), the accounting department costs first would be allocated to the other overhead pools and the projects. Then the pool that provides the next "most" service would have its costs, including the amount allocated to it by accounting, allocated to the remaining pool and the projects. Finally, the last pool costs, now increased by their share of the other two overhead pools, would be allocated to the projects. In this example, human resources costs are allocated following the accounting department costs, and the maintenance costs are allocated last.

Using the data from Figure 9.5, the costs would be distributed as follows using the step-down allocation method:

Overhead Pools			Projects		
Accounting	Human Resources	Maintenance	1	2	3
$80,000	$60,000	$40,000			
($80,000)	8,791	879	$35,165*	$14,066	$21,099
	($68,791)	2,698	33,721	20,233	12,140
		($43,577)	15,453	18,543	9,581
- 0 -	- 0 -	- 0 -	$84,339	$52,842	$42,819

*20,000 / (5,000+500+20,000+8,000+12,000) * $80,000 = $35,165

Notice that once again a total of $180,000 ($84,339 + $52,842 + $42,819) ended up in the project accounts. The amounts, however, are slightly different from those found using the direct method. Whereas the differences in allocations between the two methods in this example may not appear to be material, it should be clear that under certain circumstances the amounts allocated using the two methods might be significantly different. Also, the choice of which overhead pool to begin the step-down allocation procedure is somewhat arbitrary and performing the allocation using a different sequence would result in different allocations to projects.

Reciprocal Allocation Method

Both the direct and step-down methods of allocation of overhead pool costs are susceptible to charges of bias, whether intentional or unintentional. The only equitable method of overhead pool cost allocation is where each area pays for exactly what it uses in providing its service—including consumption of services provided by other overhead pools. The *reciprocal allocation method* fulfills this requirement. It uses a set of simultaneous equations to determine total costs of an overhead pool that includes its fair share of other overhead pools' costs.

Before the widespread availability of personal computers and spreadsheets, this method, while theoretically superior, required mastery of some formidable mathematics involving the inverting of a sometimes sizable matrix. With a spreadsheet such as Microsoft Excel,™ however, the mathematics are inconsequential. An example of the application of the reciprocal method applied using the same example as for the direct and step-down methods is presented in Appendix 9-A at the end of this chapter.

Whereas the allocated costs using the reciprocal method in this simple example do not differ significantly from the theoretically unsupportable direct method, it should be obvious that the reciprocal method can be logically defended as the method that is most fair to all parties. Once the matrices are established, only the current department costs and possibly the usage quantities must be changed to find the appropriate allocations for a new period.

Activity-Based Costing Method

Besides the standard overhead pool costs (purchasing, personnel, information systems, etc.), there may be other indirect activities that need to be applied to functional areas or overhead pools as well as to projects.

Implementing ABC

ABC is a method of applying indirect costs by establishing multiple cost pools, each of which contains the costs of certain activities. By carefully selecting an activity driver whose use causes the pool costs to increase, a pool's costs can be allocated to entities using the activities provided by the pool.

The activities captured in a pool, such as material movement or engineering services, might span the entire organization. Because this allocation procedure appears to charge indirect costs on the basis of "only users pay," the federal government encourages its use. For example, based on time spent on each activity, an engineering resource might be allocated to three activity pools: design and design changes, maintenance repairs and modifications, and a lead time reduction program (see Figure 9.6). Other costs, such as supplies, also would be allocated to these pools. Once the costs are accumulated in the pools, projects using the activities provided by the pools would be charged based on their use of the selected activity drivers.

Problems of ABC and Other Indirect Allocation Methods

A detailed discussion of ABC is beyond the scope of this book. However, several caveats concerning ABC and other indirect allocation methods are in order.

First, the activity and other overhead pools typically contain both variable and fixed costs. The *fixed costs* represent the costs that must be incurred in lump sums to support the provision of the activity while the *variable costs* are incurred as the activities are provided. Computing one rate for the entire pool treats all costs as if they were variable with consumption of the pool driver.

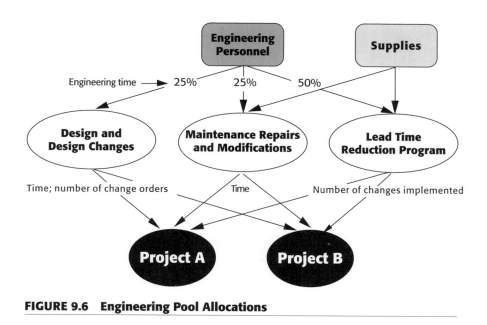

FIGURE 9.6   Engineering Pool Allocations

The pool must be geared up to provide for demand for its activities based on projected demand. Because details of projects, as well as details of individual project tasks, are inherently uncertain, over-capacity and under-capacity conditions occur frequently. Further, allocating pool costs based on driver quantity consumed means that one project's costs are influenced by the use of the pool by other projects. One way to eliminate this bias is to separate each pool into two sub-pools—one containing the variable costs of the pool and the other containing the fixed costs. Then the variable cost sub-pool can be allocated based on actual use and the fixed cost sub-pool can be allocated based on original projected demand.

Finally, the project budget will reflect the portion of overhead that is planned for allocation to the project. The allocation will be based on some cost driver or allocation base as described above. The rate is usually predetermined for a particular accounting period. Since there are usually several cost pools, there will be different rates for each pool. Two very important points for EVMS is that an appropriate allocation rate is established and that the rate used in the budgeting process is the same as the rate used in the operating cycle.

EVMS CRITERION 20

Identify unit costs, equivalent units costs, or lot costs when needed.

For projects with a manufacturing component with multiple units being produced in a production or similar-type environment, a contractor may be required to have an accounting system that is capable of providing unit costs, equivalent unit costs, or lot costs.

Unit costs consist of direct costs (e.g., materials and perhaps labor) plus indirect (overhead) cost. The cost of one unit, therefore, includes direct materials and direct labor for the unit, plus manufacturing overhead.

Computing unit costs in some production environments, specifically those on a continuous production or accelerated assembly line basis, is extremely difficult. This situation also might occur where substantially comparable units are produced for more than one customer. In these situations, it is acceptable to use *equivalent unit costs* (a quantity of units produced during a single period by assuming a particular flow of units) as computed in a process-costing environment where production consists of basically fungible (identical) units. In this situation, direct costs (materials and labor) are traced to the process, and indirect (overhead) costs are allocated to the process. The total process costs for the period then are divided by the equivalent whole units of production for the period to find the unit cost.

Where units are produced in batches or lots, the total costs (materials, labor, and overhead) of the batch or lot are traced or assigned to the group of items produced. Then the total cost of each batch or lot is divided by the number of good units to yield a unit cost.

EVMS CRITERION 21

For EVMS, the material accounting system will provide for:
  (1) Accurate cost accumulation and assignment of costs to control accounts in a manner consistent with the budgets using recognized, acceptable, costing techniques
  (2) Cost performance measurement at the point in time most suitable for the category of material involved, but no earlier than the time of progress payments or actual receipt of material
  (3) Full accountability of all material purchased for the program, including the residual inventory.

Criterion 21 establishes recording and reporting requirements for materials to ensure that data used in the computation of project performance, including cost and schedule variances and other metrics, in addition to being accurate, are assigned to appropriate periods. Without proper alignment in time, interpretation of performance metrics is extremely difficult if not impossible.

The first part of this criterion is designed to ensure that generally recognized and acceptable costing techniques are followed and that actual material costs are posted in the same CAs for which amounts were budgeted. There also should be adequate internal control procedures in place to find and correct any errors made in postings, either in amount or to appropriate accounts. While this responsibility belongs to the accounting department, the project manager should make every effort to see that they are provided accurate and timely information and he or she should review accounting reports for reasonableness.

The second part covers the timing for expensing project material. Should actual costs not be available in a timely manner, the project manager should assign estimated costs. When actual amounts become known, the estimated amounts can be corrected, if necessary. In order to recognize a material cost for which an invoice has not been received, however, the goods must be received. There is some latitude in the timely costing of material—it may be recognized when it is accepted from the supplier or when it is consumed—as long as the system is consistent. Indirect material and other costs are addressed in Criterion 19.

The value and significance of materials should determine detailed procedures followed, with this information formally documented. Because the significance and materiality of various types of material purchases can vary dramatically, it is permissible to follow different procedures for different values of materials. There is considerable variation, in practice, concerning when material costs are recognized. The time most suitable for the type of material involved is acceptable. Formal entry into the accounting system, however, should occur no earlier than when the material is received or progress payments are made.

A critical issue is making sure the cost of the materials is recorded no later than when the materials are used. Otherwise, the earned value metrics may be meaningless. Chapter 10 discusses variances of actual material costs from those planned in the budget as well as projections of future material requirements.

The third part of Criterion 21 requires full accountability of all material purchased for the program. In many organizations, project managers are permitted to borrow (or "steal") material that was ordered for another use. Construction-type industries, in particular, find this a common problem. This practice, if not controlled, makes it extremely difficult to track the inventory and consumption of materials.

If materials are purchased for one program or project, any amounts not used for their intended purpose must be tracked. This residual inventory may or may not have a market value; nevertheless, it should be tracked and reported. The *Material Management and Accounting System* (Department of Defense 2004) documents some detailed instructions on a material loan/payback technique that might be useful if borrowing materials is common in your organization.

Should a project manager or someone in your organization's accounting department desire additional information, it is readily available on the Internet. The Association for the Advancement of Cost Engineering (AACE) provides definitions of cost components and professional advice, publications, professional certification, and tools. AACE's members include cost management professionals: cost managers and engineers, project managers, planners and schedulers, estimators and bidders, and value engineers. The AACE home website is www.aacei.org.

ACCOUNTING AND EARNED VALUE SOFTWARE

Even small companies now have access to sophisticated accounting software. Just as accounting is no longer a manual operation, EVMS also can be automated to remove much of the drudgery of keeping track of performance.

Because the software industry is expanding and developing at such a hectic pace, it would be ineffective to review accounting and/or earned value software here. Most *enterprise resource management* (ERM) programs now include optional earned value modules. In addition, there are many stand-alone software programs capable of sophisticated drill-down access to detailed earned value performance. Most project management scheduling and control programs also deal more or less successfully with earned value metrics. A simple Internet search for *EVMS software* will provide sufficient leads to occupy several hours of investigation.

The six criteria on accounting covered in this chapter closely follow the principles of the budgeting criteria presented in the previous chapter. EVMS makes a very strong statement that the actual project expenses must be charged in accordance with the principles used in the planning process. EVMS accounting provides information to make management decisions; moreover, it does so in a more objective way than subjective progress estimates.

Direct costs and *indirect costs* make up the two general cost categories. Direct costs can be specifically identified with a particular activity, but even direct costs may need to be apportioned if the direct activity is shared by multiple users or cost objects.

Criterion 16 deals with direct costs. It requires that the EVMS accounting be accurate, timely, and consistent with the organization's formal accounting system. Criteria 17 and 18 prevent the duplication of entries and summarization errors by prohibiting the allocation of control accounts (CAs) to more than one work breakdown structure (WBS) or organization breakdown structure (OBS) element.

Criterion 19 regulates indirect cost allocations. It, too, stresses following processes and procedures established during the budgeting phase. Indirect costs cannot be identified with a particular activity and are generally allocated through cost pools based on rational, but arbitrary, cause-and-effect determinations (cost drivers). Overhead can be allocated using one of the three basic methods: *direct*, *step-down*, or *reciprocal*. Many government agencies and private organizations highly regard a specific allocation system known as *activity-based costing* (ABC).

Criteria 20 and 21 establish standards for two areas not involving direct and indirect costs specifically, but rather procedures. Criterion 20 relates to projects with manufacturing components and stipulates the generation of *unit costs*, *equivalent unit costs*, or *lot costs* when appropriate. The details necessary for an appropriate material accounting system are specified in Criterion 21.

Professional accountants, of course, will provide the actual accounting work, but the project manager's cooperation will ensure not only that criteria are followed but that information will be provided to all project stakeholders, including the project team, on a timely basis.

DISCUSSION QUESTIONS

1. Why should a project manager be concerned with criteria devoted to work that is the primary responsibility of others in the organization?

2. Summarize, in your own words, the four criteria dealing with assignment of costs to project elements.

3. When may Criterion 20 safely be disregarded? When not?

4. Under what circumstances might a project manager "borrow" materials designated for another project?

5. Describe your organization's system for assigning costs to projects.

6. Comment on the following statement: "Once the budget has been prepared and approved, there is nothing a project manager can do but use the dollars allocated without deviation."

7. What are a project manager's responsibilities for establishing communication links with accounting?

8. Describe some of the problems you have encountered with subcontractors.

9. How might the accounting department make your life easier?

10. Describe the three basic overhead cost allocation methods.

11. Briefly describe an activity-based costing system.

12. Describe your organization's overhead allocation method.

Appendix 9-A. Reciprocal Allocation of Overhead Costs

For convenience, the details of this example are the same as those used to illustrate the direct and step-down methods for allocation of indirect costs, repeated here as Figure 9-A.1.

	Overhead Pools			Projects		
	Accounting	Human Resources	Maintenance	1	2	3
Costs	$80,000	$60,000	$40,000			
Driver	work hours	# employees	sq. ft.			
Quantity						
hours	1,000	5,000	500	20,000	8,000	12,000
employees	2	10	20	250	150	90
square feet	250	500	100	2,500	3,000	1,550

Figure 9-A.1   Reciprocal Example

Forming equations for the total cost of an overhead pool (its own cost plus its share of the other overhead pool costs), where its use of another overhead pool is the ratio of its use of that pool's driver divided by the total use of the driver by all other pools, we have the following system:

A = Accounting
HR = Human Resources
Mnt = Maintenance

$$A = 80,000 \;+\; 2/512 \;\text{HR} \;+\; 250/7,800 \;\text{Mnt}$$
$$HR = 60,000 \;+\; 5,000/45,500 \;\text{A} \;+\; 500/7,800 \;\text{Mnt}$$
$$Mnt = 40,000 \;+\; 500/45,500 \;\text{A} \;+\; 20/512 \;\text{HR}$$

The next step is to rearrange these equations into matrix format (A*X=B) where each column of the A matrix represents the pools for accounting, human resources, and maintenance, respectively. (Remember that moving the coefficients to the opposite side of the equal sign reverses their values from positive to negative and that each variable has an implied value of 1.)

A			X	B
1	−0.003906*	−0.0320513	A	$80,000
−0.10989011	1	−0.0641026	HR	60,000
−0.01989011	−0.039063	1	Mnt	40,000

*−2/512

Once in this form, Excel™ matrix inversion formulas can be used to find A⁻¹, the inverted matrix. [The formula for the first row, first column below is =INDEX(MINVERSE(A49:C51),1,1), where A49:C51 locates the A matrix and 1,1 refers to row 1, column 1. (The formula for the second row, first column would be =INDEX(MINVERSE(A49:C51),2,1) and other cell locations would be identified in a similar manner.)]

The inverted matrix is displayed below, along with the variables and the original amounts of the three pools:

A Inverse			X	B
1.000924973	0.005176	0.03241272	A	$80,000
0.110974712	1.0030842	0.06785715	HR	60,000
0.015334125	0.0392399	1.00300685	Mnt	40,000

The next step is to multiply the A-Inverse matrix by the B matrix to find the amounts that must be allocated from each pool. Multiplying the A-Inverse matrix by the B matrix (EXCEL command =INDEX(MMULT($A$55:$C$57,$E$55:$E$57),1,1—where the matrix begins in column A, row 55) for the first row, first column (Accounting Pool) value results in the following enhanced costs for each overhead pool. The amounts to be allocated are:

Accounting	$81,681
Human Resources	$71,777
Maintenance	$43,701

When costs are allocated back and forth between the overhead pools and projects, the total costs of each overhead pool will equal zero. (For convenience, the allocation bases and usages by each department and project are repeated at the top of Figure 9-A.2.) Using this method, the allocations (all amounts rounded to the nearest dollar) are shown in the lower part of Figure 9-A.2.

	Overhead Pools			Projects			
Overhead Pool Drivers	Accounting	Human Resources	Maintenance	1	2	3	Totals
Accounting hours	1,000	5,000	500	20,000	8,000	12,000	45,500
Employees	2	10	20	250	150	90	512
Square feet	250	500	100	2,500	3,000	1,550	7,800
Overhead Pool Allocations							
OH Costs	$80,000	$60,000	$40,000	N/A	N/A	N/A	$180,000
Accounting allocation	–$81,681	$8,976	$898	$35,904	$14,362	$21,542	$0
Human Resources allocation	$280	–$71,777	$2,804	$35,048	$21,029	$12,617	$0
Maintenance allocation	$1,401	$2,801	–$43,701	$14,007	$16,808	$8,684	$0
Totals	$0	$0	$0	$84,958	$52,198	$42,844	$180,000

Figure 9-A.2   Reciprocal Allocations

Overhead pool costs have now been allocated to all users in a logical and defensible manner.

CHAPTER 10

Reporting Variances (Criteria 22–27)

> *"Things are going to get a lot worse before they get worse."*
>
> —Lily Tomlin

There are several assumptions underlying the material presented in this chapter. These assumptions include the following: (1) costs have been appropriately budgeted, and (2) costs incurred for project work have been accurately recorded and summarized to the proper control accounts. All the previous EVMS criteria are in place to support the next six criteria.

Criteria 22 through 27 establish specific metric reporting requirements and additional management actions triggered by those measures. Criteria 22 through 24 dictate the required basic metrics and how they should be analyzed, while Criteria 25 through 27 discuss how the basic metrics are used to gain additional performance insights.

Criterion 22 requires reporting of basic schedule and cost variances and Criterion 23 requires an explanation of reasons for the differences (variances) in planned and actual performance. Criterion 24 discusses information on project charges for indirect costs and their differences (variances) from plan.

Criterion 25 mandates that variances are summarized through the organizational structure and/or the work breakdown structure (WBS) in order to meet management information needs. Then Criteria 26 looks at the implementation of management changes required to address computed variances. Using original projections, actual results, and calculated metrics, Criterion 27 requires revised estimates of cost and expected variances at completion, as well as any additional funding requirements.

EVMS CRITERION 22

At least on a monthly basis, generate the following information at the control account and other levels as necessary for management control using actual cost data from, or reconcilable with, the accounting system:

(1) Comparison of the amount of planned budget and the amount of budget earned for work accomplished. This comparison provides the schedule variance.

(2) Comparison of the amount of the budget earned and the actual (applied where appropriate) direct costs for the same work. This comparison provides the cost variance.

The basic measurements of EVMS were introduced in Chapter 3. *Actual cost* (AC) (sometimes called *actual value* [AV]) is the cost of all work completed as of the status date. *Planned value* (PV) is the cost that was budgeted for the work that was scheduled for completion for that same period. *Earned value* (EV) is the cost that was budgeted for the work that actually was completed during the period. Confusion often arises here because the EV metric is the result of combining a planned value and an actual value while the other two values, AV and PV, are total actual or total planned amounts.

EV is a measurement of the actual work performed, but only at the amount budgeted (planned) for that amount of work, not its actual cost; therefore, EV constitutes the "earned" amount of the project budget. These relationships are easy to see in the EVMS metrics triangle (see Figure 10.1) that was first presented in Chapter 3.

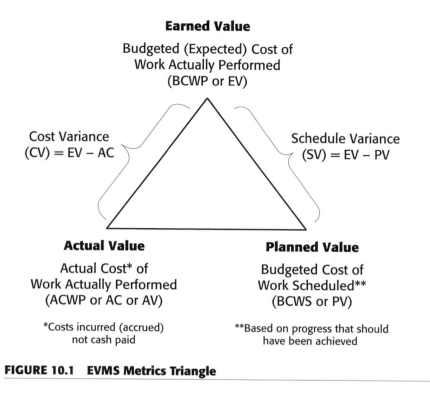

Earned Value

Budgeted (Expected) Cost of
Work Actually Performed
(BCWP or EV)

Cost Variance
(CV) = EV – AC

Schedule Variance
(SV) = EV – PV

Actual Value

Actual Cost* of
Work Actually Performed
(ACWP or AC or AV)

*Costs incurred (accrued)
not cash paid

Planned Value

Budgeted Cost of
Work Scheduled**
(BCWS or PV)

**Based on progress that should
have been achieved

FIGURE 10.1   EVMS Metrics Triangle

Criterion 22 requires information on the *schedule variance* (SV) and the *cost variance* (CV). SV is the difference between the EV and the PV (see Figure 10.1). Even though both variances are calculated in dollars, SV measures the difference between the budget for work that was *scheduled* and work that was *actually performed* since budgeted costs are held constant in both measures. The CV is the variance between the EV and the AV; it is the difference between the actual cost and the budgeted cost for the same amount of work—the work actually performed during the period being reported.

Determining the SV for the current status period, along with the cumulative SV since the start of the project, provides a valuable indicator of the project's overall schedule status in terms of dollars. However, it may not clearly indicate whether or not scheduled milestones are being met—especially if some work has been performed out of sequence or is ahead of schedule. SV does not indicate whether a completed activity is *critical* (where a positive or negative variance could affect the project's completion date) or *noncritical* (having no effect on project completion).

As we indicated earlier, this is a weakness of EVMS and it reinforces the necessity of a formal time-phased scheduling system. The status of critical activities and milestones, and therefore interpretation of variances and appropriate management response, must be determined through the diligent application of other sound project management techniques.

It is critical that the same basis used in budgeting be used for accumulating AVs. In Chapter 8, we stressed the use of a cost estimation package that includes the basis of the cost estimates as well as the cost baseline. In order to ensure valid comparisons to the baseline, the objective methods used during the estimation process must be employed during the project's progress. The accounting department should confirm that any estimates and assumptions used to accrue estimated costs for the budget baseline, such as indirect allocations, also are used in accruing AVs.

Determining the earned value of work packages that are only partially completed at the time of the project status may pose some difficulty. There are many ways to estimate how much work has been completed; however, none of them is very defensible. Work packages generally encompass one to two weeks of work, which minimizes this estimation problem, but some may be longer. Accurate progress will be easier to measure if there are discrete milestones imbedded in larger work packages so that you need not use an algorithm to determine the percent completed.

Actual cost data from the organization's accounting system, or data that can be reconciled with the accounting system, must be used for the calculation of the EVMS metrics. Analyzing the CV in detail can reveal factors causing the variance, such as a higher cost for labor and materials, a requirement for additional resources, lower than expected efficiencies, the use of different budget and actual rates, or even poor budget estimates. The budget amounts should be scheduled in conjunction with project events and then earned and actual costs applied when the event occurs. A problem often is encountered when there are delays between the end of a project status period and the availability of cost data from the accounting system. In that case, estimates must be used so that artificial variances are not created solely due to lags in recording transactions.

Correct data availability for variance computations is the key to complying with Criterion 22. Once the variances are identified, they must be analyzed. Criterion 23, discussed in the next section, requires this natural follow-up.

EVMS CRITERION 23

Identify, at least monthly, the significant differences between both planned and actual schedule performance and planned and actual cost performance, and provide the reasons for the variances in the detail needed by program management.

EVMS provides the evaluation and feedback loop for management action, so that management can evaluate variances and make informed decisions for corrective action. There may be activities that can bring a project back on plan or compensate in other ways for the variances in cost, schedule, or project scope. Sometimes the management decision may be to discontinue the project if the deviations are great enough and compensatory actions are not deemed viable.

This criterion requires the identification of significant variances and their reasons. Determination of *significant* depends on the organization, the size of the project, task and project risk, and a number of other factors. The amount of detail required for the variance report depends on the margin of deviation from the plan.

Schedule Variance

Comparing the project schedule with milestone completion reports, critical path or critical chain data, and other information such as the WBS is sufficient to discover the reasons for schedule variances. The perceived significance of the variance will depend on its severity and expected schedule impact. Even severe variations in individual task durations may not be considered significant if they are caused by factors that will not delay the project or increase costs.

If subcontractors are involved in the project, the primary organization must have processes in place that will check and verify the subcontractors' progress. It is good practice to have a responsible manager in the primary organization who reviews and analyzes the subcontractors' reports. The information then must be integrated into the primary progress report and earned value data. In EVMS, the subcontractors' progress payments will usually depend on EV calculations that must be verified by the responsible primary manager. Some items to check carefully are the use of any reserves, changes in the apportionment of manpower, or a baseline change in the subcontractors' schedules.

Cost Variance

Material usage generally accounts for a major part of a project's cost variance. Analysis of material accounts should focus on *significant* variances and may include variances above or below the expected usage as well as above or below the expected cost per item. For example, comparing budget and AC information on material usage should enable you to determine whether the variance results from a change in material cost (usually called a *price variance*) or a change in consumption (sometimes called a *quantity* or *efficiency variance*). Often, a project will require more material than was expected because of unexpected destruction during testing and scrap resulting from quality problems. Complete variance records with identification of causes will help significantly in providing accurate estimations for future project plans.

The accounting department will compute these price and efficiency variances, but you might be wise to consider keeping a journal record of selected (major) situations of rising costs or more than expected usage to aid in explaining variances that may not be computed until weeks after the events occurred.

Explaining Variances

First, be aware that Criterion 23 does not require an explanation for every variance in the EVMS calculations. Note that the criterion specifically mentions the "reasons...in the detail needed by...management"; management's interest should always be one of the guiding factors. Other factors include the level of risk in achieving the project's technical objectives and significant variances in high-cost elements.

U.S. military and security agencies prepared a joint guide for a cost/schedule report that lists five methods for setting variance reporting thresholds (Joint U.S. Defense Agencies 1996, Chapter 3). The guide reiterates that variances can be positive, negative, cumulative, current, or at completion. The authors consider these three to be the most helpful:

1. Analyze any variance that exceeds a predetermined threshold in dollar or percentage terms. This method usually results in more variance analyses, particularly as the project progresses.
2. Analyze the top 5 or 10 (or any number) largest dollar variances. This method usually reduces the number of variance analyses and focuses attention on the most significant problems.
3. Pre-select high-cost or high-risk areas for analysis. As the project progresses, the risk areas will change so the areas selected for analysis also should change.

EVMS CRITERION 24

Identify budgeted and applied (or actual) indirect costs at the level and frequency needed by management for effective control, along with the reasons for any significant variances.

The differences in and examples of direct and indirect costs were presented in the last chapter. In general, direct costs are those that can be directly traced to a project (materials and labor, for example) while indirect costs are shared overhead-type costs that must be allocated. Criterion 24 requires a thorough examination of the entire process for establishing and allocating indirect costs to individual projects. Indirect cost allocation will apply more often in organizations that do not have a project-oriented organizational structure (see Chapter 6) because the organization that is structured around projects will incur most of its costs by project and will have lower overall shared indirect expenses.

Indirect costs may be variable with some level of activity, fixed regardless of activity, or some combination of the two. For example, the human resources (HR) department may be able to handle a 10 percent increase in the current level of employees with its current staff but if additional project workers are required, HR must hire additional staffers.

Indirect fixed costs are planned and experienced based primarily on the passage of time; there should be little variance between project budgets and actual allocations with the exception of changes in costs (such as an unexpected change in the local property tax rate). Some other causes for variances include changes in corporate structure, changes in number of projects using the same organizational elements, and differences between the timeframe or driver used for planning and that used for the allocation.

The variances must be reported accurately so that they can be analyzed and the project manager can determine appropriate corrective action. Sometimes, corrective action is not appropriate, but the variance report also is important for developing revisions to the *estimated cost at completion* (EAC) and for more accurately estimating future indirect project costs.

EVMS CRITERION 25

Summarize the data elements and associated variances through the program organization and/or work breakdown

structure to support management needs and any customer reporting specified in the contract.

The summarized data elements and associated variances should include all the points shown on the EVMS metrics triangle (see Figure 10.1). Calculations for PV, AV, EV, and the two variances should be made at appropriate levels and summarized (aggregated) for the entire organization involved in the project.

The level of summarized data for a contractual report is usually well defined in the contract. The more difficult aspect of this criterion is ascertaining the level of information required for internal management needs. Management reports generally are considered adequate when constructed from the summary information at level two or three of the WBS. However, reporting must recognize that a high-level manager may have a large oversight scope where positive and negative variances at lower levels cancel each other in the manager's summarized report and may not indicate a problem. That does not necessarily mean that managerial action is not required.

The appropriate summarization starts at the control account level. Control accounts have been established in conjunction with the accounting department at the lowest level of the organization where a specific organizational unit was responsible for a specific piece of the WBS (see Control Accounts in Chapter 5). As a requirement of Criterion 25, this summation must continue upward through both the *organization breakdown structure* (OBS) and the WBS, but the summations must reconcile. That is, the total variances must be the same whether summarized through the WBS or OBS.

Management needs are satisfied and appropriate corrective actions can be identified when all levels of management receive and evaluate EVMS metrics at their level. This approach also will allow an appropriate evaluation in cases where small variances at lower management levels may not merit attention, but cumulatively signal a problem.

EVMS CRITERION 26

Implement managerial actions taken as the result of earned value information.

This criterion generally requires that management at the various levels of the organization has authority for corrective action. As pointed out earlier, a significant variance at the control account level may be cancelled out by other variances when it is included in the summarized report. Corrective actions may not be taken at the various levels at which problems have occurred unless the managers at those levels of responsibility have commensurate authority. The control account level can be the primary management control point for the project.

Caveat: This is an excellent time to review the CAUTION expressed in Chapter 3. EV metrics are *informational* as opposed to *motivational*—they may indicate a problem, but they do *not* pinpoint the reasons for the problems. Project decisions must be based on sound project management practices *and* personnel evaluations should not be based on EV metrics. The practice can elicit unproductive responses. EV metrics, however, *can* give a fairly reliable forecast of the project's final performance.

EVMS CRITERION 27

Develop revised estimates of cost at completion based on performance to date, commitment values for material, and estimates of future conditions. Compare this information with the performance measurement baseline to identify variances at completion important to company management and any applicable customer reporting requirements, including statements of funding requirements.

This criterion states three considerations in developing revised cost estimates at completion (EAC). They are "performance to date, commitment values for material, and estimates of future conditions." Those three elements will be examined first and then the second part of this criterion, reporting, will be discussed.

Performance to Date

Performance to date is primarily a calculation of EV metrics and a review of how well the technical requirements are being met.

Earned Value Measurements

One way to develop an EAC is first to calculate an *estimate to complete* (ETC) with the formula stated in Chapter 3. You must know the total *budget at completion* (BAC), the current EV, the *cost performance index* (CPI), or alternatively, the CPI and the *schedule performance index* (SPI). The CPI is the EV divided by the AV. The SPI is the EV divided by the PV. (Review the EVMS metrics triangle in Figure 10.1.)

To calculate the ETC, subtract the EV from the BAC and divide the result by the CPI. Alternatively, if both the CPI and the SPI are taken into consideration, the result would be divided by the CPI times the SPI. Once the ETC has been calculated, it is easy to develop an EAC by simply adding the ACs and the calculated ETC. The formulae are:

Estimate to Complete:

$$\text{ETC} = \frac{Budget\ at\ Completion - Earned\ Value}{Cost\ Performance\ Index} \quad \text{or}$$

$$\frac{BAC - EV}{CPI} \quad \text{(for an "optimistic" estimate) or}$$

$$\frac{BAC - EV}{CPI * SPI} \quad \text{(for a "pessimistic" estimate).}$$

Estimate at Completion (revised total estimated final cost): EAC = Actual Cost (to date) + Estimate to Complete, or EAC = AC + ETC.

To discover what level of performance must be achieved on the remaining project work in order to complete the project within some specified financial goal such as the original budget, the total project price, or another maximum amount, a *to complete index* (TCI), may be computed. This ratio, when greater than 1, reflects performance at a higher level than previously demonstrated is required; when less than 1, it means that performance can be less than previously experienced and still meet the desired goal. This index is computed by dividing the value of the remaining work by remaining funds. *Remaining funds,* however, may be defined in several ways: BAC less costs incurred to date, EAC less ACs incurred, or total contact price less ACs incurred.

Here is one commonly used version where funds are limited to those originally budgeted:

$$\text{TCI} = \frac{Remaining\,Work}{Remaining\,Funds} =$$

$$\frac{Budget\,at\,Completion - Earned\,Value}{Budget\,at\,Completion - Actual\,Costs\,Incurred}$$

To demonstrate these computations, we will use the simple example from Chapter 3, repeated here as Figure 10.2.

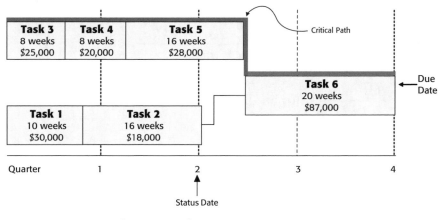

FIGURE 10.2   A Project Network

Assume the status date is now the end of the second quarter. By this date, Tasks 1, 3, and 4 should have been completely finished, along with about 93 percent of Task 2 and 57 percent of Task 5. While Tasks 1, 3, and 4 are finished, however, Task 2 is only 75 percent complete and Task 5 is estimated at 25 percent complete. Materials are added only in Tasks 1, 3, and 6; costs for other tasks are incurred uniformly over time. Costs incurred thus far total $101,500. Figure 10.3 displays this situation on the EVMS metrics triangle and Figure 10.4 contains EVMS calculations for the sample project.

We can see from the sample calculations in Figure 10.4 that the project is estimated to complete at a cost of $221,181 (or $235,973) rather than $208,000, as originally budgeted. It also is clear from the TCI that future efforts must be more productive than exhibited thus far for it to be completed within the original budgeted amount.

At each status reporting date, a schedule variance and cost variance should be calculated for each control account before being rolled up for the entire project. Control account managers need

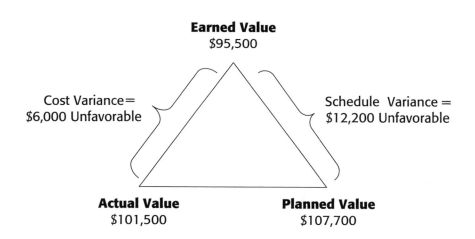

Earned Value
$95,500

Cost Variance=
$6,000 Unfavorable

Schedule Variance =
$12,200 Unfavorable

Actual Value
$101,500

Planned Value
$107,700

FIGURE 10.3   EVMS Metrics Triangle for Sample Project at Halfway Point

A status is taken at the end of 6 months for a 1-year project. The total planned budget for the project is $208,00,000. The project staff has completed Tasks 1,3, and 4 but only 75 percent of Task 2 and 57 percent of Task 5. Expenditures to date equal $101,500:

BAC = $208,000 = $30,000 + $25,000 +$18,000 +$20,000 + $28,000 + $87,000

AC = $101,500.

PV = $107,700 = $30,000 + $25,000 + $20,000 + (.93 x $18,000) + (.57 x $28,000)

EV = $95,500 = $30,000 + $25,000 + $20,000 + (.75 x $18,000) + (.25 x $28,000)

CV = $6,000 Unfavorable = $95,500 − $101,500 = ($6,000)

$$CPI = 0.94 = \frac{\$95,500}{\$101,500}$$

SV = $12,200 Unfavorable = $95,500 - $107,700 = ($12,200)

$$SPI = 0.89 = \frac{\$95,500}{\$107,700}$$

"To complete" calculations considering only the CPI ("optimistic" estimate):

$$ETC = \$119,681 = \frac{\$208,000 - \$95,500}{0.94}$$

EAC = $221,181 = $119,681 + $101,500

$$TCI = 1.06 = \frac{\$208,000 - \$95,500}{\$208,000 - \$101,500} \text{ using BAC}$$

$$or = 0.94 = \frac{\$208,000 - \$95,500}{\$221,181 - \$101,500} \text{ using EAC}$$

Alternative "to complete" calculations taking into account both the CPI and the SPI ("pessimistic" estimate):

$$ETC = \$134,473 = \frac{\$208,000 - \$95,500}{0.94 \times 0.89} = \frac{\$112,500}{0.8366}$$

EAC = $235,973= $134,473 + $101,500

$$TCI = 1.06 = \frac{\$208,000 - \$95,500}{\$208,000 - \$101,500} \text{ using BAC (no change from the "optimistic" estimate)}$$

$$or = 0.84 = \frac{\$208,000 - \$95,500}{\$235,973 - \$101,500} \text{ using EAC (with extra funding)}$$

FIGURE 10.4   Sample EVMS Calculations

to be aware of variances that will affect the EAC because authority and responsibility for corrective action begin at that level.

Interpreting the Variances

It is obvious that the second quarter results are continuing the trend established in the first quarter: cost and schedule variances remain negative. While the cost variance remains unchanged at $6,000 unfavorable, the schedule variance has increased an additional $2,200 unfavorable. However, the EAC has decreased by a minimum of $7,390 from the first quarter (from $228,571 and $265,781 to $221,181 and $235,973 for optimistic and pessimistic estimates, respectively). Thus, performance is improving.

Nevertheless, to complete the project on budget, performance must increase by a factor of .06. Or, negotiations may be entered to increase the baseline budget to a more realistic amount closer to the current estimate at completion.

Technical Performance

Variances in cost and schedule are often caused by technical problems; however, the absence of significant budget variances does not mean that the project necessarily is achieving its objectives. The quality of the project work can be determined with appropriate testing, inspections, and mechanical measurements. A narrative report by the project members sometimes can be helpful in determining the technical performance status. Reports from team members, whether solicited or not, should be read carefully and suggestions given special attention.

One problem we have encountered repeatedly is that a project manager belatedly will discover a lack of required resources. The project is rolling along right on schedule and suddenly there is no one available for the next critical task. Project managers must be aware of remaining work on the project and predict both the requirements for and availability of resources.

We absolutely believe in a project management technique called *Critical Chain*. This tool is an approach that not only overcomes certain understandable but undesirable behaviors, but also utilizes several protection buffers, including a resource buffer that provides an early warning device for critical resources (Goldratt 1997). Implementation of Critical Chain, however, must be on an organizational level for the entire portfolio of projects and is extremely difficult and risky to apply on an individual project without strong support from top management.

When corrective action or necessary project changes are required, project managers should carefully consider the alternatives. Some work-a-rounds or fixes for a technical problem may involve substantial changes in the project cost and schedule. If changes are considered necessary and an alternative action is chosen, the changes must be reflected in the project plan. New work packages may need to be added or existing packages altered.

Our experience indicates that projects get into the most trouble when changes are not fully documented and communicated. Project managers must be certain that all project changes are fully authorized, accounted for, and clearly shown in a revised project baseline (see Chapter 11 for Criteria 28 through 32 and a more thorough discussion of project revisions).

Updated Values for Materials

For each periodic EVMS measurement, there is a requirement to determine the amount and cost of materials needed to complete the project. This estimate becomes a part of the estimate to complete and should be based on the actual costs to date, actual usage to date, estimates of future usage, commitments for additional material, and projections of future prices. Any variance with the material budget must be documented and reported for possible corrective action. Just as a project manager must be concerned with provision for future human resource requirements, he or she must also be concerned with the future material requirements and must communicate and coordinate updated information in a timely manner with the organization's purchasing department.

Estimates of Future Conditions

When considering "performance to date" and "commitment values for materials" cited in this criterion, some additional facets of future conditions must be taken into account in developing the most accurate estimate at completion. For example, the estimates made from performance to date should acknowledge probable changes in future performance. The cost of materials should include both future price changes and future changes in usage. This criterion, however, adds a further general category of "future conditions."

This might be considered an unnecessary catch-all category, but there are some conditions outside the project parameters that might not be considered if it were omitted. Some examples of possible factors include the following:

- Overall anticipated business volume
- Estimates of general economic changes
- Organizational changes contemplated by management.

Performance Reporting

The second part of Criterion 27 requires the generation of information important to management and any reporting required by the contract. In order to maintain a cost-effective system, the federal government encourages contractors to report only enough information for adequate management control. While we have tried to present all the standard metrics, it is possible that particular contracts might require additional measures, such as quality performance, time required to implement approved changes, or number of changes accepted versus those requested. The project manager must be alert to these requirements and ensure that data are recorded so contractual obligations are met.

The use of *electronic data interchange* (EDI) is recommended (mandatory in many cases), using the American National Standards Institute (ANSI) Accredited Standards Committee (ASC) X.12 standard for EDI. Requirements for submitting reports by electronic means may be included in the contract (Department of

Defense, FAA, and NASA 1997, Section 2-4.d). The primary report for EVMS projects has been the Cost Performance Report (CPR); however, a proposed EVMS revision now includes the *Integrated Master Schedule* (IMS).

Cost Performance Report

The *Cost Performance Report* (CPR) (Defense Acquisition University 2004, Chapter 11.3.2.2) is a contractually required report, prepared by the contractor to provide a status of progress on the project. The report, sometimes referred to as the Contract Performance Report, must be made for all contracts that require compliance with EVMS, but it also may be requested on contracts that fall below the dollar thresholds for EVMS compliance. It is intended to provide an early indication of cost and schedule problems and show the effect of any management actions that were implemented to correct such problems.

The CPR is subject to tailoring by the contracting agency, but basically details the project's cost/schedule status and trends using five formats. A government agency may request data in Formats 1 through 4 from the contractor in order to "get the numbers" while the narrative (Format 5) is being prepared. In some cases, such as when a narrative is given during regular project status reviews, the agency may forgo Format 5.

Sample formats can be seen on the Department of Defense's website for the Directorate for Information Operations and Reports (DIOR):

1. Format 1 reports EVMS metrics on elements of the work breakdown structure (http://www.dior.whs.mil/forms/ DD2734-1.pdf).
2. Format 2 is a similar report from the viewpoint of organizational categories (http://www.dior.whs.mil/forms/DD2734-2.pdf).
3. Format 3 reports performance data concerning the performance measurement baseline (http://www.dior.whs.mil/forms/DD2734-3.pdf).

4. Format 4 deals with performance data and forecasts for staffing (http://www.dior.whs.mil/forms/DD2734-4.pdf).
5. Format 5 is a narrative that reports explanations and problem analysis (http://www.dior.whs.mil/forms/DD2734-5.pdf).

Integrated Master Schedule

A section of the Defense Acquisition University's *Defense Acquisition Guidebook* (2004, Chapter 11.8) concerns *Integrated Product and Process Development* (IPPD), which is the Department of Defense management technique that simultaneously integrates all essential acquisition activities through the use of multidisciplinary teams called *Integrated Product Teams* (IPT). These teams coordinate all the activities related to a product. The primary documents of IPPD that are now being implemented on all Department of Defense acquisitions are the *Integrated Master Plan* (IMP) and *Integrated Master Schedule* (IMS).

The IMP describes the events, significant accomplishments, and accomplishment criteria for all the activities that were specified in the Contract Work Breakdown dictionary and other documents that were a part of the government solicitation. The completed IMP then usually becomes the defining project document and part of the final contract.

The IMS places the Events and Significant Accomplishments (the Accomplishment Criteria specify the conditions for completion of a Significant Accomplishment) on a timescale as schedule milestones. Tasks are added to the IMS to support the Events and Significant Accomplishments (milestones). The tasks and milestones are linked to produce the IMS. EVMS metrics can then be generated from the IMS to provide the required performance measurements.

Other Requirements

Criterion 27 also requires the reporting of contract funding requirements. The *Contract Funds Status Report* (CFSR) (DD Form

1586) is designed to supply funding data about defense contracts to program managers for:

- Updating and forecasting contract funds requirements
- Planning and decision making on funding changes to contracts
- Developing funds requirements and budget estimates in support of approved programs
- Determining funds in excess of contract needs and available for deobligation
- Obtaining rough estimates of termination costs.

See Figure 10.5 for a sample form provided by the Defense Acquisition University.

Your project may not require the formality of the various government report formats, but these reporting criteria were designed so that the reported information is meaningful. Any report that is prepared must provide accurate and timely information that can inform management decisions. It should be noted that the previous admonition is also an excellent guideline for nongovernmental projects.

Four primary characteristics of significant information are:

1. *Relevance:* The information has accurate, confirmatory, and predictive value.
2. *Reliability:* The information is complete and as error-free as possible.
3. *Comparability:* A strict following of the requirements of EVMS will ensure that report information has a base with which current performance can be compared.
4. *Comprehensibility:* Information is fully explained and free of biased or misleading representations.

CLASSIFICATION

CONTRACT FUNDS STATUS REPORT *(Dollars in)*

1. CONTRACT NUMBER	3. CONTRACT FUNDING FOR FOR FY	5. PREVIOUS REPORT DATE	7. CONTRACTOR *(Name, address and zip code)*	9. INITIAL CONTRACT PRICE a. TARGET b. CEILING
2. CONTRACT TYPE	4. APPROPRIATION	6. CURRENT REPORT DATE	8. PROGRAM	10. ADJUSTED CONTRACT PRICE a. TARGET b. CEILING

11. FUNDING INFORMATION

LINE ITEM/WBS ELEMENT	APPRO-PRIATION IDENTI-FICATION	FUNDING AUTHORIZED TO DATE	ACCRUED EXPENDITURES OPEN COMMITMENTS TOTAL	CONTRACT WORK AUTHORIZED			FORECAST			TOTAL REQUIRE-MENTS	FUNDS CARRY-OVER	NET FUNDS REQUIRED
				DEFINITIZED	NOT DEFINITIZED	SUBTOTAL	NOT YET AUTHORIZED	ALL OTHER WORK	SUBTOTAL			
a	b	c	d	e	f	g	h	i	j	k	l	m

12. CONTRACT WORK AUTHORIZED *(With Fee/Profit)* - ACTUAL OR PROJECTED

	ACTUAL TO DATE									AT COMPLETION
a. OPEN COMMITMENTS										
b. ACCRUED EXPENDITURES										
c. TOTAL *(12a + 12b)*										
13. FORECAST OF BILLINGS TO THE GOVERNMENT										
14. ESTIMATED TERMINATION COSTS										

15. REMARKS

Page ______ of ______ Pages

CLASSIFICATION

SAMPLE FORMAT 1. Contract Funds Status Report Page 7 of 7

Source: Defense Acquisition University 2004, *Defense Acquisition Guidebook*, Chapter 11.3.2.4.

FIGURE 10.5 Contract Funds Status Report

This chapter presents the results of establishing all the EVMS metrics—the performance reports that reveal the differences between projected and actual performance. All previous criteria were established to ensure that reliable data are recorded and summarized so that reliable variances can be reported, analyzed, and addressed.

Criterion 22 stipulates that cost and schedule variances must be computed and reported at the control account and other levels necessary for management control. Criterion 23 requires that variances between planned and actual schedule and cost performance, combined with reasons for the variances, be described at a level of detail that will satisfy management and contractual needs.

Criterion 24 prescribes that differences in budgeted and applied indirect costs, as well as reasons for significant variances, must be reported at the level and frequency needed by management. These are costs that cannot be directly traced to a project and must be allocated using some rational and reasonable formula. They pose a bigger problem for functional organizational structures than project-oriented structures.

Criterion 25 requires that data elements and resulting variances must be associated with the work breakdown structure or organizational structure to support management's need for information or to comply with contractual obligations. The amounts thus associated then are combined for all elements to generate project totals.

Actions to remedy unfavorable variances are stipulated by Criterion 26 while Criterion 27 requires revised estimates of cost at completion, estimates of future conditions, comparisons with the project baseline, and implications of funding sufficiency. The Cost Performance Report and the Integrated Master Schedule are the primary reports for federal EVMS contracts.

EXERCISE 1

1. Assume the following project is being prepared for progress review at the end of the third quarter.

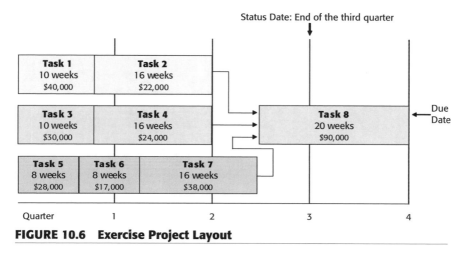

FIGURE 10.6   Exercise Project Layout

According to the budget baseline, all tasks should be completed except Task 8, which should be about one-third complete at this time. The project manager reports, however, that all tasks are finished except the last one, which is about 50 percent complete.

Required: Assuming that actual costs to date total $240,000, compute the following:

a. Budget at Completion (BAC)
b. BCWS (PV)
c. EV
d. AC (or AV)
e. Cost variance and CPI
f. Schedule Variance and SPI
g. ETC and EAC
h. TCI.

EXERCISE 2

Evaluate the variances computed in Exercise 1.

See Appendix B for solutions to Exercises 1 and 2.

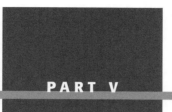

PART V

Handling a Project's Changes and Termination

The final two chapters cover the criteria for handling project changes and an important part of the project life cycle that is not covered by EVMS—terminating a project. Because every project is a unique event, meeting the project's objectives of schedule, cost, and quality is a very risky proposition. The uncertainties always result in some project modification, but managing risk can mitigate the probabilities and consequences of major change. The last five criteria detail the requirements for controlling, making, and documenting project changes.

Because finishing a project is sometimes difficult and almost always precipitates undesirable effects, Chapter 12 covers project termination. The project must first be completed and its objectives met before initiating the activities and reports that will officially close the project. One of the important documents of project termination that will help guide future projects is the "lessons learned."

CHAPTER 11

Time for a Change (Criteria 28–32)

The last five EVMS criteria cover change—how and when to change, what to change, controlling change, and reporting change. Because the need for change results from the high degree of risk involved in projects, we begin with a look at the implications and ramifications of risk. Then we address the management of change, present a formal change control process, and finish with some specific information about each of the criteria.

UNCERTAINTY MAY BE THE ONLY CERTAINTY

You probably have heard about the 1995 Standish Group's study of information technology projects and their horrendous failure rate (Standish Group International 1995). Even though a 1999 update showed only a little improvement (Standish Group International 1999), we would like to think that more professional practices, such as using EVMS, are contributing to better project success rates. Yet if anything can go wrong during the project's life span, it will. This is Murphy's Law in action. We can minimize the frequency of Murphy's visits by addressing and managing risk.

Risk management is a very complex process and is really the responsibility of the entire organization. If the organization has an enterprise risk management process or practice, the project manager should be able to align the project's risk management with the organization's risk activities. If not, the project manager should promote an enterprise risk management framework. However, the project manager must operate solo for the current project.

We will provide some suggestions and tools, but risk management depends on several key factors such as the level of the organization's capacity for risk tolerance. Therefore, please keep in mind that our suggestions and examples will need to be modified for your specific organization's environment.

If your organization would like assistance in establishing an enterprise risk management practice, we highly recommend *Enterprise Risk Management—Integrated Framework* authored by PricewaterhouseCoopers, LLP (Steinberg et al. 2004). The framework was commissioned by the Committee of Sponsoring Organizations[1] of The Treadway Commission, commonly referred to as COSO. The framework is designed to assist organizations in determining how much risk their entity is prepared to accept and how it may proceed to handle risks and opportunities effectively. This analysis and a companion document, "Applications Techniques," are available at https://www.cpa2biz.com.

UNDERSTANDING THE ELEMENTS OF RISK

> *"I know you think you understand what you think I said, but I'm not sure you realize that what you heard is not what I meant."*
>
> —Unknown

The Department of Defense (DoD) defines *risk* as: "a measure of the inability to achieve overall program objectives within defined

---

[1]COSO members include the American Accounting Association, American Institute of Certified PublicAccountants, Financial Executives Institute, Institute of Management Accountants, and Institute of Internal Auditors.

cost, schedule, and *technical* constraints and has two components: (1) the *probability* of failing to achieve a particular outcome and (2) the *consequences* of failing to achieve that outcome [emphases added]" (Department of Defense 2003, *Risk Management Guide for DoD Acquisition,* 7). An investigation of project risk should include a statement of the risk event and a categorization of its probability and consequence; for example, a computer failure is only a concern and cannot be considered a risk unless the event's probability and consequence can be specifically defined.

Another misunderstanding often occurs when someone talks about *high* risk. They may mean there is an increased probability for the event to occur or they may mean that the consequences will be severe. It is a *combination* of these two factors of probability and impact that determines the overall level of risk. Figure 11.1 illustrates four levels of probability and impact for the acceptability of project risk (left half) or the potential contribution of an

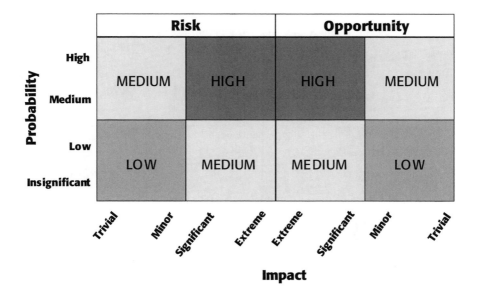

FIGURE 11.1   Probability and Impact Matrix

opportunity (right half). If the risk event's probability and impact intersect in the lower-left quadrant, the risk would be considered a low-risk event. The determination of the ratios of low, medium, and high risk could be adjusted to reflect the organization's overall risk tolerance. Similarly, if an opportunity's probability and impact intersect in its far-right lower quadrant, it would not warrant further attention. Thus, the four side-by-side quadrants are mirror images of each other and the probabilities and impact that intersect in either of the "high" regions require careful follow-up.

RISK MANAGEMENT

Our general model of risk management includes the three phases of risk assessment, disposition, and monitoring (see Figure 11.2).

FIGURE 11.2   Elements of Risk Management

Risk Assessment

Risk assessment is a multiphase process of examining the three project *constraints* (cost, schedule, and technical requirements) and other areas and factors surrounding a project in order to *identify* and *evaluate* potential problems. Identifying every possible problem is virtually impossible, but by using a variety of techniques, most of the significant project risks can be exposed. It is helpful to combine some elementary assessment during the identification phase so that immaterial problems quickly can be eliminated.

One of the major difficulties in risk identification is surfacing all the possibilities because there are so many subconscious assumptions we never question in planning a project. In the section, Identifying Risk, some techniques are described that are specifically designed to surface and explore assumptions.

The Department of Energy requires project management personnel to "demonstrate the ability to prepare a project risk assessment" (U.S. Department of Energy 1995, paragraph 4.9). DOE lists the ability to perform the following activities as evidence of this ability:

a. Perform an assessment of project risk that identifies critical systems subsystems and other factors that require focused work and resolution.
b. Identify the types of risk that are addressed in a project risk assessment.
c. Evaluate the assessed level of risk.
d. Describe the basis for the risk assessment.
e. Identify the critical project elements that contribute to the risk.
f. Identify the consequences of the risk.
g. Develop activities and alternatives to minimize the risk.
h. Identify the stage(s) of the project in which the risk exists.

Identifying Risk

Risk identification will be more complete by including in this activity as many appropriate stakeholders as possible, including the project manager, all members of the project team, end users, and outside experts concerning the project deliverables or risk management.

The following techniques have proven useful for identifying risk:

- *Brainstorming.* A trained facilitator should lead this group activity in an unrestrained atmosphere. The idea is to generate as many ideas of risks (and opportunities) as possible, with no "idea ownership," so group members can feed off one another. The contributions should be made without judgment—at least in the beginning—so that potential ideas are not suppressed. The real challenge comes in validating the items from an unrestricted list so that only the best ones survive.
- *Surveys.* This technique is a great way to solicit a lot of input, but it has at least two weaknesses. One is that many people simply do not respond to surveys while others tend always to do so, biasing the results. Another problem is that survey results are often tainted by the way the survey is presented, the way questions are asked, or the fact that questions contain various ambiguities subject to different interpretation by respondents.
- *Checklists.* A checklist of previous risk events can be very helpful when the organization has managed projects similar to the one being assessed. Be sure to allow room for additions because reviewing previous events likely will trigger thoughts about additional possibilities.
- *Personal interviews.* This technique can elicit many possible risk events if the interview is conducted in a relaxed environment by a trained facilitator, but it has weaknesses similar to the survey. In addition, the facilitator must be knowledgeable about the project because there will be no other assistance in the one-on-one situation of an interview.
- *Lessons learned (previous projects).* This technique is very similar to the risk checklist in that it presents a starting point. It differs in that it is not specific to risk events and therefore

allows for more freedom of thought; however, it may lead to some irrelevancy.

* *Examination of the work breakdown structure (WBS) elements.* This is a very thorough but time-consuming way to assess the project for potential risk. The examination should be done in stages corresponding to the levels of the WBS. Major risk events may be associated with the top levels of the WBS, but the "devil" is usually in discovering the detailed information so a solution strategy can be formulated.

We found an amusing, but effective, technique for identifying risk proposed by Dr. David Hillson (the "Risk Doctor") in his Internet briefings (2004, 9). He suggests encouraging the imagination through the use of *fantasy questions* to expose risks in a nonthreatening way. One of his fantasy questions is, "If you were dreaming about your project and it turned into a nightmare, what would be happening?" He notes that "this question encourages people to talk about perceived threats" that would not be articulated with more conservative thinking.

Evaluating Risk

Although some risk analysis is done while identifying potential project risk, a more thorough evaluation must be completed after the risks have been recognized. The process begins by expanding the depiction of the risk to establish its probability of occurrence and the possible severity of its consequences (see Figure 11.1). Identifying probable causes for each event will help with the process and provide additional insight. Since there are always a great number of potential events, they cannot all be handled in the same manner or with the same level of effort. They must be differentiated. The risk analysis process will provide a basis for determining the priority and disposition method for each event.

Categorizing risks according to sources of the risk, which portion of the project is affected, or which resources might be involved may assist in the risk evaluation process. Grouping risks according to common causes also helps generate some focused and creative responses.

Although analyzing a risk's probability and consequences, which produces the comparative level of risk, is a difficult process, it can be made somewhat easier with the use of a rating scheme. The rating should include the probability of the event's occurrence and the possible consequences for the three project constraints of schedule, cost, and specifications.

An example of a matrix utilizing a rating scheme to prioritize potential risks is provided in Figure 11.3. Each of the descriptions can be assigned a weighting factor and a matrix can be used to assess the overall threat the risk poses to achievement of the project's objective and to assist in prioritizing the risk events to facilitate the selection of appropriate disposition methods.

One complex but productive method particularly useful for analyzing risk is the *Delphi technique* developed by Brown and Dalkey of the Rand Corporation during the 1960s. It is a method of achieving consensus through an iterative and anonymous survey of experts. One of its first applications was technological forecasting, but it can be a valuable tool for analyzing possible risk and consequence. The method is "commonly used when a group must develop a consensus concerning such items as . . . uncertain future conditions or events" (Meredith and Mantel 2003, 77).

Risk Disposition

Once the risk events have been identified, analyzed, categorized, and prioritized, the next activity in risk management is to decide on an appropriate disposition method for at least the medium and high risks. Evaluation parameters should include the cost/benefit tradeoffs, the potential effectiveness of the method, and the consequences for the project's schedule and deliverables.

The Project Management Institute devotes an entire chapter to project risk management in *A Guide to the Project Management Body of Knowledge*. The *Guide* is an invaluable tool for project management and we recommend it for all project team members. When it comes to the disposition of project risk events, it describes four terms that are often misunderstood or misap-

Risk Event	Occurrence	Schedule	Cost	Specs
Vendor fails to deliver software	Remote	Major slip in project date	Initial monetary problem	Some adjustment to specs
Loss of in-house trainer (resignation, illness, etc.)	Unlikely	Some project delay	Low monetary consideration	Minor adjustment to specs
Loss of network server	Unlikely	Some project delay	Some monetary consideration	No change in specs
. . .	. . .	. . .	. . .	. . .

FIGURE 11.3   Risk Rating Form

plied—*Avoid, Transfer, Mitigate,* and *Accept* (Project Management Institute 2004, 261–262):

1. *Avoid:* "... changing the project plan to eliminate the threat posed by an adverse risk, to isolate the project objectives from the risk's impact, or to relax the objective that is in jeopardy, such as extending the schedule or reducing scope." This method will require cooperation and acceptance from the project's end users.

2. *Transfer:* "... shifting the negative impact of a threat, along with ownership of the response, to a third party." This is a form of risk sharing that is most effective in dealing with financial risk since the risk itself is not eliminated. While contracts may be used to accomplish the transfer, a risk premium generally is required. Transfer also may apply to elements within the organization such as transferring a function from hardware to software in the event of a failure.

3. *Mitigate (sometimes referred to as Control):* "... implies a reduction in the probability and/or impact of an adverse risk event to an acceptable threshold." This method usually

requires additional time and resources, such as operating a parallel plan or running modeling and screening processes.

4. *Accept (sometimes referred to as Assumption):* "... indicates that the project team has decided not to change the project plan to deal with a risk or is unable to identify any other suitable response strategy." Risks for which an appropriate disposition method cannot be determined until they occur generally fall into this classification. The most planning that may be done is to arrive at some estimate of the resources that might be required if and when the risks occur.

Any of these methods, or some combination of them, may be used in response to risk exposure. The most important point is that a risk plan must be developed prior to initiation of the project and it must be continuously updated as the project progresses.

Risk Monitoring

Risk monitoring is intended to provide a warning of impending risk events and to provide a basis for improving the risk management process. Effective risk monitoring should identify the weak and strong points of the risk management plan and forecast new risk events. It depends on a comprehensive risk plan and a reliable cost, schedule, and performance evaluation system. Fortunately, we know of such a system.

"Earned value (EV) ... is useful in monitoring the effectiveness of risk-handling actions in that it provides periodic comparisons of the actual work accomplished in terms of cost and schedule with the work planned and budgeted" (Department of Defense 2003, 79). The periodic cost/schedule variances supplied by the EVMS status data can provide for both the detection of risk events and an assessment of the effectiveness of the disposition methods. The data can be analyzed to determine the cause of variances and suggest improvements for risk handling.

There are two additional important points in risk monitoring and for risk management in general. The first is that all monitoring activity and results should be documented. A requirement for formal documentation will encourage a more comprehensive effort and provide a history for future risk management activities. The documentation is most important because it records the circumstances of risk events and provides substantiation for risk decisions. The second point is that risk monitoring and the entire risk management process must be continuous.

Continuous Risk Management

Although no longer used, a former DoD website illustrated the concepts of risk management. The site had an animated logo with the four words "Plan, Assess, Handle, and Monitor" emphasized around the center of a circle containing the word "Document." That DoD logo seemed to encapsulate the fact that risk management must be continuous. We have attempted to model that theme of continuous risk management in Figure 11.4.

The Software Engineering Institute of Carnegie Mellon University published the *Continuous Risk Management Guidebook*

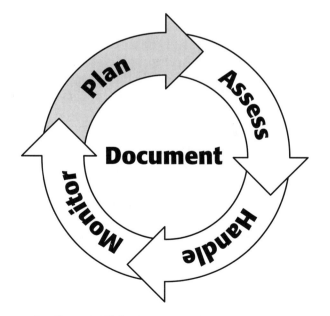

FIGURE 11.4   Continuous Risk Management

(Murphy et al. 1996). In the information on risk management the guide adds such primary words as "control, track, identify, and communicate." It all comes down to constantly being aware of and planning for the inherent risks in project management.

Risk Management Tools

There are both government and commercial tools available that can assist in risk management activities. We'll mention a few, but even a cursory search will find several.

- *@RISK for Project*© is a tool we have used frequently for modeling project schedules. It is a risk analysis and simulation add-in for Microsoft Project.® There is also a module for Microsoft Excel® that is useful in analyzing probability/impact matrices. @RISK is a product of the Palisade Corporation (http://www.palisade.com/).
- The *Program Evaluation and Review Technique* (PERT) (described in Chapter 7 as a project network representation) was originally developed as a risk management tool. It uses a probabilistic model based on three time estimates of "optimistic, most likely, and pessimistic" to plan and control a project. This technique generally has been eclipsed by newer methods, but is still favored by some. (Most project software will generate a PERT chart automatically, but the minimum and maximum times may need to be added.)
- *Critical Chain* (also described in Chapter 7) is a project management system with one of its features being an attempt to reduce the risk of project overruns. To control task completion risk, Critical Chain removes individual protection time built into task estimates—where it is often wasted—and strategically relocates it to protect critical points (project completion and feeding path mergers) in the overall project schedule.
- The Defense Acquisition University features a risk management website, http://acc.dau.mil/simplify/ev.php?ID=1203_201&ID2=DO_COMMUNITY, with links to various systems and tools.

- You can find a full list of guidebooks at: http://akss.dau.mil/ guidebookalphabeticLinks.do. The risk guidebook references such tools as *Risk Management Guide for DOD Acquisition* (5th ed.). Its second chapter, "Risk and Risk Management," is completely general and applies to all companies.
- The Mitre Corporation developed a Risk Matrix that helps to identify, prioritize, and manage key risks, but it is only available to employees of the federal government and contractors under a current government contract. If you have or expect to have a government contract, check with Mitre.
- The U.S. Army Communications Electronics Command (CE-COM) Software Engineering Center (SEC) developed the Software Insight Tool for Risk Mitigation. It has an Assessment Questionnaire with detailed questions to identify software acquisition program risks (http://www.sed.monmouth.army.mil/sit/).
- Carnegie Mellon University, Software Engineering Institute, has developed acquisition risk management practices, processes, methods, and tools (http://www.sei.cmu.edu/programs/sepm/risk/).

Risk management tools may assist in addressing and controlling risk, but they do not lighten the burden of responsibility. Nor do these activities eliminate the need for change and a formal change control process.

WHEN CHANGE BECOMES NECESSARY

We have encountered very few projects that did not require some changes to the budget, schedule, and/or objectives. Whenever changes are authorized, they should be made within a control account and first attempted within the constraints of the original control account budget and schedule. If the changes cannot be done within the original budget, then management reserve may be used. When work must be transferred between control accounts (other functional units), the transfer must be carefully controlled and documented, making sure that the budget amount also is transferred along with the scheduled work.

Project changes must not be done for work already completed and can be performed only for future work. Because of the pressure to circumvent change procedures, even changes for effort scheduled in the near future should be discouraged. Government agencies encourage *replanning activity* that is designed to reduce costs, improve efficiency of operations, or otherwise enhance the completion of the project. Appropriate replanning can be the consequence of several factors:

- A review of project specifications that modifies the objectives
- A major change in resource availability that will affect the schedule
- Budgetary restrictions that necessitate a change in resources or deliverables
- Significant changes in the rates that were utilized to calculate the original cost.

Replanning should never be done just to eliminate variances or to change a cost or schedule index. Generally, replanning is permitted to internally revise the project plan as long as it is within the original baseline. Inappropriate replanning will terminate the project's status as an EVMS-compliant system. Even when change appears to be valid, if it is excessive, it indicates a lack of sufficient initial planning and can cause the entire system to be suspect.

EVMS CRITERION 28

Incorporate authorized changes in a timely manner, recording the effects of such changes in budgets and schedules. In the directed effort prior to negotiation of a change, base such revisions on the amount estimated and budgeted to the program organizations.

EVMS Criterion 8 required the establishment of a time-phased budget baseline, which we described in Chapter 7 as the *performance measurement baseline* (PMB). Criterion 9, discussed in Chapter 8, required the establishment of budgets for all the authorized work of the project.

Both the PMB and the authorized budget are critical for valid EVMS metrics. When changes are authorized, they must be incorporated into the PMB and the project budget as soon as possible in order to maintain legitimate EVMS measurements and reporting. Other documents, such as work authorization forms, also may be affected.

If feasible, the change should be detailed at the work package level, but at the very least within a control account in order to maintain reporting integrity. Changes that encompass more than one control account should be documented by writing multiple change requests.

Authorized Changes

Any interested party should be allowed to initiate a change request, but changes must be authorized. An item in the project charter should cite the organization's change control system and specify how changes may be requested and on whose authority changes may be made. The documentation should also have specific limitations for the scope of any change authorization. The limitations can be set at different levels for different levels of authority and can be expressed in both dollars for budget changes and time for schedule changes. Change authority usually is not vested in any one person, but is the franchise of a small group of people in the organization.

Change Control Board

With one exception, every organization with which we have worked had a formal change control process and a Change Control Board or change review committee. The committees were a functional mix of organizational personnel who were primarily from the upper management level.

In one large organization, different committees reviewed potential project changes within their own structural elements. The committees were charged to review and either approve or reject requests for project changes. In most cases the change control system allowed emergency changes and other minor plan modifications without committee review. When such changes were made, the committee still reviewed and endorsed the change or recommended additional activity and/or documentation.

The duties and responsibilities for reviewing, approving, and documenting change requests vary a great deal, but Figure 11.5 illustrates the activities and decision results of a typical Change Control Board or committee.

The committee is charged with an immediate inspection of all change requests to check for emergency needs or minor modifications that will not require changes to the project budget or baseline. The committee prepares the initiating documentation and if the change is an emergency or involves only minor modification, it sends the change request directly to the project team for implementation. Otherwise the committee requests a change implementation plan from the project team. The committee then reviews the plan with other stakeholders for feasibility and acceptance.

If the plan is not acceptable, the committee notifies affected stakeholders and documents and logs the change request denial. A new change request with some modifications can always be resubmitted for consideration. If the plan is acceptable, the project team will implement the plan and modify the project plan accordingly. When the changes are complete, the team notifies the committee, which can notify stakeholders and document and log the change request results.

Documentation of Change

We cannot overemphasize the need to have standard forms for change requests and to authorize budget and schedule changes. The documentation can include change request forms, budget revision records, change authorization records, change control documents, and logs to maintain traceability of all change documentation.

A log of every change request form (CRF) should be maintained in order to schedule and monitor the change requests. While we

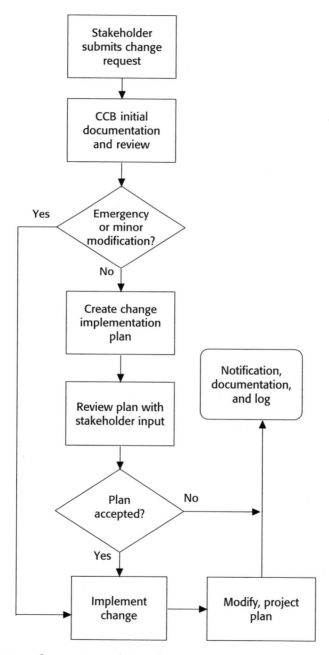

FIGURE 11.5 Change Control Board

have seen many formats for a CRF, and its design will depend on the environment of each organization, the form should have at least the following elements:

- CRF number or identification and date
- Project identification
- Identification of the affected WBS element and control account (number and title)
- Description of the change and a revised control account plan
- Reason for the change request
- Requested cost and schedule changes and their impact
- Signatures of the requestors with dates
  - —At a minimum, the signatures should include those of the control account manager, a functional or business unit manager, and the project manager
  - —Signatures also may be requested from one or more of the following: an accounting department manager, a scheduling department manager, and a Project Management Office manager
- List of documents to be changed and the impact
- Supporting documents as attachments to the request form
- Rejection or approval, with authorized signature and date.

After a CRF has been approved, several other documents must be generated, modified, and tracked. Budgets must be revised, work authorization forms modified or generated, notifications sent to all parties involved, and logs updated.

Directed Effort

Sometimes, project changes will be directed by the customer (or other stakeholder) before the impact to cost, schedule, or requirements can be fully determined. These directed changes are usually emergency reactions to cost pressures, but will certainly impact the schedule and other planning and reporting elements. The final effect of such changes must be negotiated with the customer, but estimates of the change impact should be used until replanning can be completed. The intent is to always maintain an accurate and legitimate PMB.

EVMS CRITERION 29

Reconcile current budgets to prior budgets in terms of changes to the authorized work and internal replanning in the detail needed by management for effective control.

Because of imperfect views of the future or changing conditions, making project plan adjustments is a normal process. One of the most important EVMS requirements for change is that the overall project objectives be supported in a way that the performance metrics are not compromised. The documentation must be detailed enough to track the current project values back to the original plans. A formal change control process is necessary to ensure proper control of replanning and to enable accurate reconciliation.

The original budget is the target against which project progress is measured and this base can be modified only by authorized changes. When changes have been detailed, negotiated with project sponsors, and authorized, the target is adjusted by the authorized amount. For detailed changes that have been authorized, but for which a final cost has not yet been fully negotiated, the target may be adjusted by a reasonable estimate. Special care must be exercised for adjustments when a "not-to-exceed" amount has been contracted for the project. Adequate documentation must be maintained so that reconciliation is both possible and valid.

EVMS CRITERION 30

Control retroactive changes to records pertaining to work performed that would change previously reported amounts for actual costs, earned value, or budgets. Adjustments shall be made only for correction of errors, routine accounting adjustments, effects of customer or management directed changes, or to improve the baseline integrity and accuracy of performance measurement data.

Earlier we warned that changes should not be made to work that has been completed, but there are a very few cases where retroactive changes can be made. An organization must be able to correct errors and make routine accounting adjustments. Accounting adjustments are often made when performance estimates had to be used before actual data were available. Corrections can and should be made if incorrect data are hampering management decisions, but constant change is an indication of an improperly planned or managed project. This is doubly true when changes are made to previously published historical data.

EVMS CRITERION 31

Prevent revisions to the program budget except for authorized changes.

Some rescheduling in future or current work packages is expected and acceptable, but the organization must have a change control procedure that limits changes to be made to the original budget baseline. The accounting department should record any changes in the project budget log. A budget base change should not be made without an accompanying contract modification, project charter revision, or authorization of the change control committee. Any baseline change, especially a budget change, should be limited to certain ranges as established in the change control process.

EVMS CRITERION 32

Document changes to the performance measurement baseline.

When we defined PMB in Chapter 7, we likened it to a baseline in a sporting event where it is used to measure progress. If the baseline kept moving, we would never be able to tell who was "in bounds" or who was winning or losing. The same is true of the project PMB. The validity of the performance measurement baseline must be maintained or EVMS metrics become meaningless. The PMB is a reflection of management's current plan to achieve project objectives. All changes must be documented and the links for all changes must be derivable.

The Department of Defense (Department of Defense, FAA, and NASA 1997, par. 3-7.g) requires internal procedures to "clearly delineate acceptable and unacceptable practices." DoD has established discussion points to maintain change traceability and the validity of the performance measurement baseline. They include:

- Budgets are assigned to specific segments of work.
- Work responsibility should not be transferred without transferring the associated budget.
- A budget assigned to a future specific task should not be used to perform another task.
- When management reserve is used, records should clearly indicate when and where it is applied.
- When undistributed budgets exist, records should clearly identify their amount, purpose, and to which efforts budgets are issued.
- Budgets that are assigned to work packages should not be changed once effort is started unless the scope of work is affected by contractual change or project internal adjustments that enhance management of the effort.
- Retroactive changes to budgets or costs for completed work or to schedules are not made except for correction of errors, normal accounting adjustments, revisions to reflect the formal negotiated value of completed tasks, and revisions to improve the integrity and accuracy of the baseline.

We all know Murphy's Law will strike—we're just never quite sure where, when, and how. Nevertheless, it is imperative to have risk management plans in place and risk planning should be an effort throughout the entire organization. Projects often involve opportunities as well as threats and a process similar to that of risk analysis should be designed to position the organization to take advantage of opportunities that become feasible and desirable.

No project plan can be considered complete and reliable unless it at least has a risk management component. The first task must be to ensure that risk is understood. Risk events must be defined in terms of their probability of occurrence and the severity of their impact. In consideration of these two characteristics, the intensity level of each risk, and an appropriate reaction, can be determined in line with the risk tolerance of the organization.

The method for handling a risk when it occurs can be formulated from one of four general risk disposition categories: avoidance, transference, mitigation, or acceptance. EVMS is a very effective risk management instrument, particularly for risk monitoring. Risk monitoring should be a continuous activity in order to warn of impending risk events and to improve the risk disposition methods.

Not meeting the completion date is one of the most reccurring project risks and we can recommend the Critical Chain process as an effective solution. The total risk management process must be continuous and there are many available tools to help.

Changes become necessary because of many factors; however, replanning should be done cautiously. Changes should first be attempted within the original parameters and never done just to eliminate plan variances. When changes are authorized, they must be incorporated in a timely manner and their effects recorded in the project plan. The use of a Change Control Board or a Change Review Committee is a good way to authorize changes and enforce change controls.

All changes must be reconciled from the original plan to the revised plan and any retroactive changes must be tightly controlled. In fact, all changes must be controlled to prevent unauthorized changes and to ensure appropriate documentation. DoD requires internal procedures to establish acceptable practices and established discussion points for use in maintaining the validity of the PMB.

DISCUSSION QUESTIONS

1. Describe the three major activities of risk management.

2. Discuss the following statement: "Since project problems are only potential events, it is much more profitable to spend time on man-

aging the project for success and not worry about risk management."

3. What are the parts of a complete risk description?

4. Describe some risk identification techniques and identify the most likely effective method for your organization.

5. What kind of risk rating system is in use or what kind would you like to see in use for your organization?

6. Describe the four general categories for risk disposition.

7. Why is EVMS useful in risk monitoring?

8. When is replanning appropriate and when is it not?

9. What kind of documentation would you recommend for project changes?

10. What retroactive changes can be made to project records?

CHAPTER 12

Are We There Yet?

Whew! Now that the project is complete and everyone is totally exhausted, one important final task remains: formally closing the project. No EVMS criteria require a closing process—instead, the impetus is common sense and the desire to continuously improve.

This final chapter deals with project termination. It is often said that all things must end, but that saying doesn't seem to apply to all projects. Some old projects that should have been terminated long ago are still hanging around on the books of many organizations. On some projects, work slows down to an eventual crawl, but never quite ends completely. Unless the organization is intentional, they may never disappear.

Evaluation of the many reasons for terminating a project, and when to do so, is beyond the scope of this book. Instead, we will focus on covering the important steps required to close a project properly. Without carefully monitoring the project plan and properly closing the project, the organization may suffer several adverse effects and lose an important improvement opportunity.

Recently we worked with an organization that had many inactive projects that were still on the books years after their inauguration. Many staff members were reluctant to start work on yet another project that might also just run off into the sands of time. Other staff members were grateful that they were never accountable for the project deliverables. In other cases, we have seen old projects carry over into new projects without the original project ever "finishing." In all of these circumstances, the consequences are the same: low morale, no acknowledgment of effort, and the loss of many valuable lessons.

PROJECT TERMINATION

One of the primary calculations in EVMS is the *estimate at completion* (or the estimate to complete). This periodic measurement is helpful in focusing attention on project completion and ensuring that the project is "finished"—either completed and delivered or prematurely terminated for cause. Without appropriate controls, a project may drift into unintended (and unnoticed) overspending or the unused funds from an incompletely closed project may be misapplied to other projects. It is not unusual for us to find charges to a project continuing long after it has ended.

Some government units dictate the full and appropriate termination of projects. The Department of Energy (DOE), for example, published a statement that "project management personnel shall demonstrate the ability to manage the close-out phase of a project and to bring the project to an orderly close" (1995, Paragraph 4.20). This requirement applies to specific DOE personnel, but the statement emphasizes the importance of the project closing. Figure 12.1 illustrates the main closing activities and their relationships.

We like to divide the project closing into two primary functions: (1) ensuring that the project is complete and is ready to be accepted by the owner or customer, and (2) conducting some post-project activities.

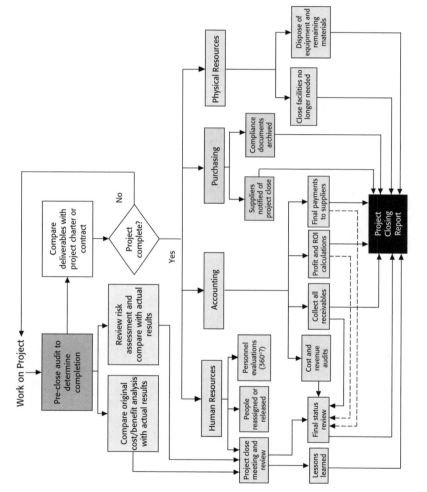

FIGURE 12.1 Project Closeout

Completing the Project

We emphasize that the project closing is a major phase of a project's life cycle and consists of all the activities and events that must occur before the project is considered complete. Figure 12.2 illustrates the project's cycle (discussed in Chapter 2, in which the importance of the project closeout is recognized). The arrows from "Closeout" to "Execution" and back indicate the recycling activity frequently required between the major phases of a project.

Closing tasks begin with a pre-close audit to determine the completion of project deliverables and to review actual performance compared to the estimates generated to justify the project. If the project is not complete, additional work must be done. If the project is complete, various resources must accomplish a whole series of actions, culminating in a project closing report, which includes a history of the project.

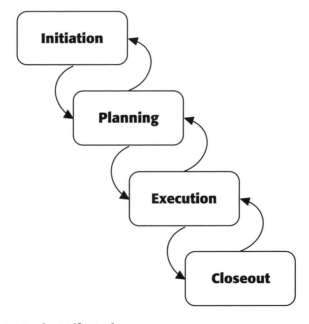

FIGURE 12.2   Project Life Cycle

Project Review

A project should not be considered complete until a physical, financial, and functional audit is performed that compares the expectations of the project charter or contract to the actual project deliverables. As well as ensuring that the project delivered on its expected objectives, this audit should examine the original cost/benefit analysis and the original risk assessment against the actual project results. The results of the final assessment (sometimes referred to as the postmortem autopsy) should be documented in the project closing report.

While the project team is still intact, all members should be involved in the final project review. A group discussion will elicit the most information with contributions by some team members stimulating thought among others. We highly recommend a period for individual reflection prior to the meeting. A questionnaire distributed before the review discussion should generate some helpful participation. We have used several versions of project review questionnaires, but one we found especially interesting from Chris Everett Project Management (info@cepm.co.uk) is included as Appendix 12-A.

The object of the review is twofold: (1) to gather data for a complete and accurate final status report, and (2) to document the lessons learned (good and bad) in this project in order to improve future projects. There are many topics to examine during the project review. Some items are required, such as the financial data, but the team group discussion can generate several more. We suggest that meeting agenda items include the following to be sure that all aspects of the project are addressed:

- How well the project objective was met
- Resource availability and utilization
- Means and effectiveness of communications
- Usefulness of project meetings
- Work that went well and why
- Work that didn't go well and why
- Any disasters, what caused them, and how they might have been avoided (or how they can be avoided in the future).

Reporting

The project closing report signifies the formal end of the project and is the final status report. The report should be sent to the project sponsor, all other project stakeholders, and especially the accounting department. The accounting department will have been involved in generating the final metrics and closing the control accounts, but there should be a formal notification to terminate any further entries for this project.

The report should document what worked well and what processes could be improved. It needs to specify the level of success in meeting the project goals and relate the impact of management activities, variances, and changes during project execution. It should also identify the items that will be a part of the operation and maintenance of the project's deliverables. The end users should have details of their responsibilities after their acceptance of the deliverables. The report should be in the same format and follow the same processes as all the preceding project reports.

Many organizations, including several state agencies, require a *Post Implementation Evaluation Report* (PIER) at the conclusion of a project. The PIER usually provides a picture of the project management results. It will cover such issues as staffing, scheduling, and the management of cost, risk, quality, communications, and user expectations. The report will often have sections for lessons learned and all the project sign-offs; if a formal PIER is not required, we recommend separate activities and reports to complete these latter elements.

Also in separate reporting, performance evaluations should be completed for all project team members. Sometimes we have seen evaluations performed by each team member for each of the other members, including the project manager. This "360-degree" approach provides a wealth of feedback that can be used to improve future performance. Most often, however, the project manager prepares evaluations for each team member. Especially in functionally structured organizations, copies of evaluations usually are sent to the member's direct supervisor.

Project Deliverables

Another task for project closeout is to ensure that all contracts and subcontractor contracts have been completed and acceptance signatures obtained. There may be some claims or outstanding issues that will need to be settled before the final report is prepared. The accounting department also will be involved as final postings are made, accounts are reconciled, and all control accounts are closed. The final status report should disclose the degree of variance from the planned schedule, budget, and technical scope, along with a brief description of causes.

Several project objective concerns should be addressed before the project is considered complete. First, the project deliverable must be transitioned to complete and successful use by the end user, and second, there should be evidence that the user can depend on and maintain usage of the deliverable. Sometimes, especially for government contracts, signoffs and clearances must be executed to ensure that all the project's terms and conditions have been met before the end user issues a formal acceptance of the project deliverable. Even without contractual obligation to do so, these final steps build significant good will for future endeavors and are good policies to have in place.

Lessons Learned

Documenting lessons learned in the management of a project is one of the most important contributions that can be made to the success of future projects. Some of the best practices that might be identified in the lessons learned document are:

- Effective communication with project stakeholders
- Ways to obtain support for the project
- Team building and consensus building techniques
- Improved cost and schedule processes
- Effective ways to identify and obtain resources
- Determining an appropriate balance between the need for detailed plans and the cost of producing the detail
- Effective scope and change management systems

- Vendor management techniques
- Ways of disseminating project knowledge.

A lessons-learned review with all project stakeholders present is the best way to get a complete picture of the project's successes and problems. Attendees at a review meeting should include the project team, executive management, external audit or oversight personnel, end users, and operations staff. This lessons-learned meeting is sometimes combined with a closing or celebratory event (described in the next section, Post Project Activities).

On large projects, if too many people are involved for an effective meeting, the meeting can be held with a representative from each major group. If for some reason a meeting is deemed not appropriate, the review can still be conducted through the use of surveys. In any case, there must be a broad and inclusive view from all perspectives in order to provide the most value for future projects.

Post Project Activities

Once the project is considered having met its goals, a few more tasks should be performed for the project to contribute to meeting future needs. These activities include acknowledging the efforts of the project staff, releasing project resources, and archiving project documents.

Holding a Closing Event

A celebration of the project's completion can be an excellent way to notify everyone of the official close of the project and recognize the team members. Many team members will be going back to functional assignments or starting new endeavors. Positive reinforcement is an effective management tool and the closing event presents an opportunity to carry a positive attitude into new engagements. Many organizations host a celebratory dinner or party; however, even recognition for the team at a regular meeting provides some incentive and reinforcement for team members.

Even if the project was not considered a success, there must be some recognition of its completion. We heard of one group that held a "wake" for its project. It's true that most of us do not want to reward failure, but we should take the time to recognize effort and learn what we can from the experience. Thomas Edison is well known for the invention of a commercially successful light bulb, but few know about the thousands of failed attempts, his many other unsuccessful ventures, or his fervent denial that his unsuccessful endeavors were failures. The most important thing is to take away lessons learned from this project that will help us with our next project.

There are several ways to reward team members for a job well done. Money always works! Although financial compensation is important, recognition can be equally effective—sometimes even surpassing monetary reward. If executive management shows its appreciation, it not only rewards the project participants but also reinforces the organization's emphasis on effective project management. Recognition is most effective when it is shown at a key organizational meeting or any large gathering. (When you have a celebratory party, be sure to invite the accounting department.)

Releasing Resources

The redeployment of project resources may begin even before the project is complete. As the project winds down, fewer staff and less space and equipment may be required. It is important that the project manager release unneeded resources as soon as possible without adversely affecting the project schedule and technical requirements. Project team members can be assigned to other projects or continue their functional assignments. At the end of a project, one of the final steps is to make sure that remaining resources are put to other use or appropriately discarded.

For government projects, these final activities may include the de-commitment of unused funds and the proper disposal of government-furnished property. Government contracting officers may also need assistance in checking the conditions of the contract, settling any unresolved issues, and completing the contract documentation.

Archiving Project Documents

All projects, especially EVMS projects, accumulate a flood of reports, documentation, and correspondence. All the essential records of a project need to be securely stored in a manner that will allow reasonable access when information is required. There may be inquiries concerning the project decisions or business audits that will necessitate the retrieval of project records. Part of the initial project plan should detail the organization, storage, retention schedule, and retrieval strategy for project documents.

The amount and type of archival records will vary from project to project depending on size and complexity. The accounting department will archive the detailed accounting records, but a usual list of other documents would include:

- RFPs, proposals, and procurement documents
- Project plans (work breakdown structure, organization breakdown structure, performance measurement baseline, etc.)
- Contracts and invoices
- Technical documents specifying design and test details
- Change request and change order documents
- Critical correspondence
- Minutes of project meetings
- Copies of reports and logs
- Lessons-learned document
- Audit results.

Most organizations have a record retention center and record retention guidelines. The project archive should include a list (with brief descriptions) of the documents that are held in the archive and contact information if further inquiry is needed. The project records can be invaluable as a training tool for project managers and in planning new projects. While retaining some document hard copies may be desirable, most information is more easily accessed in a computer database.

Because the last days and weeks of most projects are chaotic and hectic, it is tempting to do a quick wrap-up and move on to the next challenge. A formal closing process led by the project manager will avoid the loss of extremely valuable information that can greatly enhance future performance of the project team and the organization. Formal notification to all interested parties of project closing also can prevent future unauthorized charges to projects.

A pre-closing audit to determine project completion and to review and compare project results with those planned can improve planning processes. If the project is complete, four areas—accounting, purchasing, human resources, and physical resources—are involved in closing out the work and archiving records.

Accounting must wind up its project work by auditing all accounting, collecting receivables, paying suppliers, and computing profit and return on investment. All or major portions of this work are shared with the project team so they can analyze project performance.

One of the most critical areas of closing concerns human resources. People who have worked on the project have the best intuition for analyzing their performance. If they have access to financial information, they are in a position to evaluate the entire project and document lessons learned for the organization as well as for themselves. Feedback is essential for team members' personal growth; appreciation of their efforts provides motivation for future productivity.

Duties for the purchasing department include notifying suppliers of the project's close so they will not expect future orders. Purchasing also has the responsibility of archiving any required compliance documents.

Finally, physical resources must be detached from the project. Facilities no longer needed must be closed or returned. Also, any equipment and remaining materials must be disposed of properly. All information pertaining to the project is accumulated in the project's closing report. This report then is distributed to all interested parties to formally notify them of the project's close.

In effect, closing a project provides an excellent opportunity for a project health check that addresses the level of project control, compliance with contractual obligations or company policies, and validation of the original business case. It also enables examination of team interactions, including communication success. Risk issues shrouded in uncertainty at the beginning of the project now can be compared with actual results.

All this ensures that mistakes will not be repeated and that even unsuccessful efforts can contribute to future success.

DISCUSSION QUESTIONS

1. Discuss the best example of how you have closed a project in the past. Was this project labeled as a "success" or a "failure"? Did the close change this perception?

2. Closing a project appears to be a project in itself. Discuss the characteristics of this closing project and how it is different from other projects.

3. Describe some common effects of not properly closing a project.

4. Would use of a closing process template be beneficial for all projects? Why or why not?

Appendix 12-A. Project Review Questionnaire

Project Review Questionnaire

Project:

Name:

Date:

Dept/Section(s) Represented:

Position Held: Team Member/Team Leader/Project Leader/ Product Manager/Project Manager

The objectives of the project review are:

- To learn from our experiences
- To repeat successes in future
- To handle less successful aspects differently in future
- To provide data which others may benefit from
- To identify various aspects of the methodology which we may wish to change in the future

Please complete the questionnaire and return it to your Project Manager. If a question is not appropriate to your role in the project, simply mark N/A.

There is a section at the end to add any new questions which you think are appropriate to your project and which should be considered for future amendments to the questionnaire.

1. How could the product and project objectives have been better defined?
2. What areas were not well defined?

Source: Courtesy of Chris Everett Project Management at http://www. spottydog.u-net.com/guides/close/frameset.html. Reprinted with permission.

3. Were the roles of the Project Manager/Project Leaders/ Product Managers/Team Leaders understood?
4. What would you have liked the following to have spent more time on

Project Manager:

Project Leader:

Product Manager:

5. What changes would you recommend to the project organization structure and why?
6. What (if any) were the major omissions or inaccuracies in your part of the Product Definition (PD)?
7. What would you have liked to have seen in the PD which would have been beneficial to your responsibilities?
8. How could the process for pulling the PD together have been improved?
9. Was the method of planning adequate? How well was the plan monitored, maintained, and communicated?
10. Do you have any suggestions for improving the planning process? Consider: Construction of the plan, communication, monitoring, maintenance.
11. What were the factors which caused deviations from the plan? How could the original plan have been improved?
12. How did the cost of the project (in your area) compare with what was planned? What were the costs which hadn't been anticipated?
13. How good were the communications during the course of the project? Which areas worked well? Which area could have been improved upon? Consider: Department, Project Team, Other.
14. How useful were the meetings? What would you have liked them to have spent more/less time on?

Department Team Meetings:

Project Team Meetings:

Steering Team Meetings:

Informal Meetings:

15. How useful were the minutes you received? How do you feel they could have been improved? (If several, i.e., Progress, Steering, please state which).
16. How well did the decision making process work? How could it have been improved?
17. What did you enjoy most on the project?
18. What did you find the most frustrating?
19. What did you perceive to be the most successful on the project?
20. What did you perceive to be the least successful on the project?
21. What are the things that we intended to do but didn't achieve?
22. What changes would you recommend to the product development methodology, and why?
23. What are the specific recommendations that you would like to make for future (similar) projects?
24. With the benefit of hindsight, what would you have done differently?
25. What could have been done to reduce the time to first shipments?
26. What are the key areas which you think would benefit from reviewing further? (List up to 5 and indicate who you think should attend the review).

Your suggested questions/answers here

Epilogue

EVMS is a great tool for measuring and reporting the status of a project. Adhering to its 32 criteria may fit the letter of the law, but that alone will not guarantee a successful project. The project manager must have good management tools and skills and then use them to integrate and implement these criteria. That is the primary reason we have touched on so many basic project management elements.

Our basic intent has been to lead you through a project manager's view of EVMS, providing the detail you need to appreciate and support the system. We cordially invite you to contact us if you have questions or suggestions for improvement of the material.

Glossary of Key Terms

The following represents our definitions of key terms; the military acquisition website at http://www.acq.osd.mil/pm/faqs/glossary.htm is another good source. Similar definitions can be found at an Australian website, http://www.defence.gov.au/dmo/esd/evm/DefAust5655.pdf. A very extensive list of project management terms appears in the "Wideman Comparative Glossary of Project Management Terms" at http://www.pmforum.org/library/glossary/index.htm.

Acquisition Program—A directed, funded government effort that provides a new, improved, or continuing material, weapon, or information system or service capability in response to an approved need.

Activity—A self-contained effort or task that occurs over a period of time and consumes resources.

Activity-Based Costing (ABC)—An accounting technique that computes the cost of resource consumption for each product in order to determine its profitability.

Actual Cost—An incurred cost as distinguished from a forecasted, estimated, or budgeted cost.

Actual Cost of Work Performed (ACWP)—Actual Value. The costs actually incurred and recorded in accomplishing the work performed within a project status time period.

Actual Value—See Actual Cost of Work Performed.

Administrative Contracting Officer (ACO)—The individual in the government Contract Administration Office responsible for ensuring that the functions described in DFARS 242.302 are completed by the contractor in accordance with the terms and conditions of the contract.

Advance Agreement (AA)—An agreement between the contractor and the Contract Administration Office concerning the application of an approved integrated management system for a contracted project.

Algorithmic Method—Creating an estimate by the use of mathematical formulas. The formulas may be derived from research and/or historical data and use known cost driver attributes. Parametric cost estimating is considered an algorithmic method.

Allocated Budget—Also referred to as Total Allocated Budget.

Analogy Method—Creating a cost estimate by deriving cost factors from a similar project that has been completed and for which the cost and schedule are known.

Applied Direct Costs (ADC)—The actual direct costs incurred during the status time period without regard to the date of commitment or payment. These costs are associated with the consumption of labor, material, and other direct resources, and are to be charged to work in process when any of the following takes place:

- Labor, material, or other direct resources are actually consumed.
- Material resources are withdrawn from inventory for use.
- Material resources are received that are uniquely identified to the contract and scheduled for use within 60 days.

- Major components or assemblies are specifically and uniquely identified to a single serially numbered end item that are received on a line flow basis.

Apportioned Effort—Effort that is not readily divisible into work packages, but is proportionately related to another discrete effort that is measured.

Arrow Diagramming Method—A project network design to depict task sequence or precedence relationships of project activities. The design uses nodes (events) connected by lines with arrows to show the flow of activity. The activities may be shown on the node (AON) or on the arrow (AOA).

Audit—The systematic examination of records and documents to determine the adequacy and effectiveness of budgeting, accounting, financial, and related policies and procedures. The audit determines compliance with applicable statutes, regulations, and prescribed policies and procedures, and determines the reliability, accuracy, and completeness of records and reports.

Audit Trail—Information allowing record and report data to be tracked back to the original source for verification.

Authorization to Proceed (ATP)—Official authority, usually from the Procuring Activity, for the contractor to begin work.

Authorized Work—All effort performed by the contractor, conforming with the contract and within the contract price.

Authorized Unpriced Work (AUW)—Includes work that is outside the scope of the contract but that is planned and/or performed by the contractor in advance of a formal contract amendment.

Bar Chart—A presentation of data using horizontal or vertical bars to represent values of the data. For projects, the horizontal bars on a time scale represent project tasks, their duration, and sometimes their relationships.

Baseline—See Performance Measurement Baseline (PMB). Also sometimes used as an abbreviated reference to an Integrated Baseline Review (IBR).

Basis of Estimate—Documentation describing the primary methods, ground rules, models, assumptions, and data sources used to estimate the project cost.

Benefit Cost Ratio—The ratio of a project's total return to its total cost.

Bill of Material (BOM)—A listing of material items required to complete the production of a single unit.

Bottom-Up Method—A method of cost estimating characterized by a thorough, detailed analysis of all tasks, components, and assemblies and rolling the results up to summarize an estimate of the entire project. This method may be referred to as "detailed" or "grass-roots" estimating.

Budget at Completion (BAC)—The total of all budgets for the contract. See also Performance Measurement Baseline and Total Allocated Budget.

Budgeted Cost of Work Performed (BCWP)—Earned Value. The sum of the budget amounts (not actual amounts) for completed work packages and completed portions of open work packages, plus the applicable portion of the budgets for level of effort and apportioned effort.

Budgeted Cost of Work Scheduled (BCWS)—Planned Value. The sum of the budgets for all work packages (or portions thereof), planning packages, etc., scheduled to be accomplished, plus the amount of level of effort and apportioned effort scheduled to be accomplished within a given time period.

Calibration—A process of adjusting a commercial parametric model by a specific organization to its own cost experience and business culture.

Contingency Costs—An amount to be included in a project budget that represents costs that may result from incomplete design, unforeseen and unpredictable conditions, or uncertainties within the defined project scope.

Contract Administration Office (CAO)—The organization assigned responsibility for ensuring that the contractor complies with the terms and conditions of the contract.

Contract Budget Base (CBB)—The negotiated contract cost plus the estimated cost of authorized unpriced work. The CBB is equal to the Total Allocated Budget unless an Over Target Baseline has been implemented.

Contract Data Requirements List (CDRL)—A list of all data elements that the contractor is obligated to submit to the government. Each task on a Statement of Work (SOW) is associated with a CDRL. The CDRL identifies a document or other data along with specific information about that document (e.g., schedule, number and frequency of revisions, distribution). A Data Item Description specifies the content and format of the document.

Contract Target Cost—The total of all cost accounts plus undistributed budget and management reserve.

Contract Work Breakdown Structure (CWBS)—The complete hierarchal graph of the activities or intermediate deliverables necessary to complete a contract (including the DoD-approved work breakdown structure for reporting purposes and its discretionary extension to the lower levels by the contractor). The CWBS includes all the elements for the hardware, software, data, or services that are the responsibility of the contractor.

Control Account (Cost Account)—A management control point at which actual costs can be accumulated and compared to earned value. A cost account is usually defined as the intersection of the program's work breakdown structure (WBS) and organization breakdown structure (OBS). In effect, each cost account defines what work is to be performed and who will perform it.

Control Account Manager (CAM)—A member of a functional organization responsible for cost account performance and the management of resources to accomplish the control account effort.

Correlation—A statistical technique used to determine the degree to which variables are related or associated. Correlation does not prove or disapprove a cause and effect relationship.

Cost Analysis—The accumulation and analysis of actual costs, statistical data, and other information on current and completed contracts or programs. Cost analysis also includes comparisons and analyses of these data, as well as cost extrapolations of data for future projections of cost. In Department of Defense procurement organizations, cost analysis is the review and evaluation of a contractor's cost or pricing data and the judgmental factors applied in projecting from the data to the estimated costs. Cost analysis is performed to establish an opinion on the degree to which the contractor's proposed costs represent what the performance of the contract should cost, assuming reasonable economy and efficiency.

Cost Drivers—The characteristics of a system or item having a major effect on the system's or item's cost.

Cost Estimating Relationship (CER)—A mathematical expression of varying degrees of complexity that expresses cost as a function of one or more cost driving variables. See Parametric Cost Estimating.

Cost Performance Index (CPI) —The cost efficiency factor representing the relationship between the actual costs expended and the value of the physical work performed. The CPI is calculated as BCWP/ACWP or Earned Value divided by Actual Value.

Cost Performance Report (CPR)—A project report required in some government contracts, prepared by the contractor and containing information derived from the internal management system to provide a status of progress on the contract.

Cost or Pricing Data—All facts that, as of the date of the price agreement, prudent buyers and sellers would reasonably expect to affect price negotiations significantly. Cost or pricing data require certification in accordance with Federal Acquisition Regulation (FAR) 15.406-2. Cost or pricing data are factual, not judgmental, and verifiable. Cost or pricing data are all facts that can be reasonably expected to contribute to the soundness of estimates of future costs and to the validity of determinations of costs already incurred.

Cost/Schedule Control Systems Criteria (C/SCSC)—In 1967, 35 defined standards were established for private contractor management control systems to ensure that government cost-reimbursable and incentive-type contracts were managed properly. These 35 criteria have been reduced to 32 and the standards are now known as the Earned Value Management System (EVMS).

Cost/Schedule Status Report (C/SSR)—A performance measurement report established to capture information on smaller government contracts when the Cost Performance Report is not required.

Cost Variance—A metric for cost performance on a contractor project:

$$\text{Cost Variance} = \text{Earned Value} - \text{Actual Value}$$
$$(\text{or CV} = \text{BCWP} - \text{ACWP}).$$

A positive value indicates a favorable position and a negative value indicates an unfavorable position.

Critical Chain—A project scheduling system that identifies the longest path of resource-dependent activities. It attempts to provide a realistic project network by addressing the adverse effects of human behavior and using a buffering technique to protect the estimated project completion date.

Critical Path—The longest path of interdependent activities through a project network. See Network Schedule.

Data Item Descriptions (DID)—A description of a document on a Contract Data Requirements List (CDRL) that specifies the document's content and format. Government agencies maintain standard sets of DIDs.

Defense Acquisition Executive (DAE)—The individual who has responsibility for supervising the Defense Acquisition System. The DAE takes precedence on all acquisition matters after the Secretary and the Deputy Secretary.

Defense Acquisition System—The management process by which the Department of Defense provides effective, affordable, and timely systems to the users

Defense Contract Audit Agency (DCAA)—The organization tasked with monitoring a contractor's design and implementation of an acceptable accounting system.

Defense Contract Management Agency (DCMA) (formerly Defense Contract Management Command)—An independent combat support agency within the Department of Defense (DoD) that serves as the department's contract manager, responsible for ensuring that federal acquisition programs, supplies, and services are delivered on time, within cost, and meet performance requirements. The DCMA usually participates in Government Contract Quality Assurance (GCQA).

Defense Federal Acquisition Regulation Supplement (DFARS)—Department of Defense (DoD) regulations governing DoD acquisitions. A supplement to the Federal Acquisition Regulation (FAR).

Delphi Technique—A technique for applying the informed judgment of a group of experts without direct confrontation and using feedback from multiple rounds of investigation for the solution of problems.

Deterministic Model—A model that predicts an inevitable consequence based on the sufficiency of antecedent events.

Direct Costs—Costs, such as labor and materials, that can be directly related to a specific item of work.

Discrete Effort—Tasks that have a specific measurable end product or end result. They are ideal for EVMS because their measurement is based on objective indicators of accomplishment, such as project milestones.

Earned Value—Budgeted Cost of Work Performed. The value of completed work in terms of the planned (not actual) cost of that work.

Earned Value Management System—A management system that integrates project scope, schedule, and cost and establishes a baseline plan for the accomplishment of the project deliverables. The system uses earned value to measure performance progress objectively.

Earned Value Management System Criteria—The set of 32 guidelines, established by DoD 5000.2R, that defines the parameters within which the contractor's integrated cost/schedule management system must fit.

Equivalent Units—The quantity of units produced during a single period by assuming that a particular flow of units (e.g., first-in first-out, average) and partially completed units may be netted together to find the number of equivalent full units. This equivalent number is similar to that of full-time equivalent (FTE) employees.

Estimate at Completion (EAC)—The value that, expressed in either dollars or hours, represents the projected final cost of the project (or task):

EAC = Actual Value (ACWP) + Estimate to Complete.

Estimate to Complete (ETC)—The value that, expressed in dollars or hours, represents the cost of the work required to complete the project (or task). One way to calculate ETC is to subtract the Earned Value (BCWP) from the Budget at Completion (BAC).

Executive Agent (EA)—"The Head of a DoD Component to whom the Secretary of Defense or the Deputy Secretary of Defense has assigned specific responsibilities, functions, and authorities to provide defined levels of support for operational missions, or administrative or other designated activities that involve two or more of the DoD Components." (Department of Defense 2003, 3.1)

Expert Judgment Methods—Uses the experience and understanding of experts to develop cost estimates for a project

Federal Acquisition Regulation (FAR)—Regulations governing all federal acquisitions.

Fixed Costs—Costs that do not vary with the volume of business, such as facility and equipment depreciation and property taxes.

Fixed-Price Contract—A contract for which the total cost is all-inclusive and not dependent on contractor expenses or other variables.

Focal Point—The principal point of contact with a government agency for coordination and exchange of information related to acquisition contracts. Focal points will provide EVMS policy and guidance. A table of DoD focal points is available from the Defense Contract Management Agency (DCMA).

Forward Pricing Rate Agreement (FPRA)—A written agreement negotiated between a potential contractor and the federal government to make certain rates available during a specified period to price contracts. Such rates represent reasonable projections of specific costs that are not easily estimated.

Frontloading—Unnecessarily performing work out of sequence in order to obtain credit in a period earlier than the one in which it was scheduled for completion. The practice can cause distortions in EVMS measurements for both periods.

Full Time Equivalents (FTE)—A measurement of staffing units usually expressed as the number of persons employed full time per month.

Functional Organization—An organization in which the staff is arranged in a hierarchal structure by functional specialty (e.g., accounting, manufacturing, marketing).

General and Administrative (G&A)—A grouping of indirect costs that are distributed to all units within a business entity, such as corporate headquarters expenses.

Government Contract Quality Assurance (GCQA)—A review that determines if contractual requirements have been met prior to the acceptance of supplies and services.

Indirect Costs—Costs that are not directly identified with a single work element, such as for overhead and G & A. These costs are allocated to individual work elements by a selected arbitrary process.

Initial Compliance Review—A federal government review done at a contractor's facility to assess contractor application of EVMS principles.

Integrated Baseline Review—A joint review of the contractor's performance measurement baseline by the federal government and contractor to determine if the baseline captures the entire technical scope of work consistent with contractual schedules and if the baseline has adequate resources assigned.

Integrated Management System (IMS)—A management system and related subsystems that establish the relationship between the cost, schedule, and technical aspects of the project. An IMS should be designed to measure progress, accumulate actual costs, analyze deviations from plans, forecast completion of contract events, and make contract changes to the project in a timely manner.

Integrated Product Team (IPT)—Representatives from all appropriate functional disciplines working together to build successful processes and make sound and timely decisions. The IPT participants are empowered, to the maximum extent possible, to make commitments for the area they represent.

Integrated Surveillance Team (IST)—A selected grouping of individuals from participating agencies involved in the surveillance of the contractor's EVMS implementation.

Internal Replanning—Replanning actions performed by the contractor for remaining effort within the recognized contract value and schedule.

Level of Effort (LOE)—Work that cannot be effectively associated with a definable end product, such as the project manager's support activities. The earned value for LOE is measured only by the passage of time, not by any specific accomplishment.

Life Cycle—The total life span of a system, commencing with concept formulation and extending through operation and eventual retirement of the system.

Linear Responsibility Chart (LRC)—A graphical illustration of which elements of the work breakdown structure (WBS) are performed or managed by the elements of the organization breakdown structure (OBS) and to what degree.

Line of Balance—A tool for managing repetitive processes. One aspect of this philosophy is to plot activities and their planned durations across a graph as the "line." When actual completion times are plotted against this line, activities can be seen in terms of whether or not they are "in balance" and whether future task completions are behind schedule.

Management Council—A team of senior representatives involved with business activities at a particular contractor facility, generally including representatives from the contractor, major customers, the Defense Contract Management Agency (DCMA), and the Defense Contract Audit Agency (DCAA). The council serves as a forum to discuss, coordinate, and resolve issues of common concern affecting the efficiency and effectiveness of contractor operations and to facilitate the coordination of business and manufacturing process reengineering initiatives.

Management Reserve (MR)—An amount of the total allocated budget withheld for management control purposes rather than designated for the accomplishment of a specific task or set of tasks. It is not a part of the performance measurement baseline (PMB).

Matrix Organization—An organization structured so that project managers share management responsibility with functional managers. A weak matrix style puts almost all of the management authority with the functional manager.

Memorandum of Agreement (MOA)—An agreement between a government program manager and a Contract Administration Office (CAO) establishing the scope of responsibilities for contract audit services.

Milestone Decision Authority (MDA)—The designated individual with overall responsibility for a program. The MDA has the authority to approve entry of an acquisition program into the next phase of the acquisition process and is accountable for cost, schedule, and performance reporting to higher authority, including congressional reporting.

Negotiated Contract Cost—The estimated cost negotiated in a cost plus fixed fee contract or the negotiated target cost in either a fixed price incentive contract or cost plus incentive fee contract.

Network Schedule—A project schedule format in which activities and milestones are represented along with the interdependencies between activities to show the logical flow of the project. Network schedules are the basis for critical path analysis, a method for identifying and assessing schedule priorities and impacts.

Normalize—To adjust data for effects such as inflation, anomalies, seasonal patterns, technology changes, accounting system changes, and reorganizations.

Order-of-Magnitude Estimates—General cost estimates that are calculated by using only very basic criteria and are not considered to be highly accurate. They may be "first-time" estimates to determine project feasibility and further study or final estimates for smaller contracts that do not require a firm cost.

Organization Breakdown Structure (OBS)—A hierarchal graph indicating the functional relationships in an organization, which is used as the framework for the assignment of work responsibilities. The OBS is broken down progressively to the lowest levels of management.

Original Budget—The budget established on or near the contract effective date based upon the negotiated contract cost.

Overhead—Costs incurred in an operation that cannot be directly related to the individual products or services being produced. See indirect costs.

Overrun—Costs incurred in excess of the contract's target cost for an incentive type contract or the estimated costs for a fixed fee contract.

Over-Target Baseline (OTB)—A project baseline that results from increasing the budgets for remaining work without a related increase in the contract value. The process of implementing the OTB is called reprogramming and results in a total allocated budget in excess of the contract budget base.

Parametric Cost Estimating—A cost estimating methodology using statistical relationships between historical costs and other program variables. This technique employs one or more cost estimating relationships (CERs) for measuring costs based on the deliverable's technical, physical, or other characteristics.

Performance Measurement Baseline (PMB)—The time-phased budget plan against which project performance is measured. It is formed by the budgets assigned to scheduled cost accounts, summary-level planning packages, and applicable indirect budgets. The PMB equals the total allocated budget minus management reserve.

Planned Value (PV)—See Budgeted Cost of Work Scheduled.

Planning Package—A logical aggregation of work within a cost account, normally the far-term effort, that can be identified and budgeted in early baseline planning, but is not yet defined in work packages.

Plant Visit—A short-duration, summary-level review of the contractor's EVMS procedures to verify that they provide timely and reliable data.

Post-Acceptance Review—A government review performed on a specific element of the contractor's EVMS that has displayed a lack of discipline in application or no longer meets the intent of the EVMS guidelines.

Procuring Activity—The military subordinate command to which the Procuring Contracting Officer (PCO) is assigned. The procuring activity is the organization that executes a project or acquisition contract. It may include the program office, related functional support offices, and procurement offices.

Program Evaluation and Review Technique (PERT)—A management technique designed for the planning and control of complex projects. PERT is utilized by constructing a network model of the project's integrated activities and periodically evaluating the time and cost implications as the work progresses. The technique requires three estimates of the expected time to complete each activity.

Program Manager—The government's designated individual with responsibility for and authority to accomplish program objectives for development, production, and sustainment of the end user's operational needs. The program manager is accountable for credible cost, schedule, and performance reporting to the Milestone Decision Authority (MDA).

Program Work Breakdown Structure (PWBS)—The work breakdown structure (WBS) that covers the acquisition of a specific defense material master item, is related to contractual effort, and includes all applicable elements consisting of at least the first three levels. These levels are then extended by the program manager and/or contractor to create the Contract Work Breakdown Structure.

Project-Oriented Organization—An organization that assigns staff primarily by projects and not by functional specialties. The project manager has full management authority for individuals assigned to the project.

Reimbursable Cost Contract—A contract on which the total cost is the sum of the contractor's expenses plus a percentage or fixed amount for contractor profits.

Replanning—The redistribution of the budget for future work. Traceability is required to previous baselines and attention to funding requirements needs to be considered in any replanning effort.

Reprogramming—The process of implementing an over-target baseline that entails restructuring the effort remaining in the contract and results in a new budget allocation that exceeds the contract budget base.

Request for Proposals (RFP)—A document that sets out the parameters of the expected deliverables of a proposed project and solicits responses from potential suppliers.

Responsibility Assignment Matrix (RAM)—A graphical depiction of the relationship between the contract work breakdown structure (WBS) elements and the organizational units that are assigned responsibility for ensuring their accomplishment.

Schedule Performance Index (SPI)—A factor representing schedule efficiency. The SPI is calculated as the earned value divided by the planned value:

$$SPI = BCWP / BCWS.$$

Schedule Variance (SV)—A metric that indicates the project's schedule performance. SV is calculated as the earned value minus the planned value:

$$SV = BCWP - BCWS.$$

A positive value is favorable while a negative value is unfavorable.

Should-Cost Estimate—An estimate of a contract price that reflects reasonably achievable contractor economy and efficiency. It is generally accomplished by a team of procurement, contract administration, cost analysis, audit, and engineering representatives. Its purpose is to identify uneconomical or inefficient practices in a contractor's management and operations by quantifying the findings in terms of their impact on cost, and to develop a reasonable price objective for negotiation.

Significant Variances—Differences between planned and actual performance that require further review, analysis, or action. Appropriate thresholds should be established at a magnitude of variances that will provide reasonable analysis.

Software Development Life Cycle—Stages and processes through which software passes during its useful life. The cycle includes requirements definition, analysis, design, coding, testing, and maintenance.

Stakeholder (Project)—An individual who will be affected by a project or who has influence over some aspect of the project. The term does not usually apply to the project team members.

Statement of Objectives (SOO)—A document identifying the high-level product-oriented goals of a proposed project. The SOO is usually part of a Request for Proposals (RFP).

Statement of Work (SOW)—Identifies the specific tasks the contractor will perform during the contract period. The SOW could include tasks such as system engineering, design, and build. For security, the SOW includes the contractor tasks necessary to achieve specific levels of assurance, including studies and analyses, configuration management, security test and evaluation support, delivery, and maintenance of the system. These work statements also specify the development of the required documentation to be provided under the Contract Data Requirements List (CDRL).

Stochastic System—Events proceeding in a probabilistic fashion. Outcomes cannot be predicted with certainty, but probabilities are known.

Summary Effort Control Package (SECP)—An aggregation of work for far-term efforts, not yet able to be defined in enough detail for the control account level, but that can be assigned to higher level work breakdown structure (WBS) elements and is therefore not "undistributed budget."

Summary Level Planning Package (SLLP)—See Summary Effort Control Package.

Third-Party Certification—Approval of an EVMS, to a standard recognized by DoD as equivalent to the EVMS criteria, by an independent organization accredited by the standards authority and recognized by DoD.

Top-Down Method—An estimating technique that calculates the overall cost and effort of a proposed project based on the global properties of a past project.

Total Allocated Budget (TAB)—The sum of all budgets allocated to the contract. Total allocated budget consists of the performance measurement baseline and all management reserve (MR). The TAB will reconcile directly to the contract budget base.

Undistributed Budget (UB)—Budget applicable to contract effort that has not yet been identified to Contract Work Breakdown Structure (CWBS) elements at or below the lowest level of reporting.

Unit Price Contract—A type of contract in which the total price of the contract will be equal to the number of units produced multiplied by a fixed-and-agreed cost per unit. This type of contract is considered a "fixed price" contract as opposed to a "cost priced" contract.

Validation—In parametric estimating, a process used to determine whether the cost estimating relationship or model selected for a particular estimate is a reliable predictor of cost for the system being estimated. For a complete validation process, the model users must also demonstrate that they have adequate experience and training and that their processes, policies, and procedures are established, documented, and enforced.

Variable Cost—A cost that varies in parallel with the volume or rate of production of goods or the performance of services.

Variance at Completion (VAC)—The difference between the total budget assigned to a contract or contract element and the estimate at completion:

$$VAC = BAC - EAC.$$

VAC represents the amount of expected overrun or underrun.

Variance Threshold—The amount of variance that determines if a variance is significant enough to warrant a variance analysis. Thresholds should be set at a level that will provide for a reasonable analysis and discernment of potential contract performance problems without unnecessarily burdening resources.

Variances—Those differences between planned and actual performance, both cumulative and at completion, that require further review, analysis, or action. See Significant Variances and Variance Threshold.

Visit Coordinator—The visit coordinator is responsible for all aspects of a plant visit, including planning, on-site activities, and visit follow-up and closure. The program manager may choose to be the visit coordinator or may delegate the responsibility.

What-if Analysis—The process of evaluating alternative strategies.

Work Breakdown Structure (WBS)—A product-oriented family tree division of hardware, software, services, and other work tasks that organizes, defines, and graphically displays the product to be developed and relates the elements of the work to be accomplished to each other and the end product. The WBS is developed into layers of more detail, with the number of layers depending on the complexity of the project and on the purpose of the WBS. See Contract Work Breakdown Structure and Program Work Breakdown Structure.

Work Package (WP)—A set of detailed jobs or material items identified by the contractor for accomplishing work required to complete the contract. A WP represents units of work at levels where work is performed and has the following characteristics:

- It is clearly distinguished from all other work packages.
- It is assigned to a single organizational element.
- It has scheduled start and completion dates (and interim milestones if applicable).
- It has a budget or assigned value expressed in terms of dollars, man-hours, or other measurable units.
- Its duration is limited to a relatively short span of time or has milestones to enable the objective determination of earned value. It may be level of effort.

- Its schedule is integrated with other related organizational schedules.

Work-Package Budget—Resources that are formally assigned by the contractor to accomplish a work package, expressed in dollars, hours, standards, or other measurable units.

Bibliography

Adams, J., and John R. Adams. 1997. *Principles of Project Management.* Newtown Square, PA: Project Management Institute.

Albrecht, W. S., and Robert J. Sack. 2000. *Accounting Education: Charting the Course through a Perilous Future.* Sarasota: American Accounting Association.

Anderson, D., D. Sweeney, and T. Williams. 2003. *Essentials of Statistics for Business and Economics.* 3rd ed. Cincinnati, OH: South-Western.

Archibald, Russell D. 1987. "The History of Modern Project Management: Key Milestones in the Early PERT/CPM/PDM Days." *Project Management Journal* 18, no. 4: 29.

Arrow, Kenneth J. 1971. *Essays in the Theory of Risk Bearing.* Chicago: Markham Publishing.

Austin, Robert D. 1996. *Measuring and Managing Performance in Organizations.* New York: Dorset House Publishing.

Badiru, A.B. 1991. "A Simulation Approach to Network Analysis." *Simulation* 57, no. 4: 245–255.

Baldrige National Quality Program. 2003. *Getting Started with the Baldrige National Quality Program.* Gaithersburg, MD: National Institute of Standards and Technology.

Batten, Joe. 1990. *Expectations and Possibilities: How to Create Your Path to Discovery and Achievement.* Vol. 1. Santa Monica: Hay House.

Bembers, Ivan, et al. 2003. *Over Target Baseline and Over Target Schedule Handbook.* In Defense Acquisition University [database online]. Washington, DC [cited 5/4/04]. Available online at http://acc.dau.mil/simplify/ev.php?ID=17993_201&ID2=DO_TOPIC.

Boehm, Barry W. 1988. "A Spiral Model of Software Development and Enhancement." *Computer* 21, no. 5: 61–72.

Budd, Charlene S. 2003. "Planning a Project: Six Steps to Success." *Today's CPA* (January-February): 20–23.

Choo, Chun W. *Motivation.* 2003. In University of Toronto [database online]. Toronto [cited 5/10/04]. Available online at http://choo.fis.utoronto.ca/FIS/Courses/LIS1230/LIS1230sharma/motive1.htm.

Christensen, David S. 1998. "The Costs and Benefits of the Earned Value Management Process." *Acquisition Review Quarterly* (Fall): 373–386.

Christensen, David, and Carl Templin. 2000. "An Analysis of Management Reserve Budget on Defense Acquisition Contracts." *Acquisition Review Quarterly* (Summer): 191–208.

Cleland, David I., and Lewis R. Ireland. 2002. *Project Management: Strategic Design and Implementation.* 4th ed. New York: McGraw-Hill.

Crawford, J.K. *Project Management Maturity Model.* 2001. New York: Marcel Dekker.

Defense Acquisition University. 2004. *Defense Acquisition Guidebook.* In Defense Acquisition University [database online]. Fort Belvoir, VA. Available online at http://akss.dau.mil/dag/.

Defense Acquisition University. 2005. *EVM (Earned Value Management).* In Defense Acquisition University [database online]. Ft. Belvoir, VA. Available online at http://acc.dau.mil/simplify/ev.php?ID=71253_201§ID2=DO_TOPIC.

Defense Acquisition University. 2005. *Risk Management.* In Defense Acquisition University [database online]. Ft. Belvoir, VA. Available online at https://acc.dau.mil/simplify/ev.php?ID=1203_201&ID2=DO_COMMUNITY.

Department of Defense. 2004. Acquisition, Technology & Logistics. *Earned Value Management.* In Office of the Under Secretary of Defense [database online]. Washington, DC [cited 04/2004]. Available online at http://www.acq.osd.mil/pm/.

Department of Defense. 2003. *DoD Directive 5101.1, DoD Executive Agent.* In U.S. Department of Defense [database online]. Washington, DC. Available online at http://www.dtic.mil/whs/directives/corres/html/51011.htm.

Department of Defense. 2003. *DoD Instruction 5000.2.* In Department of Defense [database online]. Washington, DC. Available online at http://www.dtic.mil/whs/directives/corres/pdf/i50002_051203/i50002p.pdf.

Department of Defense. 2002. *DoD Regulation 5000.2-R.* In Department of Defense [database online]. Washington, DC [cited 3/20/04]. Available online at http://dod5000.dau.mil/DOCS/master.020405. Regulation.doc.

Department of Defense. 2004. *EVMS and C/SSR DFARS Clauses.* In Department of Defense [database online]. Washington, DC. Available from http://www.acq.osd.mil/pm/currentpolicy/dfars.html.

Department of Defense. 2004. *Federal Acquisition Regulation.* In AcqNet U.S. Department of Defense [database online]. Washington, DC. Available from http://www.acqnet.gov/far/.

Department of Defense. 2002. *Interim Defense Acquisition Guidebook.* In Office of Secretary of Defense [database online]. Washington, DC [cited 4/20/04]. Available online at http://dod5000.dau.mil/DOCS/InterimGuidebook.htm.

Department of Defense. 2004. *Material Management and Accounting System (MMAS).* In Department of Defense [database online]. Washington, DC [cited 9/20/04]. Available online at http://www.acq.osd.mil/dpap/dfars/html/current/252242.htm#252.242-7004.

Department of Defense. 1998. *MIL-HDBK-881.* In Department of Defense [database online]. Washington, DC [cited 2/4/04]. Available online at http://www.acq.osd.mil/pm/currentpolicy/wbs/mil_hdbk_881/mil_hdbk_881.htm.

Department of Defense. 1998. *Notice of Earned Value Management System.* In Department of Defense [database online]. Washington, DC [cited 02/2004]. Available online at http://www.acq.osd.mil/dpap/dfars/html/current/252234.htm.

Department of Defense. 2003. *Risk Management Guide for DoD Acquisition.* 5th ed. Fort Belvoir, VA: Defense Acquisition University Press.

Department of Defense, FAA, and NASA. 1997. *Earned Value Management Implementation Guide.* In Department of Defense *(ACQ)* [database online]. Washington, DC [cited 3/20/04]. Available online at http://www.acq.osd.mil/pm/currentpolicy/jig/evmig1.htm.

Department of Energy. 1995. *Project Management Qualification Standard Competencies.* In U.S. Department of Energy [database online]. Washington, DC. Available online at http://cted.inel.gov/cted/qualstd/proj-mgt.html.

Department of Energy. 1997. *Directive DOE G 430.1-1.* In U.S. Department of Energy [database online]. Washington, DC [cited 6/4/04]. Available online at http://www.directives.doe.gov/pdfs/doe/doetext/neword/430/g4301-1toc.html.

Department of the Navy. 2001. *MIL-HDBK-3001 (AS).* In Department of Defense [database online]. Washington, DC [cited 2/4/04]. Available online at http://casstps.nawcad.navy.mil/reference/MIL-HDBK-3001.pdf.

Department of the Navy. 1997. *MIL-DTL-81927C (AS).* In Department of Defense [database online]. Washington, DC [cited 2/4/04]. Available online at http://assist.daps.dla.mil/docimages/0000/92/48/81927C.PD6.

Dettmer, H.W. 1997. *Goldratt's Theory of Constraints.* Milwaukee: ASQ Quality Press.

Electronic Industries Alliance. 2002. *Earned Value Management Systems.* Arlington, VA: Electronic Industries Alliance.

Federal Acquisition Regulations. 2004. *Contingencies in General Contracting Requirements.* In U.S. Government Printing Office [database online]. Washington, DC [cited 6/4/04]. Available online at http://farsite.hill.af.mil/reghtml/regs/far2afmcfars/fardfars/far/31.htm#P437_90744.

Federal Aviation Administration. 2003. *Documentation Guidance for FAA Cost Estimates.* In U.S. Federal Aviation Administration [database online]. Washington, DC [cited 5/4/04]. Available online at http://fast.faa.gov/investment/cboe.htm.

Flamholtz, E.G. 1979. "Toward a Psycho-Technical Paradigm of Organizational Measurement." *Decision Sciences* 10, no. 1: 71–84.

Flannes, Steven W., and Ginger Levin. 2001. *People Skills for Project Managers.* Vienna, VA: Management Concepts.

Fleming, Quentin W., and Joel M. Koppelman. 2000. *Earned Value Project Management.* 2nd ed. Newtown Square, PA: Project Management Institute.

Glickman, Rosalene. 2002. *Optimal Thinking.* New York: John Wiley & Sons.

Goldratt, Eliyahu M. *Critical Chain. 1997.* Great Barrington, MA: North River Press.

Goldratt, Eliyahu M., and Jeff Cox. 1992. *The Goal: A Process of Ongoing Improvement.* 2nd rev. ed. Great Barrington, MA: North River Press.

Gutierrez, G.J., and P. Kouvelis. 1991. "Parkinson's Law and Its Implications for Project Management." *Management Science* 37, no. 8: 990.

Herzberg, F., B. Mausner, and B.B. Snyderman. 1959. *The Motivation to Work.* 2nd ed. New York: John Wiley & Sons.

Hillson, D. 2004. *Risk Doctor.* In Risk Doctor and Partners [database online]. Hampshire, UK. [cited 4/4/04]. Available online at http://www.risk-doctor.com/.

Hughes, Thomas P. 1998. *Rescuing Prometheus.* New York: Pantheon.

Humphreys, Gary C. 2002. *Project Management Using Earned Value.* Orange, CA: Humphreys & Associates.

Institute of Electrical and Electronic Engineers, Inc., and Electronic Industries Alliance. 1996. *IEEE/EIA 12207.0-1996.* New York: Institute of Electrical and Electronic Engineers, Inc.

International Organization for Standardization. 2004. "ISO 9000 Quality Management Principles." In *The International Organization for Standardization* [database online]. Geneva, Switzerland [cited 3/15/04]. Available online at http://www.iso.org.

Joint U.S. Defense Agencies. 1996. *Cost/Schedule Status Report Joint Guide.* In Office of the Secretary of Defense [database online]. Washington, DC [cited 9/4/04]. Available online at http://www.acq.osd.mil/pm/newpolicy/c_ssrupdate/cssr_fnl.html.

Keefer, D.L., and W.A.Verdini. 1993. "Better Estimation of PERT Activity Time Parameters." *Management Science* (September): 1086–1091.

Kerzner, Harold. 2003. *Project Management: A Systems Approach to Planning, Scheduling, and Controlling.* 8th ed. New York: John Wiley & Sons.

Klingel, A.R. 1966. "Bias in PERT Completion Times: Calculations for a Real Network." *Management Science* 13, no.4: 476–489.

Lencioni, Patrick M. 2002. *The Five Dysfunctions of a Team.* New York: John Wiley & Sons.

Lewis, James P. 2000. *The Project Manager's Desk Reference.* Boston: Mc-Graw-Hill.

Locke, Edwin A., Gary P. Latham, Ken J. Smith, and Robert E. Wood. 1990. *A Theory of Goal Setting and Task Performance.* Upper Saddle River, NJ: Prentice Hall.

Management Technologies. 2004. "The Earned Value Management Maturity Model." In *Management Technologies* [database online]. Brea, CA [cited 9/21/04]. Available online at http://www.mgmt-technologies.com/evmtech.html.

Meredith, Jack R., and Samuel J. Mantel, Jr. 2003. *Project Management: A Managerial Approach.* 5th ed. New York: John Wiley & Sons.

Murphy, R.L., Christopher J. Alberts, Ray C. Williams, Ronald P. Higuera, Audrey J. Dorofee, and Julie A. Walker. 1996. *Continuous Risk Management Guidebook.* In Carnegie Mellon University [database online]. Pittsburgh [cited 7/4/04]. Available online at http://www.sei.cmu.edu/publications/books/other-books/sample.pdf.

National Aeronautics and Space Administration. 2002. *NPD 9501.3A. Earned Value Management.* In NASA Online Directives Information System Library [database online]. Washington, DC [cited 7/4/04]. Available online at http://www.ksc.nasa.gov/procurement/kics/docs/npd95013a.pdf.

National Aeronautics and Space Administration. 1996. *Parametric Cost Estimating Handbook.* In National Aeronautics and Space Administration [database online]. Washington, DC [cited 5/4/04]. Available from http://www1.jsc.nasa.gov/bu2/PCEHHTML/pceh.htm.

National Defense Industrial Association. 2005. *ANSI/EIA-748-A Standard for Earned Value Management Systems Intent Guide.* Arlington, VA. Available from http://www.ndia.org/Content/ContentGroups/Divisions1/Procurement/PDFs10/NDIA_PMSC_EVMS_IntentGuide_Jan2005.pdf.

National Security Industrial Association. 2003. *Industry Standard Guidelines for Earned Value Management Systems.* In Department of

Defense [database online]. Washington, DC. Available online at http: //www.acq.osd.mil/pm/newpolicy/indus/evms_gde.htm.

Neave, Henry. 1990. *The Deming Dimension*. Knoxville: SPC Press.

Peterson, Rein. 1985. "Critical Path Scheduling." *Business Quarterly* 30, no. 2: 70.

Parkinson, C.N. *Parkinson's Law*. Boston: Houghton Mifflin, 1957.

Pritsker, A.A.B., and W.W. Happ. 1966. "GERT: Graphical Evaluation and Review Technique. Part 1: Fundamentals." *Journal of Industrial Engineering* 17, no. 5: 267–274.

Project Management Institute. 2000/2004 (3rd. ed.). *A Guide to the Project Management Body of Knowledge (PMBOK® Guide)*. Newtown Square, PA: Project Management Institute.

Project Management Institute. 2003. *Organizational Project Management Maturity Model (OPM3™)*. Newtown Square, PA: Project Management Institute.

Rouse, Margaret. 2004. *Gantt Chart*. In *TechTarget* [database online]. Needham, MA [cited 7/5/04]. Available online at http:// whatis.techtarget.com/definition/0,,sid9_gci331397,00.html.

Rumsey, D. 2003. *Statistics for Dummies*. New York: John Wiley & Sons.

Sarbanes, Paul S., and Michael G. Oxley. 2002. *Sarbanes-Oxley Act of 2002, H.R.3763*. Washington, DC.

Schulte, Ruthanne. 2004. *Is Poor Project Management a Crime?* http: //www.welcom.com/content.cfm. Houston: Welcom.

SETI@home. 2004. "Ksetiwatch." in *The Planetary Society* [database online]. Berkeley [cited 5/6/04]. Available online at http://ksetiwatch.so urceforge.net/.

Slemaker, C.M. 1985. *The Principles and Practice of Cost/Schedule Control Systems*. New York: McGraw-Hill.

Software Engineering Institute. 2004. *Capability Maturity Model® (SW-CMM®) for Software*. In Carnegie Mellon University [database online]. Pittsburgh [cited 6/16/04]. Available online at http: //www.sei.cmu.edu/cmm/cmm.sum.html.

Standish Group International. 1999. *Chaos: A Recipe for Success*. West Yarmouth, MA: Standish Group International.

Standish Group International. 1995. *Chaos: Charting the Seas of Information Technology.* West Yarmouth, MA: Standish Group International.

Steinberg, Richard M., Miles E.A. Everson, Frank J. Martens, and Lucy E. Nottingham. 2004. *Enterprise Risk Management—Integrated Framework.* Jersey City: American Institute of Certified Public Accountants.

Stevenson, James P. 1993. *The Pentagon Paradox: The Development of the F-18 Hornet.* Annapolis: Naval Institute Press.

Stewart, R.D., R.M. Wyskida, and M. Richard. 1995. *Cost Estimator's Reference Manual.* New York: John Wiley & Sons.

U.S. Securities and Exchange Commission. 2003. "Management's Reports on Internal Control Over Financial Reporting and Certification of Disclosure in Exchange Act Periodic Reports," in U.S. Securities and Exchange Commission [database online]. Washington, DC [cited 7/03]. Available online at http://www.sec.gov/rules/final/33-8238.htm.

Verma, Vijay K. *Organizing Projects for Success.* 1995. Newtown Square, PA: Project Management Institute.

Verma, Vijay K., and Hans J. Thamhain. 1996. *Human Resource Skills for the Project Manager.* Vol. 2. Newtown Square, PA: Project Management Institute.

Vroom, Victor H. 1964. *Work and Motivation.* New York: John Wiley & Sons.

Wake, Stephen F.R. 2003. *Earned Value Analysis.* Buckinghamshire, UK: Stephen Wake.

Westney, R.E. 2001. "Risk Management: Maximizing the Probability of Success." In *Project Management for Business Professionals,* edited by Joan Knutson. New York: John Wiley & Sons.

Wideman, R.M. 2004. *The Role of the Project Life Cycle (Life Span) in Project Management.* In R. Max Wideman [database online]. Vancouver, BC [cited 3/15/04]. Available online at http://www.maxwideman.com/papers/plc-models/intro.htm.

The 32 EVMS Criteria

The 32 EVMS criteria are grouped in the five areas of Organization, Planning and Budgeting, Accounting Considerations, Analysis and Management Reports, and Revisions and Data Maintenance. The information in the guide was developed jointly by DoD, FAA, and NASA (DoD, FAA, and NASA 1997). Note that the criteria are numbered consecutively, but start with the section number 2.

2.0. The Department of Defense [DoD] has formally recognized 32 Criteria as defining acceptable Earned Value Management Systems Requirements. The Criteria are those from the industry standard *Earned Value Management Systems Guidelines*, August 1996, and are published in DoD 5000.2-R, Appendix VI. Contractors with systems formally recognized by the DoD as meeting the 35 Cost/Schedule Control Systems Criteria prior to December 1996 will be considered as compliant with the 32 EVMS criteria.

Organization

2.1. Define the authorized work elements for the program. A work breakdown structure (WBS), tailored for effective internal management control, is commonly used in this process.

2.2. Identify the program organizational structure including the major subcontractors responsible for accomplishing the authorized work, and define the organizational elements in which work will be planned and controlled.

2.3. Provide for the integration of the company's planning, scheduling, budgeting, work authorization and cost accumulation processes with each other, and as appropriate, the program work breakdown structure and the program organizational structure.

2.4. Identify the company organization or function responsible for controlling overhead (indirect costs).

2.5. Provide for integration of the program work breakdown structure and the program organizational structure in a manner that permits cost and schedule performance measurement by elements of either or both structures as needed.

Planning and Budgeting

2.6. Schedule the authorized work in a manner which describes the sequence of work and identifies significant task interdependencies required to meet the requirements of the program.

2.7. Identify physical products, milestones, technical performance goals, or other indicators that will be used to measure progress.

2.8. Establish and maintain a time-phased budget baseline, at the control account level, against which program performance can be measured. Budget for far-term efforts may be held in higher level accounts until an appropriate time for allocation at the control account level. Initial budgets established for performance measurement will be based on either internal management goals or the external customer negotiated target cost including estimates for authorized but undefinitized work. On government contracts, if an over target baseline is used for performance measurement reporting purposes, prior notification must be provided to the customer.

2.9. Establish budgets for authorized work with identification of significant cost elements (labor, material, etc.) as needed for internal management and for control of subcontractors.

2.10. To the extent it is practical to identify the authorized work in discrete work packages, establish budgets for this work in terms of dollars, hours, or other measurable units. Where the entire control account is not subdivided into work packages, identify the far term effort in larger planning packages for budget and scheduling purposes.

2.11. Provide that the sum of all work package budgets plus planning package budgets within a control account equals the control account budget.

2.12. Identify and control level of effort activity by time-phased budgets established for this purpose. Only that effort which is unmeasurable or for which measurement is impractical may be classified as level of effort.

2.13. Establish overhead budgets for each significant organizational component of the company for expenses which will become indirect costs. Reflect in the program budgets, at the appropriate level, the amounts in overhead pools that are planned to be allocated to the program as indirect costs.

2.14. Identify management reserves and undistributed budget.

2.15. Provide that the program target cost goal is reconciled with the sum of all internal program budgets and management reserves.

Accounting Considerations

2.16. Record direct costs in a manner consistent with the budgets in a formal system controlled by the general books of account.

2.17. When a work breakdown structure is used, summarize direct costs from control accounts into the work breakdown structure without allocation of a single control account to two or more work breakdown structure elements.

2.18. Summarize direct costs from the control accounts into the contractor's organizational elements without allocation of a single control account to two or more organizational elements.

2.19. Record all indirect costs which will be allocated to the contract.

2.20. Identify unit costs, equivalent units costs, or lot costs when needed.

2.21. For EVMS, the material accounting system will provide for:

(1) Accurate cost accumulation and assignment of costs to control accounts in a manner consistent with the budgets using recognized, acceptable, costing techniques.

(2) Cost performance measurement at the point in time most suitable for the category of material involved, but no earlier than the time of progress payments or actual receipt of material.

(3) Full accountability of all material purchased for the program including the residual inventory.

Analysis and Management Reports

2.22. At least on a monthly basis, generate the following information at the control account and other levels as necessary for management control using actual cost data from, or reconcilable with, the accounting system:

(1) Comparison of the amount of planned budget and the amount of budget earned for work accomplished. This comparison provides the schedule variance.

(2) Comparison of the amount of the budget earned and the actual (applied where appropriate) direct costs for the same work. This comparison provides the cost variance.

2.23. Identify, at least monthly, the significant differences between both planned and actual schedule performance and planned and actual cost performance, and provide the reasons for the variances in the detail needed by program management.

2.24. Identify budgeted and applied (or actual) indirect costs at the level and frequency needed by management for effective control, along with the reasons for any significant variances.

2.25. Summarize the data elements and associated variances through the program organization and/or work breakdown structure to support management needs and any customer reporting specified in the contract.

2.26. Implement managerial actions taken as the result of earned value information.

2.27. Develop revised estimates of cost at completion based on performance to date, commitment values for material, and estimates of future conditions. Compare this information with the performance measurement baseline to identify variances at completion important to company management and any applicable customer reporting requirements including statements of funding requirements.

Revisions and Data Maintenance

2.28. Incorporate authorized changes in a timely manner, recording the effects of such changes in budgets and schedules. In the directed effort prior to negotiation of a change, base such revisions on the amount estimated and budgeted to the program organizations.

2.29. Reconcile current budgets to prior budgets in terms of changes to the authorized work and internal replanning in the detail needed by management for effective control.

2.30. Control retroactive changes to records pertaining to work performed that would change previously reported amounts for actual costs, earned value, or budgets. Adjustments should be made only for correction of errors, routine accounting adjustments, effects of customer or management directed changes, or to improve the baseline integrity and accuracy of performance measurement data.

2.31. Prevent revisions to the program budget except for authorized changes.

2.32. Document changes to the performance measurement baseline.

On August 3, 2002, NASA issued some modifications to the criteria in Directive: NPD 9501.3A. The most significant change was the addition of another criterion at the end of the section on Analysis and Management Reports. That criterion reads, "Maintain, manage, and safeguard all records/reports, when appropriate, according to the guidance provided in NPG 1441.1, NASA Records Retention Schedules, and dispose of the records according to these schedules (National Aeronautics and Space Administration 2002, 1).

APPENDIX B

Answers and Solutions

CHAPTER 3

Exercise Solutions:

1. TV = $289,000. ($40,000 + $30,000 + $28,000 + $17,000 + $22,000 + $24,000 + $38,000 + $90,000)

2. PV = $178,540. ($40,000 + $30,000 + $28,000 + $17,000 + $21,120 + $23,040 + $19,380)

3. AV = $137,500.

4. EV = $129,800. ($40,000 + $30,000 + $28,000 + $17,000 + $11,000 +$0 + $3,800)

5. CV = ($7,700) unfavorable. ($129,800 - $137,500)

   CPI = .944 project over budget. ($129,800 / $137,500)

6. SV = $(48,740) unfavorable. ($129,800 - $178,540)

   SPI = .727 project behind schedule. ($129,800 / $178,540)

7. "Optimistic" EAC = $306,144. ($289,000 / .944)

   "Pessimistic" EAC = $421,106 ($289,000 / (.944 * .727))

CHAPTER 4

1. c.

2. b.

3. d.

4. b

5. d.

6. a.

CHAPTER 10

Exercise 1 Solution

a) BAC = $289,000 = ($40,000 + $22,000 + $30,000 + $24,000 +$28,000 +$17,000 + $38,000 + $90,000).

b) BCWS (PV) = .$229,000 = [$40,000 + $22,000 + $30,000 + $24,000 +$28,000 +$17,000 + $38,000 + (.3 X $90,000)].

c) EV = $244,000 = [$40,000 + $22,000 + $30,000 + $24,000 +$28,000 +$17,000 + $38,000 + (.5 X $90,000)].

d) AC (or AV) = $240,000.

e) Cost variance = $4,000 Favorable = $244,000 - $240,000;

$$CPI = 1.02 = \frac{\$244,000}{\$240,000}.$$

f) Schedule Variance = $15,000 Favorable = $244,000 - $229,000;

$$SPI = 1.07 = \frac{\$244,000}{\$229,000}$$

g) $ETC = \$44,118 = \dfrac{\$289,000 - \$244,000}{1.02};$

$EAC = \$284,118 = \$44,118 + \$240,000$

h) $TCI = 0.92 = \dfrac{\$289,000 - \$244,000}{\$289,000 - \$240,000}$

Exercise 2 Solution

All variances in Exercise 1 are favorable. As of the end of the third quarter, the planned value of work that should have been completed is $229,000, but the project team has completed work with an earned value of $244,000, generating a favorable schedule variance of $15,000, an SPI of 1.07, and indicating that the project is ahead of schedule. Whereas the earned value is $244,000, actual costs are only $240,000, resulting in a $4,000 favorable variance and a CPI of 1.02, both indicating very good performance.

At this point the estimate to complete is $44,188, meaning that the estimated total cost at completion is $284,118. This compares favorably with the original budget at completion of $289,000. From this point to the end of the project, the team needs to exert only 92 percent of the effort expended thus far to complete the project on budget.

Because the schedule variance also is favorable, the estimate to complete, estimate at completion, and the to-complete index would only become more favorable if the SPI were included in these measures. The project team has done an outstanding job!

CHAPTER 11

Discussion Points

1. **a.** Risk assessment. **b.** Risk disposition. **c.** Risk monitoring.

2. **a.** Problems will occur; it's not just a possibility. **b.** Risk management is crucial for project success. **c.** Risk management must be considered an integral part of the project plan.

3. **a.** A statement about the potential event, including cause. **b.** A rating of its probability of occurrence. **c.** The severity of the consequence of the occurrence.

4. Possibilities include: fantasy questions, brainstorming, surveys, checklists, interviews, lessons learned from previous projects, and the examination and evaluation of each work breakdown structure element.

5. Several possibilities, but should include ratings for probability and the three project constraints of schedule, cost, and performance.

6. Avoidance, transference, mitigation, acceptance.

7. It provides periodic comparisons of actual accomplishments with the plan that will provide evidence of risk events and the effectiveness of risk handling.

8. **a.** Replanning is appropriate when the project objectives have been changed, a major resource has changed, budgetary restrictions occur, and/or significant changes have occurred in the basis of the original plan. **b.** Replanning is not appropriate just to eliminate variances.

9. Change Request Form, budget revision records, work authorization records, change control documents, notification lists, and logs.

10. Only for correction of errors, routine accounting adjustments, effects of customer- or management-directed changes, or to improve the baseline integrity and accuracy of performance measurement data.

Index